Once again, to Kathryn

Table of Contents

Preface

In the early 1920s, a seismic shift occurred in the business of making movies in America. Eyeing huge new revenue opportunities, film studios increasingly adopted the big business strategies and structures similar to those of the U.S. automotive and other manufacturing industries. To maximize output, they created assembly-line production operations and pressured behind-the-camera filmmakers—then accustomed to wearing multiple hats—to specialize in producing, directing, writing, editing, and other capacities. As these work roles became more specialized, they also—and very curiously—became more "gendered." Women, who until this point had been key contributors to the young industry's success, increasingly heard that they were too fragile, gentle, or otherwise poorly suited for this tough new high-stakes game and soon found work difficult to find. With only rare exceptions, female film directors—who had numbered in the dozens in the 1910s—virtually disappeared for the next 60 years. Female producers faced a similar fate. And female film editors and assistants, who could easily land jobs in cutting rooms during the 1910s, were told that this work was now too taxing for them physically, passed over for advancement, and urged to give up their jobs so men could have them.

For these female film editors, however, there was one notable difference: a small, tenacious, and extremely talented number remained; rose to the top of their profession; and in some cases held positions of considerable power and influence within the industry for decades. By doing all of this, they also served as role models to another generation of women who entered the editing profession in the middle of the 20th century. These women, in turn, played critical roles in revolutionizing and revitalizing U.S. filmmaking in the 1960s and 1970s and inspiring hundreds of other women to become editors in the years that have followed.

Today, while female film producers, directors, cinematographers, and others remain relatively scarce in mainstream U.S. moviemaking, female film editors are plentiful, prominent, and proud heirs to a rich professional heritage. And, unlike their colleagues who produce, direct, or work as cinematographers, they have numerous female role models and the great advantage, to paraphrase Isaac Newton's famous line, of standing on the shoulders of the giants who came before them.

This naturally leads to some tantalizing questions. How—even as women were pushed out of most other key behind-the-camera roles—did a number of early female film editors manage both to survive and to thrive in an environment increasingly hostile to their gender? Who were these women? What drove them? What did they accomplish? How did they influence the development of filmmaking in the U.S.? And who were some of the younger women they inspired that came into their own during the mid–20th century? What drove them? What did they accomplish? How did they influence filmmaking? And how did they, in turn, inspire many of the female film editors working today?

This little known but still very important story in the history of the U.S. film industry is what this book is about. The principal focus is on nine legendary women who played (and, in a couple of cases, still play) major roles in shaping the ways films have been made over the last 100 years. In addition, the book touches briefly on nine other women editors who also warrant special recognition for their distinctive and influential contributions to film.

By no means is this book intended to be the last word on these women in particular or on female film editors in general. It confines itself only to female editors working in the U.S. for all or much of their careers and to those working primarily on mainstream feature films produced either in Hollywood or in New York. Needless to say, there have been and are many other women working outside the U.S. and/or mainly on documentary films that have made major contributions as well.

Finally, this book is not a primer on the often misunderstood and greatly underappreciated art of film editing. Instead, it is mainly a collection of stories about accomplished, influential, and, in many cases, sadly overlooked female film editors intended for readers with a general interest in film and/or gender studies. Many good books have been written about the editor's art, and 10 of the more popular and widely respected are listed at the back of this book. Those interested specifically in learning more about film editing are encouraged to check them out.

~

Although a book may only have one "official" author, numerous people help in many ways to bring each book project to completion. And again, I would like to thank my "kitchen cabinet" of friends and family members who have offered everything from their cogent insights on film to their great listening skills as this book development process has moved from conception to completion. Specifically, I would like to single out Elliot Lavine, Bob and Melanie Ferrando, Jimmy Meuel, Annette Hulbert, Peter Nelson, Natalie Varney, Joe Ercolani, Jim Daniels, and Paul Bendix. I'd also like to extend a very appreciative thanks to Photofest, the New York–based photo source that has helped me choose images for this and my last two film books. Finally, I would like to give a very special thanks to my long-time friend Scotty Martinson for devoting both her expertise and many hours of her time to editing the manuscript.

⁓

Long neglected, the contributions of women to the development of film as one of today's most powerful and pervasive communication mediums are finally—and with great energy and enthusiasm—being recognized, studied, and discussed. Yes, it is about time that many of these women, especially the female film pioneers, get their due. And, in recent years, a number of new books focusing on women in directing, producing, screenwriting, and other behind-the-camera professions throughout film history have been released and well received.

Now, I believe it is time to turn the spotlight on the female editors. As film studies, their stories offer strikingly different perspectives from what we normally hear about how great movies are made and how the feature film has evolved over the last 100 years. As gender studies, they offer captivating and often rousing examples of strong, capable women who were determined to play important, influential roles in a male-dominated industry and, despite the odds, actually did it.

Introduction

Today, it's difficult for most of us—even many film students steeped in what we now call the "classic" Hollywood period of the 1930s, 1940s, and 1950s—to imagine that there was a thriving, multi-million-dollar-a-year U.S. film industry well before the rise of the studio system in the 1920s. This industry had grown out of the success of the short "novelty" films shown mostly in the world's first indoor film exhibition spaces: the modest, often seedy nickelodeons that flourished from about 1905 to 1915. Beginning in 1910, it quickly shifted its production center from the East Coast to Southern California, and particularly to a sleepy little town a few miles north of Los Angeles named Hollywood. About this time, it was also helping to turn actors performing in these films—most notably a short, spunky Canadian-born actress named Mary Pickford—into full-fledged media sensations, the world's first movie stars. And, beginning about 1915, it was overseeing a major transformation in product as the short films, which had been its bread and butter, quickly gave way in popularity to the "feature," a film of approximately an hour or more that allowed for the telling of more complex, nuanced stories.

It's even more difficult for many of us to imagine that, during much of this time—from the early 1910s to the early 1920s, to be exact—this was an exceptional period not only for female stars such as Pickford but also for women who worked *behind* the camera. For various reasons—from the adoption of a more theatrical organizational model to tell feature-length stories to a demand for morally uplifting stories at which women were perceived to excel—women found work with relative ease. These women were not merely in support roles, either. Frequently, they worked as producers, directors, screenwriters, and editors. In fact, virtually the only major creative role that remained almost exclusively a male enclave was the cinematographer, the cameraman.

5

Often these female producers were stars who leveraged their fame and power to assure that they had final say over all aspects of the films they chose to do. Among the most successful of these actress-producers was Pickford herself. A shrewd businesswoman who (along with director D.W. Griffith, comic actor Charlie Chaplin, and her husband, actor Douglas Fairbanks) went on to co-found United Artists in 1919, she oversaw virtually every aspect of the films she starred in starting in the mid–1910s. Soon, other stars such as Lillian Gish and Gloria Swanson were following her lead. In addition, many more women ran small production companies or headed up production units within larger companies. In fact, film historian Jane Gaines has noted that, between 1916 and 1923, "women were more powerful in cinema than any other American business—to the point that more women than men owned independent production companies in 1923."[1]

In addition to producing, numerous women—at least 25, according to various sources—directed films during this time. Prominent among them was Mabel Normand, a comedienne who also starred in her films and who had an enormous influence on the young Chaplin. Another was Alice Guy Blache, who, before coming to the U.S. in the 1910s had made some of the very first films ever, beginning in 1896. Still others included Ida May Park, one of Universal's most prolific directors in the late 1910s; Ruth Ann Baldwin, who in 1916 was singled out by *Photoplay Magazine* as "one of the most capable" directors at Universal at the time[2]; Cleo Madison, whose 1916 film, *Her Bitter Cup*, is now regarded as one of the earliest feminist classics; and Nell Shipman, whose 1916 hit, *God's Country and the Woman*, established her as a leading independent producer/director.

Often, as was also true of Chaplin and other male filmmakers of the time, many of these women wore multiple hats, sometimes producing, scripting, starring in, and editing in addition to directing their films. Among all these women, perhaps the most financially successful and critically acclaimed was Lois Weber, a social moralist whose films tackled such subjects as birth control, child labor, capital punishment, and spousal abuse. In 1916, for example, Weber was the top-salaried director in the film industry, making $5,000 a week at Universal. And, after the success of her film *Where Are My Children?* that year, Universal's cost-conscious studio head Carl Laemmle was moved to say, "I would trust Miss Weber with any sum of money that she needed to make any picture that she wanted to make. I would be sure that she would bring it back. She knows the motion picture business as few people do and can drive herself as hard as anyone I have ever known."[3] Laemmle's counterparts at Paramount

Perhaps the most successful of Hollywood's early women film directors, Lois Weber (center, shown here later in her career) was one of many proven women filmmakers who found it increasingly difficult to find work by the mid–1920s. Unlike female directors and producers, however, a number of female film editors managed to keep working steadily and, in some cases, were recognized and praised for their contributions to filmmaking (Photofest).

apparently felt the same way, because, in 1920, they lured Weber away from Universal, offering her $50,000 per film plus 50 percent of the profits. The following year, she took full advantage of this deal, churning out five films.

While women were amply represented in the producing and directing ranks, they verged on dominance in another key filmmaking role, the editor, which was known at the time as the film "cutter." The story here, though, unfolds quite differently.

Initially, film directors did their own cutting, which in the first years of filmmaking was fairly rudimentary. Then about 1910—to sort through, organize, and assemble the growing amounts of film footage directors used in their moviemaking—a new breed of behind-the-scenes worker began to appear in the backrooms of film studios. The beginners in this field were called film "patchers," and eventually they worked their way up to jobs as "negative cutters." These jobs were usually tedious, requiring that workers sift through huge quantities of filmed footage by hand to find the shots that worked best and then put them together in the optimal ways to tell stories on film. Because the work was low paying and considered menial and monotonous (work akin to knitting or sewing), women—usually young women just out of high school with little or no professional training—were considered ideal candidates for the jobs.

These attitudes quickly changed in the late 1910s as Griffith and others transformed the perception of cutting from a tedious chore to a highly respected art that could literally mean the difference between a film's success and its failure. Along with his in-house cutters, the husband-and-wife team of James and Rose Smith, Griffith—in films such as *The Birth of a Nation* (1915) and *Intolerance* (1916)—perfected many of the film cutting techniques still popular today. These range from dynamic crosscutting to build suspense to the strategic use of close, medium, and long shots within a scene to further the story or intensify drama. A few years later, MGM's production head Irving Thalberg also acknowledged the role's growing prestige by giving these cutters the more elevated title of film "editors."

As the 1920s began, women were riding high in the film industry. Mary Pickford and other female producers wielded enormous clout. Lois Weber and other female directors were turning out successful films that also offered distinctive female perspectives on a variety of human experiences. Female screenwriters such as Frances Marion, Anita Loos, June Mathis, Grace Cunard, and Gene Gauntier were industriously developing scripts, many of them also finding writing an excellent entree into directing. And the cutting rooms were bursting with women, many with their eyes on long careers in the film business. In 1920, the work of all of these behind-the-camera females—many of them quite prominent and powerful—inspired the magazine, the *Ladies' Home Journal*, to predict with great fanfare that, within five years, "the feminine influence will be fully 'fifty-fifty' in 'Studio Land.'"[4]

As the 1930s began, however, both the current reality and the future prospects for women working behind the camera on Hollywood films were—with the exceptions of screenwriters and costume designers—quite bleak. Virtually all of the female producers had disappeared. Only one—a child-actress-turned-producer named Virginia Van Upp—worked regularly, overseeing films at Columbia Pictures from the early 1930s to the early 1950s. The female directors suffered a similar fate. Between the late 1920s and the early 1940s only one woman, a one-time editor named Dorothy Arzner, regularly directed films for major Hollywood studios. Then, after Arzner's retirement in 1943, no woman directed until actress Ida Lupino helmed a handful of low-budget independent films beginning in 1949. Needless to say, no woman worked regularly as a cinematographer. And film editing, once dominated by women, was increasingly viewed as a man's job. Later in her life, for example, veteran MGM editor Adrienne Fazan recalled that, in the early 1930s, her studio "didn't want me to become a feature cutter." According to her, MGM's production head Eddie Mannix had even told her that film editing was "just too tough for women," who "should go home and cook for their husbands and have babies."[5]

There were numerous reasons for this enormous change in the fortunes of women filmmakers, but perhaps the most compelling was a fundamental structural shift that occurred within film companies in the early and mid-1920s. As the cost of film production grew, these companies increasingly needed more capital with which to work. This led to both borrowing more money from Wall Street and other investors and, as smaller independents found it more difficult to stay in the game, more consolidation. In turn, the larger companies that remained became vertically integrated, controlling all aspects of the business from film development and production to film distribution and exhibition through nationwide movie theater chains. To make the films, the companies also adopted hierarchical organization structures and "assembly line" production strategies similar to the automotive and other manufacturing industries. The scrappy independent production companies where both men and women (often wearing multiple hats) would write, produce, direct, act in, and edit films gave way to the multi-layered corporate models of senior executives, production heads, and staff producers, directors, writers, cinematographers, editors, and other personnel. Increasingly, individual roles became more specialized. Directors, for example, had less and less say over other aspects of production such as writing or editing. There were exceptions, of course. Charlie Chaplin managed to remain a viable independent "auteur" for decades, and (except for one brief period) Cecil B. DeMille ran his own semi-autonomous unit within Paramount until the 1950s. But, for the most part, filmmakers had to accept the new order of things.

One aspect of this new order that was devastating for female filmmakers was that, as various work roles became more specialized, these roles also became more "gendered." While it was all right for women to remain alongside men as scriptwriters and costume designers, for example, gender became a principal determinant in who worked in such roles as producer, director, and editor. Reflecting the masculine sensibility of the industrial business model that film companies now embraced—and cognizant of the fast-growing costs of films—the new thinking was that filmmaking had become a far more serious business, one in which strong, no-nonsense men were best suited for key management, production, and technical roles. To reinforce this stereotype, some male directors (most famously DeMille and Erich von Stroheim) even adopted overtly masculine forms of dress such as jodhpurs and high laced-up boots as well as stern, often harsh, on-set behaviors. And, as Adrienne Fazan's statement about how women editors were perceived in the 1930s confirms, attitudes towards women in the cutting room had also changed dramatically since the 1910s.

Although female producers and directors virtually vanished from the scene in the 1920s (and wouldn't start reappearing until the 1970s), however, a significant number of the pioneering women editors managed to remain and, despite the odds, often become powerful forces in the film industry.

Several of them even became—among editors in general and women editors in particular—legendary figures in the profession. Five of the most notable include Anne Bauchens, Viola Lawrence, Margaret Booth, Barbara McLean, and Dorothy Spencer.

The first woman to be nominated for an editing Academy Award (for 1934's *Cleopatra*) and the first woman to win an editing Academy Award (for 1940's *North West Mounted Police*), Bauchens (1882–1967) worked mainly with Cecil B. De Mille from 1917 to 1959. Along the way, she received the nickname "Trojan Annie" because of her enormous stamina, often working 18-hour days on DeMille's complicated large-scale epics. De Mille—as strong-willed and egocentric as they came—considered

Shown here (with an unidentified crew member) on the set of her film *Outrage* (1950), actress Ida Lupino might be the only woman who directed mainstream feature films during the late 1940s and 1950s. During this time, however, women editors such as MGM's Margaret Booth and 20th Century–Fox's Barbara McLean had assumed powerful supervisory roles in major studios (RKO Pictures/ Photofest).

Bauchens an indispensable creative partner throughout their 40 years together. In fact, she was one of the very few people, male or female, who could hold her own with him in arguments over artistic decisions.

Often referred to as Hollywood's first woman film cutter, Lawrence (1894–1973) began her career holding title cards and earning a meager $5 a week as a messenger before her future husband Frank taught her the craft and she cut her first film in 1913. Five years later, she and Frank resettled in Hollywood where, during the 1920s, she worked for Universal, First National, and the independent companies of Gloria Swanson and Sam Goldwyn. She spent the rest of her career (from the early 1930s to 1962) at Columbia, where she rose to supervising editor. A two-time Academy Award nominee for editing late in her career, she also did some of her finest work on films ranging from Nicholas Ray's brilliant, devastating film noir *In a Lonely Place* (1950) to George Sidney's musical adaptation of *Pal Joey* (1957).

Beginning her career as a patcher and then a cutter for D.W. Griffith in 1915, Booth (1898–2002) later impressed producer Louis B. Mayer with her skills, eventually joined him at MGM, edited such 1930s MGM classics as *Mutiny on the Bounty* (1935) and *Camille* (1936), became the studio's supervising editor in 1937, and stayed there until 1968. Then, in her 70s, she was hired by producer Ray Stark and served as supervising editor on his films until 1986, when she was 88 years old. Throughout her career, Booth was regarded as one of the best editors in the film business. In fact, in one 1977 poll, in which 100 leading film editors were asked to rank the top editors in the history of the medium, she placed number three. She is also the only film editor to receive an Honorary Oscar for her lifetime of work.

Nicknamed "Bobbie," McLean (1903–1996) began as an editing assistant for silent film director Rex Ingram in the early 1920s. A decade later, Darryl Zanuck called her "one of the best editors in town" and was soon her boss at the newly merged 20th Century–Fox, where she was regularly assigned to the studio's prestige pictures and received seven editing Academy Award nominations between 1936 and 1951, winning an Oscar in 1945. In 1949, she was promoted to chief of the studio's editing department and held that position until she retired in 1969. According to many accounts, McLean was considered one of Zanuck's most respected and trusted confidantes, often deferring to her opinion on controversial studio matters by beginning with the words, "Bobbie says...." As a further indication of his trust and confidence in McLean, Zanuck prohibited directors or producers from entering the studio's editing department to meddle during post-production. This was—he let it be known—McLean's domain.

Beginning as an assistant editor for Frank Capra in 1926, Spencer (1909–2002) soon graduated to editor and worked on more than 70 films until her retirement in 1979. Famous for her innovative editing techniques in John Ford's *Stagecoach* (1939) and for her tight, suspenseful editing in Ford's *My Darling Clementine* (1946), she also edited films for Alfred Hitchcock, Ernst Lubitsch, Elia Kazan, Joseph L. Mankiewicz, Raoul Walsh, and other iconic Hollywood directors. A four-time Academy Award nominee for editing, Spencer—who developed a reputation as a superb editor of action films—finished her career working on such 1970s disaster films as *Earthquake* and *The Concorde...Airport '79*.

These five were certainly not the only female editing luminaries working in Hollywood during the "classic" era from the 1920s until the 1960s. Just a few other distinguished female editors include Rose Smith (*The Birth of a Nation, Intolerance*) Dorothy Arzner (*Blood and Sand, The*

Covered Wagon), Blanche Sewell (*Grand Hotel, Queen Christina, The Wizard of Oz*), and Adrienne Fazan (*An American in Paris, Singing in the Rain, Gigi*).

～

All of these successful careers lead to an inevitable, and fascinating, question: How—even after women were systematically purged from producing, directing, and editing positions beginning in the 1920s—did a core of female film editors manage not only to survive but also to be highly successful?

While each one of these female editors has an individual story, many share similarities that can help us piece together why and how they were able to remain and, in some cases such as Booth and McLean, become powerful film industry figures.

First, several of them had established themselves as capable, respected practitioners well before woman editors were marginalized in the 1920s. This is certainly true of Lawrence, Smith, Bauchens, and Booth, who all started in the 1910s. This, however, doesn't explain why they and others remained when established women producers and directors could no longer find work. The reason here could reside in the role of the editor itself. Not nearly as visible as the director or producer, not the "auteur" (or author) of the film, and not a major management/leadership position, a woman editor was—simply put—less conspicuous and thus less threatening in the new masculine order.

Second, early in their careers several of these women won the trust, support, and protection of some of the industry's most powerful male figures. From 1917 until his death in 1959, for example, Cecil B. DeMille made it abundantly clear that he would only work with Bauchens and no one else. In fact, when he signed new film contracts, it was always spelled out that she—and only she—would edit his films. When she went to work at MGM, Booth quickly earned the respect and support of production head Irving Thalberg and studio head Louis B. Mayer. McLean found herself in a similar position with studio head Darryl F. Zanuck at 20th Century–Fox as did Lawrence with studio head Harry Cohn at Columbia.

Third, as women such as Booth, McLean, and Lawrence assumed positions of greater authority within their respective companies, they were able to mentor other women and, in the process, protect them from discrimination. Sewell and Fazan, for example, both worked for Booth for many years at MGM, and Spencer worked for McLean from the 1940s to the 1960s at 20th Century–Fox.

Fourth, these women were all extremely capable. Together, for example, Booth, Bauchens, McLean, Lawrence, Spencer, and Fazan received a total of 20 Academy Award nominations for their work. What makes this even more remarkable is that Booth, McLean, and Lawrence also spent decades in supervisory capacities guiding other editors, both men and women, to numerous additional Academy Award nominations and wins. As well as awards, another measure of the value these women brought to the filmmaking process is how often major directors sought them out to edit their films. Spencer, for example, edited multiple films for John Ford, Alfred Hitchcock, Elia Kazan, Joseph L. Mankiewicz, Fred Zinnemann, Ernst Lubitsch, Raoul Walsh, and many other highly regarded directors.

Fifth, as well as being capable, these women were extremely dedicated to their work. Bauchens' nickname "Trojan Annie," for example, was in recognition for the 18-hour days she often spent editing DeMille pictures in her early years. Even when she was in her 70s she would, when needed, put in 14-hour workdays. It is worth noting, too, that many of these women made work a higher priority than the traditional female role of motherhood. Bauchens and Booth, for example, never married, and McLean, although she married, never had children.

Finally, some of these women made special efforts to fit into the predominantly male world—to be, as Booth once described herself, "one of the boys."[6] Even though she appeared very lady-like, for example, Booth prided herself on her tough, no-nonsense manner. McLean, who could more than hold her own with Zanuck and other strong male personalities at 20th Century–Fox, went by the more masculine sounding nickname "Bobbie."

Together, these and other women also did something quite extraordinary for younger women who, in the decades that followed, aspired to be film editors. They served as role models, proving that, despite gender-based prejudices, women could nevertheless succeed and even thrive in their profession. In the 1970s and 1980s, as these gender prejudices were just beginning to break down in Hollywood and elsewhere, for example, aspiring female directors had—outside of Arzner and Lupino—virtually no role models who were working after the mid–1920s. Aspiring female editors, however, had more than a dozen who had proven that women in their profession could win Academy Awards, receive other major industry honors, make essential contributions to films that would become classics, supervise large teams of editors, and, at least within the tight-knit editing community, achieve iconic status.

~

As the studio system collapsed in the 1960s and a new film industry emerged from the old, new generations of women were entering the editing field and picking up where the older generations had left off. In many cases, they have been innovators who have brought new perspectives to the art and dramatically changed the ways films are made. Among these were—and are—women such as Dede Allen, Verna Fields, Anne V. Coates, and Thelma Schoonmaker.

One of the most influential editors of the 1960s and 1970s, Allen (1923–2010) cut such classic films as *The Hustler* (1961), *Bonnie and Clyde* (1967), *Dog Day Afternoon* (1975), and *Reds* (1981). She had an extended collaboration with director Arthur Penn and also worked with Elia Kazan, Robert Wise, and Warren Beatty. Influenced in part by the French New Wave editing techniques, Allen pioneered the use of audio overlaps and utilized emotional jump cuts—stylistic flourishes that brought energy and realism to characters. In her later years, she increasingly worked with younger editors, mentoring them in their work.

Affectionately known as the "mother cutter" for such "New-Hollywood" directors as Peter Bogdanovich, Steven Spielberg, and George Lucas in the 1970s, Fields (1918–1982) rose to prominence for her innovative work in such films as *What's Up, Doc?*, *Jaws* (for which she won an Oscar), and *American Graffiti*. Based on her work, she was named Vice President of Feature Production at Universal Studios in 1976, becoming one of the film industry's first high-level woman executives.

Beginning as a cutting room assistant in 1948, Coates (1925–) edited her first film in 1952 and her most recent, *Fifty Shades of Grey*, in 2015. Along the way, she has edited more than 50 films such as *Lawrence of Arabia* (1962), for which she received an Academy Award; *Becket* (1964); *The Elephant Man* (1980); *In the Line of Fire* (1993); *Out of Sight* (1998); and *Erin Brokovich* (2000). Relocating from London to Hollywood in the mid–1980s, Coates, like Allen and Fields, has spent many years working with and mentoring young directors.

Although she has edited films for other directors, Schoonmaker (1940–) has, since 1967, worked mostly with Martin Scorsese, receiving seven Academy Award nominations and winning three Oscars for her work on *Raging Bull* (1980), *The Aviator* (2004) and *The Departed* (2006). Known for a highly innovative, often flamboyant technique that fits Scorsese's distinctive artistic vision like a glove, she is one of the most respected editors working today.

Since the 1970s, numerous other women have shined as editors as well. Just a few of these include Marcia Lucas (*American Graffiti*, *Star Wars*),

Carol Littleton (*E.T., Body Heat, Places in the Heart*), Susan Morse (*Manhattan, Hannah and Her Sisters*), Lisa Fruchtman (*Apocalypse Now, The Right Stuff*), and Sally Menke (*Pulp Fiction, Inglourious Basterds*).

The word *numerous* is not hyperbole, either. In recent years, women have consistently made up about 20 percent of the Motion Picture Editors Guild. In 2012, for example, they represented about 1500, or 21 percent, of its 7,300 members. This is in sharp contrast to the American Society of Cinematographers, which, in the same year, had more than 330 members, only eight of which, less than 3 percent, are women.[7]

In addition, the film community has consistently recognized the high quality of the contributions women editors have made. One popular gauge of success within the industry, for example, is Academy Award nominations, and, when we break certain categories down by gender, we can make some fascinating discoveries. In the entire 88 years of the Academy Awards, for example, more than 430 Best Director nominations and 87 Oscars have gone to men while only four nominations along with one lone Oscar (to Kathryn Bigelow in 2010 for *The Hurt Locker*) have gone to women. In the Best Cinematographer category, no woman has ever been nominated, let alone won. In the Best Editor category, however, women have received nearly 70 nominations and 13 wins since this award was first presented in 1935. These include several multiple nominees such as Barbara McLean and Thelma Schoonmaker (seven each), Anne Coates (five), and Anne Bauchens and Dorothy Spencer (four each).

Instituted in 1988, the American Cinema Editors (ACE) Career Achievement Award offers another fascinating assessment. For example, in the first eight years the award was given (two are awarded each year), five women—McLean, Spencer, Booth, Allen, and Coates—were among the first 16 recipients. If they were still alive during these years, Bauchens, Lawrence, and Fazan would undoubtedly been strong candidates for the award as well.

Equally intriguing is a list the *Motion Picture Editors Guild* released in 2012 revealing the results of a members' poll of the 75 best-edited films of all time. The top eight included:

1. *Raging Bull* (1980)
2. *Citizen Kane* (1941)
3. *Apocalypse Now* (1979)
4. *All That Jazz* (1979)
5. *Bonnie and Clyde* (1967)
6. *The Godfather* (1972)

7. *Lawrence of Arabia* (1962).
8. *Jaws* (1975)

Of these eight, women edited four: *Raging Bull* (Schoonmaker), *Bonnie and Clyde* (Allen), *Lawrence of Arabia* (Coates) and *Jaws* (Fields). In addition, *Apocalypse Now* was co-edited by a woman, Lisa Fruchtman.

~

Clearly, women editors have had, and continue to have, an enormous impact both on the editing profession in particular and on the quality and character of American films in general. And just as clearly, their contributions to so many great films lead to a number of irresistible—if probably unanswerable—questions:

- Are there specific reasons why so many directors—the overwhelming majority of whom are male—have preferred to work with woman editors?
- Are there specific gender-based strengths women bring to the editing role?
- Is there a distinctive female voice in editing that ultimately influences the character of the finished film?

Tackling these questions involves a number of caveats. Certainly since the 1920s, the majority of Hollywood film editors, supervising editors, award winners, and editing icons have been men. They range from Ralph Dawson, whose brilliant editing in the classic 1938 film, *The Adventures of Robin Hood*, earned him his third editing Academy Award in four years, to Michael Kahn, whose celebrated collaboration with Steven Spielberg over more than 30 years has led to a record eight Academy Award nominations and three Oscars. And they include such other editing "greats" as Elmo Williams, Ralph E. Winters, Sam O'Steen, Walter Murch, Joel Cox, and many, many more. So, while women have been ably represented in film editing since the 1910s, they have not been dominant in the field since the 1920s. Most directors work with male editors.

Regardless of gender, directors have also forged different kinds of working arrangements with editors. Many—from DeMille to Scorsese—have preferred to work closely and collaboratively with a single editor on film after film. Others, especially during the studio system's heyday, often didn't have the luxury of choice; sometimes they were assigned an editor, and frequently they had only limited access to the editing process. Directors have varied widely, too, on the amount of creative freedom they will allow their editors to have. Dorothy Spencer, who worked with dozens of different directors during her 50-year career, once commented on this, saying that, while some directors (such as John Ford and Mark Robson) gave her a lot of room to be creative, others (whom she didn't name) could be quite autocratic and restrictive. Often, veteran editors working with younger directors, can, because of their greater experience, exert a greater influence over the process. This was certainly true of Verna Fields in the 1970s; Dede Allen in the 1980s, early 1990s, and 2000s; and Anne V. Coates in the 1990s and 2000s.

Given all these variables, let's look at the questions again.

First, are there specific reasons why so many male directors have preferred to work with female editors?

One very disarming answer came from Quentin Tarantino in a 2004 interview. "When I was doing my first movie the only thing I knew is that I wanted a female editor," he said. "Because I just felt a female editor would be more nurturing to the movie and to me…. They wouldn't be trying to shove their agenda or win their battles with me. They would be nurturing me through this process."[8] Certainly, he takes great stock in the widely accepted "feminine" qualities that make men feel more relaxed and supported when they are with women rather than other men. And curiously, Thelma Schoonmaker, who has worked closely with Martin Scorsese for decades, shares similar thoughts. "Filmmaking is a collaboration," she noted in 2013. "People have to learn how to deal with their own egos and work as partners. And I think women are probably better at that [than men]."[9]

Jason Reitman, who directed *Thank You for Smoking* (2005), *Juno* (2007), and *Up in the Air* (2009), works regularly with female editor Dana Glauberman and is also one of many directors to claim that the director-editor relationship can take on many of the characteristics of a marriage. "As a director," he has said, "you spend many months with hundreds of people, balancing everyone's ideas and dealing with constant input, and then literally overnight you're in small box—a jail cell—with one person, and the two of you have to carry the film across the finish line. And it often does feel like a marriage. Who do I want to spend all that time with? You spend more months editing than you do shooting and you do it in a tiny room sitting a few feet from each other. There are very few people on earth that you want to share that sort of proximity and time with, so you better have good chemistry."[10]

Another answer has come from several other contemporary male directors who consciously seek out women editors, citing the need for, and value of, a female perspective in the cutting room. In addition to Tarantino, Scorsese, and Reitman, these include Lawrence Kasden, who has spoken about the importance of having a woman's point of view when editing scenes involving romance or sex, and Woody Allen, who has worked with women editors (Susan Morse and Alisa Lepselter) on every one of his films since *Manhattan* in 1979.

Second, are there specific gender-based strengths women bring to the editing role?

This is always a tricky subject because it often means making generalizations. But, Dr. Michael Mills, who teaches psychology at Loyola-Marymount University in Southern California, has noted that, at first glance, editing might seem to be a slightly better fit for men. In addition to "empathizing," more of a female preference, Mills has said that editing involves working alone for long periods and constant "systematizing," both male preferences. He also notes, however, that "to be a good film editor, you need to select the best takes, and women are better at reading and interpreting facial expressions of emotions than are men. My guess is that perhaps high levels of both systematizing and empathizing are characteristic of the best film editors."[11]

Editor Mary Jo Markey, who regularly works with director J.J. Abrams, heartily agrees. "Empathy is one of the most important things I bring," she has said. "Making the action work depends on your investment in the characters. I won't say this about all women, but I do think I was raised like a lot of women in my generation, not so much to be seen and not heard, but encouraged to be observers. And I do think it creates a quality where you look at people and think about what they're thinking and experiencing, and that's kind of what I do when I'm cutting."[12]

Editor Dana Glauberman has approached this subject a bit more cautiously. "It's easy to say we, as women, are a stronger talent at it, simply because people think we are more nurturing than men are, we are more sensitive than men are," she has noted. She added that there are obviously many talented male editors, too, "some of whom I've learned a great deal from."[13]

Third, is there a distinctive female voice or perspective in editing that ultimately influences the character of the finished film?

Perhaps the most appropriate short answer is: Depending on numerous variables, yes.

When describing her work on *Up in the Air* in 2009, for example, Glauberman offered this glimpse on how her editing helped to shape the nonverbal moments in the first meeting between the two main characters played by George Clooney and Vera Farmiga, who soon become lovers. "In a scene like that, there is a sort of playfulness that goes on," she said. "There were little looks that they gave each other. Sometimes I stayed a beat longer on a take to get that little sparkle in their eyes…. You can see a lot of playfulness in the quick cuts back and forth when they are teasing each other, but then there are also certain moments that Vera would give a little raise of an eyebrow, or George would give the same thing. Those tiny nuances are really helpful to show their character and show what they are after."[14]

Here, the editor's specifically female talents for reading body language and non-verbal cues while also bringing empathy to the situation are obvious. By making the editing choices she did, Glauberman clearly influenced the character of the film by giving greater resonance to the attraction the two characters share, building in more tension between them, and even improving the quality of the two acting performances audiences ultimately saw in the finished film. Clearly a good male editor would have been able to do something similar, but editing with this kind of perspective is a talent in which many acknowledge that women have an edge.

Another variable is Glauberman's considerable talent. It is unlikely that many other editors, females included, would have been able to cut that scene quite as well.

Still another variable is the amount of creative freedom she has. While many editors have the ability to dramatically influence the character of the finished film, virtually all editors work for, and must ultimately comply with, the film's author, its director. In Glauberman's case, she regularly works with a director, Jason Reitman, who respects and supports her judgment. But, if a director—as Dorothy Spencer admitted to experiencing frequently—is autocratic and restrictive, then an editor has far less creative freedom. While a talented editor might have the ability to bring a great deal of personal insight and perspective to a film, he or she might not always have the opportunity to do so.

∼

When asked why there are so many women film editors today, Mary Jo Markey once put it in the plainest possible terms. "A lot of women go into editing," she said, "because women go into editing."[15]

And—we might add—they always have.

Since the earliest days of the film industry this has been the case, and even through many decades when women were marginalized in many key filmmaking roles including editing, this remained the case. Still, women editors resisted the pressures to quit, excelled in their work, sometimes rose to powerful supervisory positions, and served as role models for other women who came afterwards. In the process, they forged a proud tradition, one that clearly lives on in today's ranks of film editors.

The chapters that follow delve more deeply into this story by focusing in on the several of the key figures in this tradition and their professional stories. In particular, they attempt to answer such questions as:

- Just who were (and are) some of these key women, many of whom have now reached legendary status within this profession?
- What personal styles and distinctive talents did they bring to their work?
- What gender-based challenges did they have to face, and how did each of them address these challenges?
- What classic films did they work on, and how did they contribute to these films' successes?
- What impact have they had on the U.S. film industry overall?

The choices of the women featured in this book are, of course, subjective, and no doubt others familiar with this subject may question certain inclusions or omissions. That, obviously, is their privilege. Since relatively little has been written about many of these women, there is clearly a need for more research and analysis of their lives and contributions to the film industry. If someone has been omitted or not discussed to a reader's satisfaction, the opportunity to correct the oversight is always there.

~

Although several of the stories in this book begin well over a century ago and a few end more than a half-century ago, they all, in some way, resonate with us now. All focus on determined, talented, and often inspiring women who pursued challenging creative work and achieved great success in environments that weren't always hospitable toward them. In addition, all involve people whose influence is still very much with us— interpretive artists who have played pivotal roles both in making scores of classic films and in shaping the essential nature and ongoing development of the U.S. film industry. Their names might not be listed on a particular editing credit, but there absolutely is a bit of Margaret Booth, Barbara McLean, Dede Allen, and the other women featured in these chapters in every film we see today.

1

"Trojan Annie"

Anne Bauchens' Epic 40-Year Partnership with Cecil B. DeMille

In early 1914, William deMille,[1] a prominent New York playwright who had recently moved west to become part of Southern California's bustling, upstart motion picture business, took his secretary, a very proper, soft-spoken young woman named Anne Bauchens (1882–1967), to a movie screening. The film, a western called *The Squaw Man*, had been co-produced and co-directed by William's flamboyant younger brother, Cecil. Cecil's first attempt at filmmaking, it was also the first feature-length film ever made within the geographic boundaries of Hollywood. Within weeks, *The Squaw Man* would become an enormous box office hit, both launching Cecil's career and laying some of the groundwork for what would eventually become Paramount Pictures. On that particular day, however, it also had a deep impact on the impressionable Bauchens. "I was a very naïve young lady," she recalled decades later. "I had never been among the literary and more intelligent groups [so] I just thought it was the most wonderful thing I'd seen."[2]

The experience changed Bauchens' life. In addition to working as William's secretary in his new role as a writer-director, she helped out wherever she was needed and soaked up everything she could about this fascinating new art form. For a brief period, she worked as a production assistant, literally creating the position of script clerk, the person who records every detail of individual film shots so they can later be matched in the editing process. Then, more and more, she found herself drawn to the cutting room, where the finished films were actually put together. At first, she learned about cutting from William. Then, one day in 1917 in the cutting room the two brothers sometimes shared, she looked over to Cecil and said: "Some day I'm going to cut your pictures." At this, Cecil—who had little patience for what he perceived as impertinence—snapped back: "No one will *ever* cut a picture of mine, except me!"[3]

Two months later, however, Cecil asked Bauchens to replace an assistant director who had dropped out of a film, a drama called *We Can't Have Everything* (1918). As well as assisting DeMille on the production, she helped with the editing. "I made suggestions when they occurred to me," Bauchens said. "Evidently, Mr. DeMille liked them, for he said that maybe I would like to try cutting. I cut his next picture and stayed on the job."[4]

Beginning her editing career in 1917, Anne Bauchens worked mainly with producer/director Cecil B. DeMille until his death in 1959. The first woman ever to be nominated for a Best Film Editing Academy Award (for 1934's *Cleopatra*), she is also the first women editor ever to win an Oscar (for 1940's *North West Mounted Police*) (© Paramount Pictures).

And, as Bauchens added, she "stayed and stayed."[5]

For the next 40 years, from the late 1910s until the late 1950s, Bauchens and Cecil B. DeMille were joined at the hip—or maybe it would be more fitting to say, "joined at the editor's moviola." During that time, she edited every one of the 39 films DeMille made. At DeMille's request, she was also on the set constantly to watch how scenes were shot and advise on how those shots could be edited together. In between DeMille projects, she edited more than 20 films for other directors as well, including such respected figures as Victor Fleming, William Dieterle, Mitchell Leisen, and John Farrow. But, when DeMille needed her, she was always there. In fact, every time he negotiated a new film deal, DeMille made certain that Bauchens was a part of the package. He never edited, he made it clear, with anyone else or without her.

Along the way, Bauchens also earned the respect of many others in the film business. In 1935, the first year the Academy of Motion Picture Arts and Sciences presented an Oscar for editing, she was a nominee for her work on DeMille's *Cleopatra* (1934) with Claudette Colbert. Six years later, for her work in DeMille's action-adventure film *North West Mounted Police* (1940) with Gary Cooper, she became the very first woman ever to win a Best Editing Oscar. Then, in the 1950s, when she was in her 70s, she received two more Academy editing nominations for her work on two of DeMille's most ambitious films, *The Greatest Show on Earth* (1952) and *The Ten Commandments* (1956). For her work on *The Greatest Show on Earth*, she also received the very first ACE Critics Award from the prestigious film industry association, American Cinema Editors.

Along with her fierce loyalty to DeMille, Bauchens brought several other strengths to the relationship critical to their successful partnership.

One was her legendary stamina, which earned her the nickname "Trojan Annie." Because DeMille's pictures were often big, complicated spectacles that required much more editing work than most films, she often put in extremely long hours in the editing room. In the 1920s, for example, she would routinely work 16- to 18-hour days when a film was in post-production. And, even in the 1950s when she was well into her 70s, she would work 10- to 14-hour days. Rather than stoically bearing this burden, she seemed to relish the challenge, saying in an interview in the 1950s that the 14-hour days she was putting in at the time "were nothing compared to the 18-hour stints Mr. DeMille and I would chalk up."[6]

Another strength was her fearlessness in opposing the often imperious, always intimidating DeMille when the two disagreed about their work. As Charles West, who headed Paramount's editing department, once said, "Annie and DeMille did not always see eye to eye. They usually went through about five weeks of disagreement and out of it came good pictures. Annie, as everyone knew, was very strong-minded and stubborn. So was DeMille. One of them always had to bring the other around because neither of them would give in."[7] Obviously, she had earned and maintained his respect to an extent that only a handful of other people ever did.

Yet another strength, as this implies, was her ability. As DeMille noted in a memoir he wrote near the end of his life, "She is still best film editor I know."[8] And her Oscar, three additional Academy Award nominations, and recognition from the American Cinema Editors all certainly confirm the high regard of her editing peers. Only two women received Best Editing Oscars during Bauchens' long career, and she was one of them.

Assessing her, however, must also involve assessing DeMille, who worked side by side with her in the editing room on nearly all the films they did together. Although he had a genius for staging spectacle and other talents essential to telling the stories he wanted to tell, he was, according to many accounts, someone who needed a good editor. As the legendary Margaret Booth, the long-time head of MGM's editing department, noted (with characteristic prickliness) in a 1965 interview: "DeMille was a bad editor, I thought, and made [Bauchens] look like a bad editor. I think Anne really would have been a good editor, but she had to put up with him—which was something."[9] While this appraisal seems overly harsh, it clearly suggests DeMille's considerable reliance on Bauchens' editing judgment and skills. Perhaps, without DeMille, Bauchens could have been an even better editor and blossomed more on her own. But then, without DeMille, she might not have ever been challenged to the extent that she was and inspired to meet the many demands she did. In any case—and regardless of Margaret Booth's sharp words—Bauchens remains one of Hollywood's most celebrated and respected film editors from the 1920s to the 1950s.

A Life Largely Lived in the DeMille Universe

Unlike many of her fellow female film editor pioneers who started when they were quite young, Bauchens was past 30 when she first stepped into a cutting room.

Born in St. Louis in 1882 (or possibly 1881, as a few sources state), she was the only daughter of Luella McKee Bauchens and Otto Bauchens, who worked as a railroad porter. When she was a young woman, she aspired to become an actress and studied for a time under a local actor-director named Hugh Ford, while also studying gymnastics and dancing and working to support herself as a telephone operator for the city newspaper, the *St. Louis Post-Dispatch*. Eventually, she left for New York to pursue acting on the Broadway stage. Finding those jobs elusive, she went to work as a secretary for a real estate firm and, when the firm went bankrupt, was hired as William deMille's secretary. When William's brother Cecil convinced him to come to Hollywood in the mid–1910s, she came as well, and, by 1917, she had become the sole editor on Cecil B. DeMille films, a post she would hold until his death in January 1959.

Today, the DeMille name has become synonymous with the kind of ornate, sumptuously produced, and perhaps garish Biblical and historical epics such as his two versions of *The Ten Commandments* (1923 and 1956), *The King of Kings* (1926), *The Sign of the Cross* (1932), *Cleopatra* (1934), *The Crusades* (1935), and *Sampson and Delilah* (1948). Over the course of his career, however, he was far more versatile, working in various genres from contemporary melodramas to westerns, to comedies of manners, to action-dramas such as *The Greatest Show on Earth*. At the same time—like Chaplin, Griffith, Ford, Hitchcock, and a handful of other Hollywood directors whose careers overlapped with his—he was also a genuine auteur, an author whose films usually reflected his values, vision of the world, and personal style. As much as anyone, except perhaps Chaplin after 1920, DeMille also enjoyed great autonomy. A showman first, he had an excellent sense of what the public wanted and how to package it for mass consumption. With only a handful of exceptions, his films were hits, and sometimes—as in the case of his second *The Ten Commandments*—among the most popular films ever made. Because a DeMille film usually meant big box office, Paramount essentially allowed him to be an independent in-house producer for most of his career. And, at several points in the studio's history, DeMille could rightfully claim credit for singlehandedly keeping its account books in the black. For more than 40 years, he was a towering Hollywood figure.

In the decades since DeMille's films were made, however, his work has not held up as well in film studies circles as the work of other auteur directors such as Chaplin, Ford, and Hitchcock. For contemporary audiences especially, his concerns and outlook seem dated and difficult to relate to. Given this limitation, however, his films often exhibit such a passionate point of view and such daring and dynamic showmanship that they are almost impossible not to respond to. As Scott Eyman noted in his excellent 2010 biography of the director, "DeMille's movies were a pure expression of DeMille, defiant throwbacks to another century's beliefs and styles, yet too audaciously conceived and executed ever to be entirely dismissed."[10]

Like other powerful Hollywood figures, DeMille had his entourage, an inner circle of people from employees to family members and friends he repeatedly turned to for assistance and advice. Unlike most other Hollywood figures, however, most of DeMille's most trusted advisors—sometimes referred to as his "harem"—were women. In addition to Bauchens, there were (among others) DeMille's wife Constance, his daughter Cecilia, pioneer screenwriter Jeanie Macpherson, and his private secretary Gladys Rosson. The nature of these relationships differed widely. At various times, for example, Macpherson and Rosson (along with DeMille stock company actress Julia Faye) also served as DeMille's mistresses. But, whether there was a sexual component to the relationship or not, all of these women shared an intense life-long loyalty to him, and, in various ways, he reciprocated.

Despite DeMille's tendency to become involved with women in his inner circle, there is no evidence that he and Bauchens, who never married, ever shared anything more than work and friendship. In fact, in his memoirs, DeMille shared a humorous story about how—in 40 years of working together—he had only stirred her passion once. As the story went, a car DeMille was driving with Bauchens as a passenger spun out so its back end was hanging out over a cliff. "I hung onto the brake," he remembered, "and Anne threw her arms around my neck and said, 'Oh, Cecil!' That was Annie's only burst of emotion toward me in the forty years we've been working together."[11]

As DeMille's editor, Bauchens held one of the most important posts in the DeMille universe. And, considering both the scale and complexity of many of the productions they worked on together and DeMille's stubborn personality, hers was no easy task.

Given that the two nearly always edited his films together, it is almost impossible to point to specific sequences and moments and say precisely that they are the results of Bauchens' inputs or of DeMille's. But, considering the egocentric, often overbearing DeMille's enormous reliance on Bauchens for so long, it is not unreasonable to assume that she brought a great deal of value to the equation. He could not have done quite what he did without her, and he knew it.

During the 1920s, the films varied between contemporary comedies of manners to some of the first notable examples of the films DeMille would ultimately be best remembered for: his big and often very plodding and preachy Biblical epics.

One of these was his first version of *The Ten Commandments* (1923).

More than two hours long, the first one-third is a large-scale epic telling the Bible story of Moses leading the Israelites out of Egypt and receiving the commandments from God on Mount Sinai. Then, quite awkwardly, the final two-thirds is a modern day morality tale of two brothers, one who follows the commandments and becomes a poor but virtuous carpenter and the other who consistently breaks the commandments, becomes very rich, and is ultimately led to ruin and tragedy.

Another of these epics, one that is far more compelling, is *The King of Kings* (1927), DeMille's version of the last few weeks of Jesus Christ's life, culminating in the Last Supper, Crucifixion, and Resurrection. A full two hours and 35 minutes long, it is filled with moments that, while tinged with hokum, remain quite powerful, even for those who are not necessarily fans of Bible stories.

One scene, very effectively orchestrated by DeMille and Bauchens, is when Jesus gives a young blind girl sight. It begins about 16 minutes into the film. At this point, viewers have been introduced to numerous characters, but they have not seen Jesus himself.

The girl, dressed in rags and whose eyes seem eternally closed, has been led to Jesus' mother Mary, whom she asks to take her to Jesus so he can perform a miracle on her and give her sight. Mary then leads the girl to Jesus, who is still off-camera, presents her, and leaves. The film cuts to a closer shot of the girl, who says (in the inter-title): "Lord, I have never seen the flowers nor the light. Wilt thou open my eyes?" Behind her we see two apostles, both watching intently. The film cuts back to the girl, her eyes still closed. The space around her head begins to go dark. Then suddenly—and quite unexpectedly—the film cuts to total blackness. Just like the girl, we in the audience cannot see a thing. We are now effectively inside her head, seeing from her point of view. After a second or two, a light—first dim and then brightening—shines down from right to left across the screen. Then, over the light, appear the words: "I am come a light into the world—that whosoever shall believe in me shall not abide in darkness." Cut back to the girl in close-shot, now with some diffused light around her. The light becomes brighter, and she seems to recede into it. Cut back to the girl's point of view, which is now an image of diffused light filling the screen that is slowly but constantly shifting. Cut back to the girl, now filled with great excitement. Cut to an inter-title: "Oh—oh! I begin to see—the light!" Cut back to the girl, now wringing her hands with joy and excitement. Cut back to her point of view. At first we see a big, sun-like circle of light filling much of screen. Then, slowly the face of Jesus begins to appear in this light, as if emerging from it, and becomes more and more distinct. The light recedes, but not entirely. Around Jesus a halo remains. Finally, the girl—still drenched in light—opens her eyes. Cut to Jesus. He nods, smiles kindly, and holds out his hands out to her. She holds her arms out to him. Cut to the film's first two-shot of both the girl and Jesus as he holds her arms with his hands and then hugs her.

What an entrance!

While the subject matter depicted here may not resonate with many modern viewers, this remains a very moving scene 90 years after it was first screened. It owes much, of course, to the film's clever scripting, which waits until this point to introduce Jesus; DeMille's careful and very sensitive direction; and the very honest and moving acting of eight-year-old Muriel McCormac as the blind girl. But, the editing is what brings it all together and makes it work so well. While the scene, which lasts approximately four minutes, includes lots of cuts to keep the action crisp and engaging, it also includes a good share of leisurely fades and dissolves that allow the audience to fully absorb the enormity of what is happening in the young girl's life … and to visually reinforce the film's theme that Jesus is indeed the light of the world. Upon repeated viewings, the timing of every cut, dissolve, and fade seems perfect. Nothing is too long. Nothing is too abrupt.

The coming of both sound films and the Great Depression in the late 1920s presented some new challenges to Bauchens and DeMille.

Like her fellow editors, Bauchens had to learn how to cut for what was essentially a new art form, the talking picture. This meant developing new editing strategies, especially for scenes heavily dependent on spoken dialogue. The editing rhythms prevalent in silent films, which used relatively little dialogue and inter-titles, for example, had to be rethought entirely. In addition, film editors now had to work very closely with a new kind of studio employee called the sound editor, and relationships could often be highly competitive and downright adversarial.

DeMille had to stay relevant as well, and in 1932 he released *The Sign of the Cross,* a film that has in many ways defined what we today call "a DeMille picture." In keeping with what had worked for him in the 1920s, this was a lavish epic set in ancient times with a strong Christian message that also included a large cast and sumptuous, complex set pieces. But now—during what we now know as the Pre-Code Era, a brief period when filmmakers constantly pushed the envelope when it came to challenging restrictions on screen sex, violence, and other taboos—he went to new lengths to titillate as well as preach. In other words, as he extolled the Christian virtues to audiences, he also thrilled them with scenes that were more overtly sexual in nature and more brutally violent than he ever had. This was of course brazenly hypocritical, but it was also highly successful. *The Sign of the Cross* was an enormous hit with audiences who wanted to have it both ways: to be praised for their virtue while also getting a voyeuristic look at some of the very exciting things they were missing out on because they were virtuous.

This film also presented some intriguing new challenges for Bauchens, who, as usual, had to make it all work.

One involved a famous scene from the film, in which the beautiful and manipulative Empress Poppaea (wonderfully played by Claudette Colbert) bathes in asses' milk. Colbert is clearly topless, and the scene goes on for several minutes. For the entire time, the intent is to tease viewers by showing as much breast as possible without revealing Colbert's nipples. With a great deal of precision cutting, Bauchens and DeMille achieve this effect. But, more important, the cutting appears very natural and the scene flows smoothly. Combined with Colbert's fine acting, what could easily have appeared forced and silly comes off as quite credible.

Another scene involved a much-talked-about lesbian dance, in which a decadent female character sings and dances around and periodically caresses the virtuous Christian heroine's lovely body. Here, there is a dynamic quality to the cutting that gives this scene an eroticism that still holds up today. Quickly, the film cuts between the dance and the various characters watching it and, in the process, becoming quite aroused. Again, anything less than first-rate editing would have diminished the effect, making the eroticism seem silly.

Still another challenge came at the end of film when viewers are treated to grand-scale carnage and atrocities in the Roman Colosseum. Sometimes, too, this is mixed in with moments of titillation, as in a couple of scenes when beautiful young women, clothed only in slim garlands of flowers strategically wrapped around their bodies, are, first, about to be devoured by crocodiles and then accosted by a gorilla. It's all quite bizarre, but it's also clear that, without precise, quickly timed edits, the whole purpose of evoking horror would have been undermined and the film's overall dramatic impact greatly diminished.

While it has its flaws and dated aspects, *The Sign of the Cross* was nevertheless a very daring film to make. To even attempt it took a supremely confident director. But, to succeed, especially in many scenes that could easily have gone wrong, it also took a supremely capable editor.

The success of *The Sign of the Cross* led to *Cleopatra* in 1934, and throughout the 1930s and much of the 1940s, DeMille turned out films—

most of them hits—at a steady clip. Many of his better films during these years, such as *The Plainsman* (1936), *Union Pacific* (1938), and *North West Mounted Police* (1940)—for which Bauchens received her Oscar—were westerns. Even though Paramount demanded that she also edit for other directors between DeMille pictures, Bauchens remained deeply involved in every DeMille effort, observing and advising during shooting as well as editing.

After a rare box-office disappointment, an American colonial era action-adventure story called *The Unconquered* (1947), DeMille, needing a hit, returned to his tried-and-true formula of lavish, sexy Biblical epics with *Samson and Delilah* (1949). The strategy worked. Although the film seems stiff, stodgy, and a bit silly today, it was hugely successful when released, ultimately reaping box office receipts of more than $25 million on a budget of only $3 million.

By the early 1950s, both DeMille and Bauchens, who by then had both turned 70, were showing signs of slowing down (at least by their standards). They would have only two more films left: *The Greatest Show on Earth* (1952) and a remake of *The Ten Commandments* (1956). Both efforts were hugely popular, and both received numerous Academy Award nominations, especially in technical categories. Bauchens was nominated for Best Editor for her work in each film, bringing her lifetime total to four nominations with one win. And DeMille received his only competitive Academy Award, as producer of *The Greatest Show on Earth*, which won the Best Picture Oscar that year.

Both films were also filled with enormous editing challenges. In *The Ten Commandments,* for example, DeMille worked with as many as 12 cameras in some scenes, eventually shooting more than 100,000 feet of film. It was Bauchens' job to whittle it all down to 12,000 feet and a running time that still ran nearly four hours. In addition, she had to edit many of the large, action scenes and glass-and-matte shots with the utmost precision— always a tricky business in those pre-digital days. It's a testament to her skills that even the most difficult of the film's most spectacular and technically challenging scenes, such as the parting of the Red Sea, still hold up well today decades after audiences have become accustomed to far more sophisticated computer-generated effects. DeMille later noted that it was "the most difficult operation of editing in motion picture history."[12] Given that DeMille often spoke in superlatives, this may or may not be the case. The editing challenges involved in *Gone with the Wind* and other films made before 1956 were also monumental in scale and difficult to implement as well. Still, it was an enormous task.

In addition, Bauchens and DeMille make ample use of long dissolves to underscore the film's themes. One of the most powerful comes near the end of the film when Egypt's ruler, Ramses II (Yul Brynner), returns to his throne room now dark and empty except for him and his queen, Nefretiri (Anne Baxter). At this point, his arrogant defiance of the god of Moses has caused great suffering and loss for them. Both sit on their huge dark thrones in despair, and, in a final surrender, Ramses says that Moses' god "is God." At this, the film dissolves very slowly—and with great emphasis—from this scene to a scene of Mount Sinai (where the god of Moses resides). In the frame, Sinai (with a fiery light overhead) emerges between Ramses and Nefretiri and above them, visually drowning them out of the frame like the waters of the Red Sea drowned Ramses' army just minutes earlier in the film. In all, this one dissolve takes about 12 seconds, quite long—and daring—for 1956 when long dissolves were quickly going out of fashion. But, here, because it underscores meaning so dramatically, it is quite powerful.

According to Lisa Mitchell, who acted in a small role in *The Ten Commandments* and then went on to a career as a film historian, this experience was difficult in another way as well. With DeMille working on the film in Egypt and huge amounts of footage to edit, raw footage was regularly flown to Los Angeles for her to edit without him, an experience that gave the 74-year-old Bauchens considerable separation anxiety.[13]

Although DeMille considered other projects after *The Ten Commandments*, this was his last hurrah as well as Bauchens'. When he died in January 1959, she retired and lived quietly until her death at a home for motion picture retirees in Woodland Hills, California, in May 1967.

As noted earlier, Bauchens never married. She lived in an unassuming home in Los Angeles for most of her life. For a time, she shared the home with her widowed mother. Later, she had a housekeeper and a dog she credited with taking very good care of her. While she was active in her church and an enthusiastic gardener, her work with DeMille was truly her life. And, along with the stamina that earned her the nickname Trojan Annie, her loyalty to him was legendary.

Scott Eyman captured this in very poignant terms in his biography of DeMille. At a gathering the day after DeMille's funeral Bauchens told a story of how DeMille had spotted someone smoking a cigarette in the final print of one scene from the 1956 version of *The Ten Commandments*. "Bauchens believed that, if DeMille saw it, it had to be there, so she ran the footage for two days straight, over and over again," Eyman wrote. "She never found the offending shot—nobody ever has—but she had been worrying about that phantom cigarette for the last three years and would for the rest of her life.... Then she began to cry."[14]

~

Like the vast majority of her contemporaries, Bauchens embraced the traditional "continuity editing" philosophy, which espoused that editing should strive to achieve a logical coherence between shots without drawing attention to itself—by effectively being invisible. And her editing style—much like her modest, soft-spoken personal style—followed suit and stayed fairly consistent throughout her long career.

To signal scene changes in films, for example, she quickly abandoned many of the gimmicky editing techniques common in silent films such as "wipes" and "iris ins," and "iris outs" and relied heavily on the less showy and self-conscious fades and dissolves. Often, too, her fades, and especially her dissolves, are used to visually convey irony.

When cutting actual scenes, she thought along similar lines. "You must make the story flow evenly [and] splice in the close-ups and the distance shots so the audience is not conscious of any break in the story," she once noted. "Unusual angles should not be employed merely for their own interest, unless they are effective in telling the story. The moment the audience is aware of various cuts and devices used, the story will suffer."[15]

We don't know what Bauchens thought of the more stylized, self-conscious editing techniques that emerged in the 1940s in films such as *Citizen Kane* or of the "shock cuts" and other even more radical techniques the French New Wave filmmakers employed in the late 1950s and 1960s. But, since these techniques were so alien to both her personal and professional sensibilities, she most likely would not have been impressed. She was very much a person of her time.

Although she stayed within the confines of the "invisible" style, Bauchens nevertheless remains an extremely able practitioner of it. And, for 40 years, her work was invaluable in helping a sometimes ingenious but also flawed director-showman transform his lavish imaginings into consistently well-crafted, commercially successful films.

Bauchen's Work on the "Emphatically Lavish" Cleopatra

DeMille's *Cleopatra* was born out of the phenomenal popular success of *The Sign of the Cross* two years before. Delighted that they had come up with a winning swords-sandals-and-sex formula, the director and Paramount were intent on using it again to strike box-office gold. In the meantime, the times had changed and the Hollywood Production Code, which had previously been dismissed by many filmmakers, was now being enforced much more strictly. DeMille had great clout, however, and, while not quite as violent or risqué as *The Sign of the Cross, Cleopatra* is still filled with lots of action and alluringly dressed women.

The story of course is the well-known saga of the clever Egyptian queen (played by Claudette Colbert) who stayed in power largely by seducing and manipulating Julius Caesar (Warren William) and Marc Antony (Henry Wilcoxon), two of the most powerful Roman leaders during the first century B.C. Ultimately, however, Caesar's heir, Octavian, defeats Antony and Cleopatra's combined forces in the Battle of Actium and the lovers both commit suicide.

Several critics have suggested that DeMille's approach to this story bears a remarkable resemblance to Alfred Green's *Baby Face* (1933), Warner's string of "gold digger" musicals, and numerous other popular films that featured downtrodden Depression-era heroines who use sex to scheme their way to wealth and power. And they may very well have a point. DeMille was very conscious of making his historical films relevant to contemporary issues and concerns, and his take here certainly echoes the desperate mood of the times.

For this production, DeMille—already widely acknowledged as one of the kings of Hollywood spectacle—was often unabashedly over the top. The film's big showstopper, if you will, is the famous sequence on Cleopatra's barge, which culminates with her bedding Marc Antony—perhaps the most elaborate seduction in movie history. Filled with music, dance, pageantry, scantily clad women, and opulence all around, it is large enough to make a splashy Busby Berkeley dance number seem small by comparison. "Emphatically lavish" were the words Mordaunt Hall of the *New York Times* used to describe *Cleopatra* upon its release in August 1934.[16] And, to support his point, he referred specifically to this scene.

To address budget constraints while also wanting everything to appear on a grand scale, DeMille came up with some very clever solutions. In his depiction of the Battle of Actium, for example, he used scenes from his 1923 version of *The Ten Commandments, The Sign of the Cross*, and Raoul Walsh's 1925 film, *The Wanderer*, along with shots featuring major characters from *Cleopatra*. The result—a long battle montage—also presented a major challenge for him and, in particular, Bauchens as they sorted through the existing footage and cut the sequence together.

Noted for its opulent (and sometimes over-the-top) sets and costumes, Cecil B. DeMille's *Cleopatra* (1934) with Claudette Colbert (center) offered Anne Bauchens a number of major editing challenges. One is a brilliantly orchestrated battle sequence toward the end of the film, which—to save money—was made up largely of existing footage from previous films (Paramount Pictures/Photofest).

Throughout the film, the editing is quite effective in many ways.

Perhaps the most apparent is Bauchens and DeMille's handling of the "showstopper," the sequence on Cleopatra's barge. The cutting is done to maximum effect throughout. One eye-popping moment is when Antony first beholds Cleopatra reclining in splendor in the center of the proceedings. It's quite a sight, and we move back and forth between them at just the right pace—each cut long enough to see that she has really made an impact on him but also never prolonged, always crisp. Another is the cutting of various scenes involving many people. Those viewing the dancers and other performers in reaction shots are treated as central to the experience as well, people absorbing all the sumptuous pageantry.

The editing is also highly effective in more subtle ways. Particularly impressive is how Bauchens handled dissolves to visually communicate irony throughout the film. One example is a longish (six-second) dissolve from Caesar's assassination in the Senate to a close-up of a vaguely troubled Cleopatra, ornately dressed and waiting to be escorted to the Senate and named Rome's queen. Although we may have mixed feelings about Cleopatra and her motives, the timing of the dissolve makes her a particular poignant figure at this moment. We feel genuine sympathy for her. Another example is the dissolve between Octavian's call for war against Antony and Cleopatra and a scene of them in Egypt lounging in a rapturous pose, seemingly intoxicated by the love they share and listening to the sensuous strumming of a harp. Again, the dissolve is a bit longer than usual (this time about seven seconds), just long enough to let the irony sink in—that they are clueless and doomed. Incidentally, this scene is also famous for a not-so-subtle touch DeMille added to subvert the Production Code. After a few moments, the camera pans to a new angle of the lovers and Cleopatra's reclining, and provocatively clad body, which we now see through the harp strings in the foreground. As the harpist's hand (in the foreground) plays from this angle, there is the suggestion that he is also caressing Cleopatra's breasts in the background. The code, of course, would not tolerate actor Wilcoxon literally stroking actress Colbert's breasts, but, as we look through the harp strings, the suggestion is clearly communicated. Soon, however, the enforcers of the code would become more vigilant and even DeMille would not be able to get scenes such as this past the censors.

The editing is also extremely effective near the end of the film in the montage Bauchens and DeMille assembled mostly from existing footage to portray the Battle of Actium. About eight minutes long, the montage includes more than 200 separate shots, nearly all of which are three seconds or less in length. Aided by a rousing musical score, it moves with great speed and urgency. But its most impressive attribute is how artfully it conveys the complete story arc of the battle through images alone. As Antony and Cleopatra accept the fact that there will be a battle, they kiss. This kiss then dissolves into smiths forging spears in fire, suggesting a cause and effect between their fiery passion and the bloodshed it is leading toward. Then we watch the events unfold from each side: Antony and Cleopatra's forces from right to left on the screen, Octavian's forces from left to right. The horns sound, soldiers march, chariots ride out, everyone clashes, there is bloodshed and chaos, day turns to night, the battle now rages between ships on the water, ships ram each other, men struggle to survive underwater, ships catch fire, killing is widespread. Throughout we also see brief shots of Antony, Cleopatra, and Octavian in the midst of all of this. The three glimpses of Cleopatra are especially telling. First, she is riding out filled with anticipation. Next, she looks more somber. Finally, as her face is superimposed over some battling soldiers, she appears downcast, seeming to realize that her and Antony's defeat is inevitable. As well as gripping, the entire montage is extremely well organized and clear; without a single word spoken, every important facet of the battle is communicated. A great deal of effort, care, and intelligence went into its creation, and both Bauchens and DeMille deserve kudos for this often-ingenious use of mostly recycled footage.

As hoped, *Cleopatra* was a major hit with both audiences and critics. It was nominated for five Academy Awards, including Best Picture and—in the first year this contribution was recognized by the Academy—Best Film Editing. Bauchens' work—especially in assembling the Cleopatra's barge and Battle of Actium sequences—was widely praised.

Shining Brightly on Her Own

Like many of her contemporary editors, men as well as women, Bauchens' precise contribution to the films she worked on is difficult to assess. The constant use of longer-than-average fades and dissolves in the films she worked on certainly suggests her interest in keeping the flow of the story moving from scene to scene with great smoothness and reflects her sensibility much more closely than the more flamboyant DeMille's. We also can't dismiss DeMille's enthusiastic praise and lifetime commitment to using her services. He did not suffer fools, and she clearly contributed much more than her loyalty and diligence. Finally, there's the high esteem that other editors had for her. One of the first three editors ever nominated for an Oscar, she was also the first woman to win one. Then, later in her career, she was nominated twice more. This stands in sharp contrast to DeMille, who, during a long and commercially successful career, received only one Academy Award nomination for directing.

Although, as many have noted, Bauchens spent her career in DeMille's shadow, this shy, soft-spoken woman still managed to shine brightly on her own.

2

"The eyes to me are everything"

*Viola Lawrence's 47 Years of Seeing
into the Eyes of Actors to Convey
the Essence of Characters*

On Thursday, August 9, 1962, a brief item appeared on a back page of the show business news publication *Daily Variety*. Wedged in between a listing of "Amusement Stocks" and a blurb announcing that comedian Jimmy Durante would appear that evening at a Quaker Oats sales convention in Denver, the item was about a retirement luncheon held the previous day for a veteran Columbia Pictures film editor. Its first sentence noted that, at the luncheon, the retiree had received a gold lifetime membership card from the film editors' professional association, American Cinema Editors (ACE). And the four sentences that followed, which together contained 67 words—exactly one for every year of the honoree's 67 years of living up until that point—provided a few scant details about a long career.

That, in essence, was how Hollywood said goodbye to Viola Lawrence (1894–1973).

Lawrence—"Vi" to her co-workers and friends—had certainly not been forgotten. About 80 of these people had attended the luncheon, and many of them doubtlessly had glowing things to say about her and her work.

She hadn't become irrelevant, either. Just the year before, she (along with editor Al Clark) had been nominated for a Best Editing Academy Award for their work on director George Sidney's big-budget musical comedy *Pepe*, starring the popular Mexican actor Cantinflas. This honor came only three years after another Oscar nomination (shared with editor Jerome Thoms) for her work on Sidney's 1957 musical *Pal Joey* with Frank

Sinatra. This, in turn, had followed on the heels of a prestigious ACE Critics Award for her contribution to the 1956 biopic *The Eddy Duchin Story* with Tyrone Power. During the previous six years, she had clearly been at the top of her game.

Yet, Lawrence's departure garnered no more fanfare than a long-time rank-and-file employee at a bank or factory might have received. In fact, her ACE lifetime membership card, while gold, didn't even have the pizazz of a corporate-issue gold retirement watch.

At the time, no one—including Lawrence, who would save the *Daily Variety* clipping until she died—felt that she hadn't received her due. Film editing had long been called "the invisible art," and Lawrence, who had begun editing in the 1910s and along the way had cut more than 100 films, had toiled in semi-anonymity for decades. Bright lights and fanfare at this late date would have seemed out of place.

Viola Lawrence (pictured here with actor Chester Morris in 1934) edited more than 100 films in a storied career that continued from the 1910s to the 1960s. Along the way, she worked on films by such major directors as Erich von Stroheim, John Ford, Howard Hawks, Orson Welles, and Nicholas Ray (Photofest).

Despite her low profile, however, Lawrence had long since established herself as one of her profession's most accomplished practitioners. In silent films, she had edited at several studios for major directors as different (in temperament and artistic vision) as Henry King and Erich von Stroheim. When sound arrived, she quickly adapted, moving to Columbia (where she would remain for nearly 30 years) and working on films for iconic directors from John Ford and Howard Hawks to Orson Welles and Nicholas Ray. When the traditional screen format gave way to wide-screen CinemaScope in the mid–1950s, she adapted again, doing, what film writer I.S. Mowis has called, "some of her finest work"[1] on films such as *Pal Joey*. All told, she was an editor for 47 years—49 if we count a brief apprenticeship when she learned her craft while working other jobs.

Throughout her career, Lawrence excelled in virtually all facets of her art. In Hawks' *Only Angels Have Wings* (1939), for example, she cut busy crowd scenes, intimate conversations, musical interludes, and taut action sequences all with great skill and perceptiveness. In addition, she had a special gift for cutting in ways that suggest more about what is going on *within* characters—that get us, if you will, closer to their essence. "I like the use of close-ups," she once noted. "Most actors do their best work in close-ups.... The greatest emotion for everyone is realized when they look straight into the actor's face, in his or her eyes. The eyes to me are everything."[2] And in films as different as von Stroheim's *Queen Kelly* (1929) and Ray's *In a Lonely Place* (1950) she delivers on this core belief in a big way, helping to make complex, ambiguous characters startlingly compelling.

Amiable and articulate, Lawrence also prided herself on being a team player who saw her role mainly as providing support to her producers and directors. "Of course, the director is always the final authority," she staunchly affirmed later in life.[3] But, when she wasn't happy with how things were going, she could be opinionated, blunt, and—regardless of who was listening—fearless about speaking her mind. "Crusty" was another word one director's biographer used to describe her.[4]

Sometimes artistic issues would bring out this crustiness. When she began to cut *The Lady from Shanghai* with Orson Welles in 1947, for example, she felt obligated to tell studio head Harry Cohn that, even though the director was Orson Welles, the footage was still a "jumbled mess."[5] She then urged Cohn to order Welles to shoot additional shots, including close-ups, which the director was adamant about not wanting in the film. Ultimately, it was Lawrence who—for better or worse (as some Welles partisans contend)—prevailed, both in getting the additional shots and in having them included in the final cut.

Other times the subject could be an issue that had little to do with specific films. Lawrence was, for example, one of the few women editors from the 1920s to the 1960s who openly criticized the studios' systematic practice of driving—and keeping—women out of her profession. One time, she even went as far as to talk about how badly her husband, fellow editor Frank Lawrence, had treated young female editing assistants in the 1920s. And her outspokenness wasn't limited to this subject, either. She could—and often did—level pointed barbs at just about everything from the film industry's lack of respect for the craft of comedy to what she saw as the inability of Los Angeles area audiences to intelligently assess movie previews.

In the little that has been written about her, Viola Lawrence has usually been characterized as a pioneer—possibly Hollywood's first full-fledged female film editor. She was certainly that, but she was also talented and tenacious enough both to stay in a hard profession that was especially hard on women for the last 40 years of her career and—during all of that time—to thrive. Of the more than 100 films she worked on, many are forgettable, many more are solid studio efforts, and several are genuine masterpieces. Looking at films as superb and diverse as *Queen Kelly, Only Angels Have Wings*, and *In a Lonely Place*, for example, we see the work of three of Hollywood's most gifted auteur directors, each in top form. Yet, when we look at these very different films in relation to each other, we also see the distinctive creative element they all share. This, of course, is the person who pieced together the final film draft that, in each case, assured something very special—the outspoken pro people called "Vi."

"Quite naturally, I'm on the woman's side in my profession"

Viola Lawrence and the movies grew up together.

She was born Lilian Viola Mallory in Brooklyn, New York, on December 2, 1894. It was just a year after the first public demonstration of Thomas Edison's Kinetoscope motion picture projection machine was held at the nearby Brooklyn Institute of Arts and Sciences. And it would be another decade before the cramped, often dingy, and usually bustling nickelodeons would dot downtowns not only in Brooklyn but also throughout the United States.

In 1911, the year after D.W. Griffith and much of his stock company left the East Coast to make a short movie in the small, sleepy Southern

California town of Hollywood, 16-year-old Viola Mallory began her film career at American Vitagraph, a studio located in Brooklyn's Flatbush neighborhood. Initially, she worked at $5 a week both as a messenger and as the person who held up silent film title cards for the cameras. Two years later, she began to learn the craft of editing, cutting a short film based on an O. Henry short story. Her teacher was Frank Lawrence (1883–1960), a former nickelodeon projectionist, who in 1903 was hired as Vitagraph's first cutter and had subsequently become head of the studio's editing department. By 1915, Viola was a full-fledged cutter.

In the next few years, two important changes occurred for both Viola and Frank. In 1917, they were lured to Hollywood to work for Carl Laemmle at the Universal Film Manufacturing Company, Frank as the studio's supervising editor. And in 1918, they were married.

Afterwards, Viola and Frank would occasionally partner in the editing room as well. One joint effort was Samuel Goldwyn's first sound film, 1929's *Bulldog Drummond* with Ronald Colman.

More often than not, however, they worked separately. Best known today for editing Howard Hughes' 1930 adventure film *Hell's Angels*, which includes particularly impressive aerial battle scenes, Frank is also credited with creating the famous "Tarzan yell" by running the soundtrack backwards through an editor's Moviola. By the late 1930s, however, he had stopped editing, and little is known about him after that. He died in Los Angeles in July of 1960.

During the 1920s, as the studios were actively discouraging women from becoming editors, Viola was still able to find work with First National, Columbia, Samuel Goldwyn at United Artists, and Gloria Swanson's independent company. During this time, she also made major contributions to several notable films.

One of these is the 1926 Goldwyn-produced western *The Winning of Barbara Worth* with Colman, Gary Cooper, and silent screen heartthrob Vilma Banky. Directed by Henry King, who would later forge a long and highly productive professional relationship at 20th Century–Fox with another female editor, Barbara McLean, this film was an attempt to capitalize on the huge commercial success of two other silent western epics, James Cruze's *The Covered Wagon* (1923) and John Ford's *The Iron Horse* (1924).

A solid effort throughout, *The Winning of Barbara Worth* is probably best known for a beautifully conceived and executed seven-minute action sequence that Lawrence cut near the end of the film. Featuring a bursting dam, a torrent of flood waters, men on horses warning people to evacuate and seek higher ground, scores of people scrambling to do just that, and many of them being swallowed up by the flood, the sequence works on several levels. First, largely through crosscutting, it gives us a thorough account of the disaster and its impact on numerous people from the hero (Colman) to three little girls, to an old man in a wheelchair, to the crooked businessman whose desire to cut corners has led to the dam burst and disaster. Second, it mixes both long and close shots with great finesse to capture both the large-scale impact of the disaster and a wide range of intimate personal stories also taking place. Finally, the cutting on specific moments in the action and the pacing and flow of shots are pitch perfect. Watching this sequence, we can't help but feel swept away by the experience as well. It's a remarkable assemblage that's thrilling to watch even 90 years after the fact. It's also proof that—at the relatively young age of 31—Lawrence had mastered her trade.

An even more fascinating example of her work during this time was her contribution to Erich von Stroheim's strange, brilliant, and ultimately unfinished 1929 silent film, *Queen Kelly*.

A co-editor on other von Stroheim films such as *Blind Husbands* (1919) and *Foolish Wives* (1922), Lawrence was brought in to the production of *Queen Kelly* when it was in complete disarray. With only about one-third of the originally envisioned five-hour film shot and the film's budget nearly depleted, the film's producer/star, actress Gloria Swanson, and her business partner/lover, financier Joseph Kennedy, had fired the eccentric, difficult director. Desperate to recoup at least part of her considerable financial investment, Swanson then asked several filmmakers (among them producer Irving Thalberg and directors Edmund Goulding, Sam Wood, and Richard Boleslawski) to write various scripts using the existing footage. Eventually, Swanson decided on an ending in which her character commits suicide and assigned Lawrence the unenviable task of organizing the many hours of existing footage to tell a coherent story that could then be completed with a few added "bridge" scenes. Finally, with the help of cinematographer Gregg Toland, Swanson directed these scenes herself, Lawrence did a final edit, and in 1932 the film with the "Swanson ending" (as it came to be called) was released in Europe. With his remaining legal leverage, von Stroheim had managed to stop the film from being exhibited in the U.S. In 1950, however, he allowed the showing of a few scenes in Billy Wilder's film *Sunset Blvd.*, in which he—ironically—co-starred with Swanson.[6]

Despite all this dysfunction and chaos, it's startling how good the first 70 minutes of *Queen Kelly* is. Most of the credit, of course, goes to von Stroheim, whose ability to convey complex psychological detail and striking visual compositions that eloquently reinforced his themes was years ahead of his time. Yet, Lawrence also deserves credit for shaping the hours of footage she had in ways that convey von Stroheim's distinctive vision to maximum effect.

Set initially in a fictional Middle European country, *Queen Kelly* is a twisted fairy tale of a likeable but philandering prince (Walter Byron) who falls for an innocent convent girl (Swanson) to the chagrin of a jealous, depraved queen (Seena Owen). This concept was also, as film writer Michael Koller has noted, "a stroke of genius for Stroheim, as it would partially liberate him from his usual obsession with realism and allow his imagination free rein to more effectively concentrate and amplify his themes, creating an intense, stylized world."[7]

In support, Lawrence gives resonance to this "intense, stylized world" in numerous ways.

One of the most interesting is her frequent use of dissolves. Usually employed in older films to signify the passage of time from one scene to the next, dissolves are also (and often) used in *Queen Kelly* to move between items in a room and other images within a scene to heighten intensity and suggest otherworldliness. One excellent example of this technique early in the film is the scene when we are introduced to the queen. It is morning, she sits up in bed—appearing naked except for a cat she holds against her breasts—and finishes off a glass of champagne. Around her we then see several (sometimes conflicting) objects—a photo of the prince; a copy of Boccaccio's book of erotic tales, *Decameron*; a prayer book and rosary; an ashtray filled with cigar butts (yes, apparently the queen smokes cigars); an empty champagne bottle; and sleep medication—dissolving slowly from one to the other in an eerie, dream-like manner. A well as suggesting a hangover and the groggy state of mind that accompanies it, these dissolves also give the scene a more stylized, unreal atmosphere that also suggests this character's escapist, perhaps deluded, and certainly troubled state of mind.

Another way Lawrence helped to give additional resonance to the world of *Queen Kelly* is through her use of expressive, intense close-ups.

While always important to her, Lawrence depended on close-ups even more than usual in *Queen Kelly*, and the impact is often quite powerful. Particularly interesting is the way she used close-ups to show what's occurring with female characters at key moments. One remarkable scene is when the queen first confronts the prince after he's spent the night partying and womanizing. At first, she seethes with jealousy. Then, remembering that she really has the upper hand in this relationship, she coyly announces that she has a "surprise" for him that evening, one we suspect will put him in his place for good. Here, we see her as insecure, angry, spiteful, and manipulative—sometimes all at once. Another fascinating scene is when Swanson's character, the convent girl, must face the convent's mother superior after she's flirted with the prince. Swanson's close-ups are wonderful, vividly conveying both her young character's point of view when recounting the incident as well as her acceptance of the punishment she receives for her transgression. But Madge Hunt, the actress who plays the mother superior, does a fascinating job of conveying sternness, a calm composure, and great empathy in her close-ups. Apparently seeing an opportunity, Lawrence held on the close-ups of Hunt a bit longer than other editors might have, and the extra emphasis gives both her tiny role and this scene added depth and dimension.

In the early 1930s, Lawrence returned to Columbia, where she remained until her retirement in 1962. Like fellow female editors Margaret Booth at MGM and Barbara McLean at 20th Century–Fox, Lawrence eventually became a supervising editor. Unlike them, however, she continued to juggle both supervisory responsibilities and editing assignments for her entire career, and she received—over the next three decades—editing credit on more than 80 additional films.

During the 1930s, she made important contributions to several notable efforts. In Frank Borzage's Pre-Code romance *Man's Castle* (1933), for example, her cutting was instrumental in highlighting the sensitive acting performances of stars Spencer Tracy and Loretta Young. And in John Ford's social satire/romance *The Whole Town's Talking* (1935) her work played a key role in bringing out sides to actress Jean Arthur that audiences hadn't seen before and, in the process, helping to transform Arthur from a fading ingénue into Columbia's top female star.

Of all the 1930s films Lawrence worked on, however, perhaps the one that's best remembered today is Howard Hawks' 1939 story of daredevil pilots who fly the mail through the Andes in South America, *Only Angels Have Wings*. Among the film's highlights are its often-gripping flying scenes. And in many of these Lawrence does an outstanding job of putting together shots of actors in cockpit mock-ups, airplane models, and actual planes in flight to create edge-of-your-seat suspense. Among these, perhaps the best is the film's last flying sequence when two characters played by Richard Barthelmess and Thomas Mitchell are in a plane that nosedives, catches fire, manages against the odds to make a crash landing back at the runway, and—just after the two men are evacuated—explodes. Of note, too, in this sequence are the pacing and the rhythms of the editing. Throughout the flight from beginning to end, each shot is just as long as it needs to be; the cuts all happen very naturally, so naturally that we have to make an effort to notice them because they blend into the action so well. It is traditional Hollywood editing at its best.

In the 1940s, Lawrence continued to edit films for Columbia at a steady clip, sometimes working on four, five, or—as in 1941—even six films a year. Among her best efforts during the decade were Alexander Hall's fantasy-comedy *Here Comes Mr. Jordan* (1941) with Robert Montgomery and Claude Rains and Charles Vidor's musical *Cover Girl* with Rita Hayworth and Gene Kelly (1944). After helping to make Jean Arthur a top star at Columbia, Lawrence's cutting also proved to be a vital component in helping Hayworth become the studio's top star in the 1940s. Seeing this symbiotic relationship with Hayworth, the studio assigned Lawrence to cut all but three of the actress's many films during the 1940s and 1950s.

Although work on most of her 1940s films went routinely, Lawrence also faced some serious challenges in 1947 and 1948 when trying to cut one of the best-known films she ever worked on, Orson Welles' *The Lady from Shanghai*.

As they saw the film's initial rushes, both Columbia's studio head Harry Cohn and his assistant Jack Fier began to doubt whether the film could even be releasable. Their doubts were confirmed when Lawrence told them that the footage was a "jumbled mess." An added concern for all three of them was Hayworth's appearance. With her signature long red hair severely cut back and dyed blond, they felt that their studio's top star looked mousy. Finally, for artistic reasons (perhaps to create a more detached relationship between filmgoers and the film's characters), Welles had seriously limited the number of close-ups he shot, something that particularly rankled Lawrence.

Soon, Cohn ordered extensive reshooting and re-editing, which delayed the film's release for more than a year and caused the project to go over budget by more than 30 percent. In the process, Lawrence cut more than an hour out of Welles' initial edit (which the studio then destroyed). And, when the film was finally released in the U.S., just about everyone considered it a disaster.

One highlight of the film, though, is a shoot-out in a fun house hall of mirrors that has since become an iconic piece of film noir. Taking up a little more than two minutes of the finished version, Welles had originally intended it to be about 20 minutes. As it is, it's absolutely spellbinding, and it begs one to wonder what the much longer version would have been like.

Although Welles enthusiasts have roundly denounced Cohn, Lawrence, and others at Columbia for not understanding the director's overall vision and ruining his film, the situation may have been more complicated. Cohn, who was one of Hollywood's most financially savvy studio heads at the time, may have foreseen (and perhaps rightfully) a box-office failure, an art film that audiences would stay away from in droves. And Lawrence's remark that the film at one point was a "jumbled mess" cannot be immediately discounted, either. She may have been a more conventional cinematic thinker than Welles, but during her career she also worked with von Stroheim, Ray, and other cutting-edge directors and had always treated their work with great respect. Despite Welles' undisputed talent, there may have been problems with his initial cut of the film, and at least some of the concerns of Cohn, Lawrence, and others at Columbia may have been warranted. Since the studio destroyed so much of Welles' initial footage, however, we will probably never have a definitive answer.

The year after her unhappy experience with *The Lady from Shanghai*, Lawrence embarked on a partnership with Humphrey Bogart's newly formed (and, sadly, short-lived) Santana Productions, which distributed through Columbia. Over the next three years, she edited five films for the independent company, two of them (both starring Bogart), 1949's *Knock on Any Door* and 1950's *In a Lonely Place*, for the very talented director Nicholas Ray. A far better artistic fit for Lawrence than Welles, Ray offered her the chance to work on the kind of emotionally complex, deeply affecting stories she excelled at. Her work on the brilliant and emotionally wrenching *In a Lonely Place* could very well be the best of her long career.

Remaining busy throughout the 1950s, Lawrence worked on films ranging from noirs to comedies, to dramas, to musicals that featured a variety of stars from Joan Crawford and Ginger Rogers to Edward G. Robinson and Tyrone Power. She also continued to work on films starring Rita Hayworth, and, as she had done a decade before with Hayworth, she began working on films featuring another up-and-coming female star at Columbia, Kim Novak.

Of these films, perhaps the best known today is the musical *Pal Joey* (1957) that featured both Hayworth and Novak vying for the attentions of Frank Sinatra. While the story of a philandering but charming entertainer seems dated today, the film includes some memorable songs (most notably "The Lady Is a Tramp") and was quite well crafted. It received four Academy Award nominations in technical categories, including one for Lawrence and Jerome Thoms for Best Editing.

Three years later, Lawrence (this time with editor Al Clark) received her second Oscar nomination for the big-budget musical comedy *Pepe*. While not a success with critics or audiences, the film managed to receive seven Academy Award nominations, mostly in technical categories. At the time, Lawrence quipped that *Pepe* may have been her most demanding job ever because she and Clark had to pare down more than 500,000 feet (roughly 100 miles) of exposed film into about 20,000 feet (roughly four miles).[8] Even at this length, however, the sprawling film ran for more than three hours, a running time that probably further dampened its box office appeal.

After her retirement in 1962, Lawrence lived quietly in Los Angeles until her death at age 78 on November 20, 1973. A sister, Edith Bennett of Los Angeles, survived her.

~

In addition to her long, extremely productive career, part of what made Viola Lawrence special was that "crusty" character of hers. At a time when most people in the film business worked for studios and made it a point not to criticize those in power, she liked to be the provocateur, saying exactly what was on her mind no matter who heard it. Sometimes, too, she would bow to diplomacy, adding just a pinch of self-deprecating humor along with her barb to make it a little more palatable.

Often, her statements were simply quirky and challenging. Once, for example, she railed against Hollywood's lack of appreciation for the craft of comedy. "I don't understand this preoccupation with drama on the part of people of this industry who should know that comedy is far more difficult," she said. "But fun pictures never come in for Academy honors. Musical comedy, once in a while, yes … but straight comedy, never! It's the same with cutting. The editor of a comedy doesn't receive his just due."[9] She had no qualms about using her sharp tongue on the hometown audiences, either. "When we try pictures out on a New York or a San Francisco audience, we find them twice as hep, understanding, receptive, and wisely critical," she stated fervently. "It's even smarter for a studio to try pictures first up at Santa Barbara or in San Bernardino—anywhere out of this eccentric town. Hollywood people are too professional, too insular in their tastes."[10]

But she was also outspoken about more serious issues that mattered to her, and one that mattered a great deal was the industry-wide effort to discourage women from becoming film editors. Once, for example, she recalled how her husband Frank, who had taught her to cut in the 1910s, was simply "mean" to female assistants he supervised at Paramount in the

1920s. "He just hated them," she said. "If any of the girls were cutting—if they did get the chance to cut—he'd put them right back as assistants," but he "broke in a lot of boys."[11] And, even near the end of her career, the issue still riled her. "Quite naturally, I'm on the woman's side in my profession," she said at the time. "I don't think there are enough woman cutters…. If you ask me, women have more heart and feeling than men in this work."[12]

Then—no doubt with a slight twinkle in her eye—she added, "Now, listen to my masculine contemporaries yell when they hear this!"[13]

Lawrence's Contribution to In a Lonely Place

As a stylist, Lawrence closely adhered to the classical editing techniques her husband Frank taught her in the early 1910s and people such as D.W. Griffith later refined. She was not a major innovator, and, as her experience with Orson Welles may have illustrated, she could have also been resistant to certain kinds of editorial experimentation.

Yet, as her frequent use of close-ups to reveal the inner states of characters suggests, she clearly brought a humanist's sensibilities to her work. And among her talents was a special ability to bring out the humanity in characters audiences might initially find difficult to like and relate to. Ultimately, she helped to make these characters more nuanced, ambiguous, and intriguing. And, in the process, she also helped to make the actors who played these characters look better in their roles.

When these goals closely meshed with the goals of a gifted director the results could be electric. And in all of Lawrence's films perhaps the foremost example of this talent is her work on Nicholas Ray's film noir masterpiece about a troubled Hollywood screenwriter suspected of murder, *In a Lonely Place*.

In her 2000 essay on the film, writer Fiona Villella called it "one of the finest *noir* melodramas Hollywood ever produced, … a film in which all elements—performance, story, score, lighting, and editing—work in complete concert to realize the emotional weight of its drama."[14]

It's almost impossible to disagree.

Based on Dorothy B. Hughes' 1947 mystery novel *In a Lonely Place*, the film both builds on the original story and departs from it in a variety of ways to express and explore many of the preoccupations of its director, Ray, and its star, Humphrey Bogart. In the film's angry, isolated, and occasionally violent main character, screenwriter Dixon Steele (Bogart), both director and actor saw a man very much like themselves, and together

Troubled lovers Laurel (Gloria Grahame) and Dix (Humphrey Bogart) share a tense moment in Nicholas Ray's film noir masterpiece *In a Lonely Place* (1950). Later in her career, Lawrence proved herself adept at taking on new kinds of films such as noir and the lavish color musicals of the late 1950s and early 1960s such as *Pal Joey* (1957) (Columbia Pictures/Photofest).

they chose to dig deep into Steele's dark soul. The deep personal connection between artists and story didn't stop there, either. To play Steele's love interest and potential salvation, aspiring actress Laurel Gray, they initially considered Bogart's real-life wife, Lauren Bacall. Then, when they learned that Warner Brothers, where Bacall was under contract, wouldn't allow her to play the part, they turned to Ray's real-life wife, Gloria Grahame. It's a film, as director (and avid Ray fan) Curtis Hanson has noted, that's "so heartfelt, so emotional, so revealing that it seems as though both the actor and the director are standing naked before the audience."[15]

Although Ray and Bogart played lead roles in this creative process, several other people had to be both in synch with their aims and capable of achieving them for the film to succeed as well as it does. Among these people are its co-star, Grahame; its screenwriter, Andrew Solt; its cinematographer, Burnett Guffey; the composer of its dark, unsettling musical score, George Antheil; and of course its editor, Viola Lawrence.

On the film, Lawrence contributed in several ways.

Her talent in cutting action scenes, for example, is clearly in evidence in the emotionally charged sequence after the film's beach party scene, when Steele, feeling betrayed, leaves in a rage and Laurel follows. He gets in his car, she quickly hops in, he drives fast and recklessly until he almost causes an accident with another car. Steele then stops. The other driver (a young man) also stops and jumps out to start an argument. In turn, Steele jumps out of his car and attacks the other man. Finally, just as he is about to hit the man with a rock, Laurel yells at him to stop. To amplify Steele's out-of-control state of mind and Laurel's increasing anxiety and fear, the cuts are quick but very carefully chosen, moving back and forth between shots of the car driving on both sides of the road, the actors' emotionally charged faces, a speedometer approaching 70 miles per hour, and other distressing images. In its entirety, the sequence excellently conveys a sense of crazed recklessness and unpredictability. We in the audience are, in a sense, seated right in Laurel's place, and, like her, we see firsthand how terrifying Dixon Steele can be.

Lawrence also does a fine job of conveying some of the film's more expressionistic moments. One, for example, is a nightmare Laurel has late in the story shown through super-imposed dissolves of the chief murder investigator, Captain Lochner (Carl Benton Reid) and her masseuse Martha (Ruth Gillette) both warning her about how dangerous Steele is and then a super-imposed image of Steele beating the driver of that other car. Particularly effective is how all these images are positioned in relation to the sleeping Laurel, looking down from virtually the same high, imposing angle—the first two characters with commanding, authoritative expressions and then Steele hitting with rage in his eyes. In fact, the image of Steele is positioned as if he were hitting her.

Yet, by far Lawrence's most important contribution to the film is her handling of the many close-ups and close two-shots, particularly of Steele and Laurel. Both Bogart and Grahame were superb actors at conveying various states of mind with their faces, Ray obviously appreciated this about them, and, according to accounts of the filming, he frequently pushed the camera in on them to get more of what they were conveying about their characters.[16] It was Lawrence's job to bring out the very wide range of emotions the two characters feel without showing too much, a difficult feat in a film as delicately nuanced as this one. And it is amazing how well she balances the emotions of a character both with the rhythms of a particular conversation and with a film's need for economy. As viewers, we always feel that we get just enough, never too much or too little.

One wonderful example of Lawrence's using a close-up very effectively is her handling of the film's first image: a popular noir shot of a driver's eyes in a car's rearview mirror. This is such a strong image here, Steele's dark and lonely face set against the dark city night, that it doesn't need to be emphasized too much. So, Lawrence uses it as a background to the film's first credits, which introduce Bogart, the film's telling title, and Grahame. Then, as the remaining credits are shown, she cuts to a medium shot of Steele from the back driving alone in the car. Along with George Antheil's sad, unsettling score, many of the essentials of this story are established before we even get to the director's credit. It's economical without ever sacrificing emotion for economy.

As the relationship between Steele and Laurel begins to unravel later in the film, the close-ups and close two-shots of the couple become more frequent, more complicated, and more revealing. Often, they betray the words the two lovers are sharing with one another.

When Steele tells Laurel that they should get married, for example, we see two very revealing close-ups of her that amply convey her surprise, fear, dread, and hope that she can somehow talk her way out of this situation. A moment later we see Steele sitting on a sofa looking at her as she is off-camera with growing fear and insecurity of his own. Then just a few moments later, when she goes to the kitchen to check the coffee, we see that she realizes that she cannot get out of this bind—that she has to say "yes" to marriage. Throughout, we get just enough facial expression to clearly tell us what's occurring inside the two characters but never too much. It moves beautifully.

The film's last scene is another excellent blending of emotion and economy. The mutual fear and distrust has now hit a feverish pitch. Laurel definitely wants to run away from Steele. He finds out that she is planning to fly to New York, becomes enraged, forces her to her bed, and starts choking her. The phone rings, snapping him out of his rage. He goes to answer the phone—tired, now defeated—and hears the "good news" that he is innocent of the murder the police had suspected him of. Captain Lochner wants to apologize to Laurel as well. Steele calls her to the phone. She is now exhausted, too, but also senses that, finally, she may now be free of Steele.

When Lochner apologizes, we see a close-shot on Laurel. "Yesterday, this would have all meant so much to us," she says.

Then, the film cuts to a medium shot on Steele standing at her front door. He listens as we hear Laurel off camera finish her thought. "Now, it doesn't matter," she says. "It doesn't matter at all."

This line becomes Steele's cue to leave for good, and we see his reaction and acknowledgement. The film cuts to him walking down the stairs and through the apartment's courtyard, then back to Laurel who says her goodbye so quietly only she can hear it, then finally to Steele by himself in long shot at the edge the courtyard. Just as the film's titles came up over his lonely image at the film's beginning, the words "The End" come up on him, alone once again.

In her essay on *In a Lonely Place*, Fiona Villella called this last scene "a brilliantly swift and economic succession of shots [that] bring the film to closure."[17]

Again, it's almost impossible to disagree. While Ray obviously contributed a great deal to the editing process here, Lawrence's understanding of both Ray's objectives and the complex and often disturbing human emotions at the core of this film is quite remarkable. It's fun to imagine her working with Ray again on such emotionally charged films as his very moving *On Dangerous Ground* (1951) or his now-iconic *Rebel Without a Cause* (1955). But, it's also fruitless to speculate. Suffice it to say that, on this film, their talents and artistic sensibilities complemented each other extremely well.

Much More Than a Pioneer

It has been easy for people—as many have done—to view Viola Lawrence as merely a film industry pioneer, a competent editor of standard Hollywood fare, a good corporate soldier for Columbia Pictures, and little more.

It has also been simplistic and terribly unfair.

While often described as a pioneer, Lawrence was also a survivor when fellow trailblazers, including many women, left the industry in the face of growing sexism, increased competition for jobs, and changing times. In addition to surviving, she thrived, editing more than 80 films during her nearly 30 years at Columbia alone, where, for much of that time, she also served as the studio's supervising editor. She began in film when nickelodeons were still popular, and she finally retired after a six-year run in which she received two Academy Award nominations and an ACE Critics Award for her work on major big-budget studio releases.

As these last details suggest, she was also more than merely a competent editor of standard Hollywood fare. Her work on great films for directors such as von Stroheim, Hawks, and Ray is a testament to her skills as well as theirs. And her work on fine films by top directors such as Henry King, Frank Borzage, John Ford, and George Sidney is further evidence that her work was excellent far more often than it was merely competent.

Finally, while she was certainly a loyal studio employee, she was also a person who didn't shy away from controversy, even when her remarks took the film industry to task. Her early and consistent criticism of the treatment of women editors, for example, is certainly proof of her sense of fair play and her courage.

It is ironic that this film editor who so passionately believed in the power of close-ups to bring audiences closer to the essence of on-screen characters—to see, if you will, more deeply into their souls—has received so little critical attention, so few probing close-ups of her or her work. Considering both her prodigious output for nearly half a century and the high quality of much of that work, she deserves *much* more than the ACE gold lifetime membership card she received at her retirement luncheon that August day in 1962.

3

"Boy, was I tough"

The Long Reign and Lasting Legacy of MGM's Margaret Booth

In his 1995 book, *Making Movies*, director Sidney Lumet recalls a time in 1964 when Margaret Booth (1898–2002), then MGM's long-time supervising film editor, flew to England to screen three soon-to-be-released films, including Lumet's *The Hill* (1965). Then well into her 60s, and no doubt jetlagged from her long airplane flight, Booth screened all three features one after another, beginning at 8:00 the following morning. At 1:00 sharp that afternoon, she met with Lumet and his editor to inform them they needed to cut two minutes from their picture. When Lumet objected, Booth began naming shots that could be shortened. She didn't speak from notes, either: all of what she said came right off the top of her head. "Her film memory was phenomenal," Lumet recalled. "She named seven or eight moments, always perfect on where the shot occurred, what took place in the shot, how its beginning or end might be trimmed—and she'd seen the picture only once."[1]

As well as impressing Lumet, Booth had clearly ruffled his feathers. Still smarting from this and perhaps other run-ins with her, he told a group of young filmmakers four years later: "When I complete a film for Metro, I have to get blood on the floor to protect it from a lady by the name of Margaret Booth. She was Irving Thalberg's cutter, and to this day she checks every movie made for Metro-Goldwyn-Mayer and can stop you at any point, call off your mix, and re-edit herself. She *owns* your negative."[2]

Such was the power of Margaret Booth in the 1960s. And such had been her power for decades.

Petite, shy, modest about her achievements, and, according to fellow editor Dede Allen, "very much a lady-lady," Booth, as Allen also noted, "had tremendous command."[3] In fact, film writer Graham Daseler has gone as far as to call her, "a terror to directors throughout the industry, pouncing on weakly edited scenes like a ravenous jungle cat."[4]

Born in the nineteenth century and living into the twenty-first, her career as a film editor, supervising editor, and later a producer stretched a full seven decades, from 1915 until 1986. During that time, she apprenticed with director D.W. Griffith, perhaps the first person to deeply explore and exploit the possibilities of film editing; edited many of MGM's best films in the 1920s and 1930s; served as a trusted confidante as well as supervising editor for MGM's studio head Louis B. Mayer; and—in the 1970s and 1980s—worked as the supervising editor and then a producer for Ray Stark's film company, Rastar, on such films as *The Way We Were* (1973), *The Goodbye Girl* (1977), and *The Slugger's Wife* (1985). Along the way, she received several industry honors, including a Lifetime Achievement Oscar in 1978, the only film editor to be so honored.[5]

Beginning her film career as an editing assistant for D.W. Griffith in 1915, Margaret Booth (shown here in the 1930s) went on to become one of MGM's top editors before becoming the studio's supervising editor, a post she held for 30 years. Afterwards, she was the supervising editor on films produced by Ray Stark. She retired in 1986 at age 88 (Photofest).

Throughout her career, Booth kept a low profile. Outside of the film industry, few people have ever heard her name. In fact, to this day many film teachers, historians, and scholars know little or nothing about her. Yet, for decades, film producers, directors, and fellow editors both revered and often feared her for what film historian Kevin Brownlow has called "her uncanny perceptiveness" and her "immense power."[6] Within the tight-knit community of film editors, she remains an iconic figure.

Booth's editing style in many ways reflected her low-profile personal style. She was both a key developer and a stalwart champion of the "classic" Hollywood style that sought to make editing seamless, seemingly invisible, drawing as little attention to itself as possible. Yet, in her practical, no-nonsense way, she also preached that editors should be attuned to the rhythms of a film and cut to accommodate the emotion a story is conveying; she saw that there was poetry in editing, too.

A self-described workaholic and perfectionist, Booth was devoted to editing. She never married. She turned down offers to direct. Especially during her early years, she often worked all night for no extra pay just to solve problems that stumped her. And later, when she supervised editors, she exerted an enormous influence over others who were following in her profession. As one of them, Frank Urioste, who would go on to edit such films as *Die Hard* (1988) and *Basic Instinct* (1992), once said, "Margaret would tell us: 'It's your responsibility for the pace of the movie. It's your responsibility to get the best performances out of the actors. It's your responsibility to make it as good as you can.'"[7]

"One doesn't 'hire' her, one is lucky to get her."

Born and raised in Los Angeles, Booth, then 17, had just graduated from Los Angeles High School when a family tragedy occurred that, ironically, launched her in the film business.

The day was June 16, 1915. Booth's older brother Elmer, who was supporting the family through his work as an actor in D.W. Griffith's films, was killed in an automobile accident. Tod Browning, another Griffith actor who later achieved fame directing such films as 1931's *Dracula* and the 1932 cult masterpiece *Freaks*, was driving Booth and a third actor, George Siegmann, when their car hit a moving train, injuring Browning and Siegmann and instantly killing Booth.

Griffith stepped in, first to deliver a moving eulogy at Elmer's funeral and then to offer financial help to the Booth family by giving young Margaret an entry-level lab job as a film joiner, or "patcher." While Margaret appreciated Griffith's help, she never—throughout her long life—forgave Browning for her brother's death.

As a patcher and then a negative cutter for Griffith, Booth was literally present at the creation of the art of film editing. Primarily, she learned from Griffith, whose innovations in parallel cutting and other editing techniques were pushing the boundaries of the still relatively new art. In addition, she worked with two of Griffith's most trusted hands, the husband and wife cutters Jimmie and Rose Smith, who, along with Griffith, edited the epics *The Birth of a Nation* (1915), *Intolerance* (1916), and other films. But, with virtually no dedicated editing tools to work with, the work, while stimulating, could often be monotonous and wearing. As Booth later recalled: "[I]n the old days we had to cut negative by eye. We matched the print to the negative without any edge numbers. We had to match the action. Sometimes there'd be a tiny pinpoint on the negative, and then you knew you were right. But it was very tedious work. Close-ups of Lillian Gish … would go on for miles, and they'd be very similar, so we all had to help one another."[8]

By the end of the decade, Booth had moved on from Griffith's company and was working as a cutter for another legendary Hollywood figure, Louis B. Mayer, then an independent producer. At Mayer's company, she met John M. Stahl, a man she considered "a remarkable director,"[9] and became his assistant. "I used to stand by him while he cut, and he used to ask me to come in with him to see his dailies in the projection room," she once said. "This way he taught me the dramatic values of cutting, he taught me about tempo—in fact he taught me how to edit."[10]

In an interview in the 1970s, Booth recalled an incident that helped her earn her "editor's stripes" with Stahl. As much of a perfectionist as Booth, the director made it a practice to shoot many different takes of scenes from different angles and from different distances. As he edited, he routinely discarded film he no longer wanted on the cutting room floor. Then, at night after Stahl had gone home, Booth would often take the discarded film and experiment with it for hours, hoping to improve her skills. One time Stahl had spent a day trying to get a sequence of edits right and finally went home unsuccessful. That night, Booth, working only with his discarded footage, put together what she thought Stahl was looking for. The next morning she told him what she had done and showed it to him. As Booth recalled: "He said, 'I like it. I'll take that.' And he used my cut. So from then on I started to cut for him."[11]

For several years, Booth was content to work as Stahl's assistant.

Then, in April 1924, a business merger occurred that was to change the direction of her career. Marcus Loew, the owner of the Lowe's motion picture theater chain, bought and consolidated Metro Pictures, Samuel Goldwyn's Goldwyn Pictures Corporation, and Mayer's company to create a major new film company named Metro-Goldwyn-Mayer. Mayer was named head of studio operations, a post he would hold for the next 27 years. And, the following year, he made his brilliant, ambitious protégé, 25-year-old Irving Thalberg, the new company's head of production. Along with most of Mayer's employees, Stahl and Booth joined the new company.

While she continued to work with Stahl, Booth increasingly enjoyed working with many of the other talented directors on board—people such as Clarence Brown, Sam Wood, Robert Z. Leonard, and Fred Niblo. And, three years later, when Stahl left MGM and asked Booth to come with him, she declined. "I didn't want to work for just one man," she later said. "I enjoyed working for everyone.... I feel people get tired of you, and you get tired of them by the time a picture's finished.... MGM was like home to me. I started there so young. I knew everybody there, and never wanted to work any other place."[12]

Booth considered this decision to be a critical one in her career, and, in later years, contrasted her experience with that of fellow female editing pioneer Anne Bauchens, who worked primarily with Cecil B. DeMille for more than 40 years. Bauchens, Booth felt, never got out from under DeMille's imposing shadow, and, despite her talent, remained an obscure, unappreciated figure.

At MGM, Booth became a close ally of Thalberg, a person she once called "the greatest man who was ever in pictures."[13] Thalberg soon assigned her to cut many of the studio's prestige pictures and often asked her to evaluate the work of other editors and recommend changes to films. According to film historian Cari Beauchamp, "He depended on her as much as [he did on] any writer. The two of them would go to a screening and sit next to each other, making plans for how the re-shoot would be done and how it would be edited."[14]

According to numerous accounts, Thalberg was also the first to elevate the name film "cutter" to the more prestigious-sounding "editor," a term that had previously only been used in films for script supervisors. And the first person he awarded the title of film editor to—according to these accounts—was none other than Booth. In fact, Thalberg was so impressed with Booth's ability to get to the essence of problems in films and recommend solutions that he even suggested that she direct, something only one woman, Dorothy Arzner, was doing for a major Hollywood studio at the time. But, Booth's ambition was always to be the best editor in town, and, as long as she remained at MGM, that was fine with Thalberg.

When sound came into the filmmaking equation in the late 1920s, Booth was assigned to the studio's first part-talkie film, 1929's *The Bridge of San Luis Rey*. This presented a couple of challenges to Booth and her fellow editors. One was that, with the addition of sound, editors had now lost much of the flexibility they had had with silent film. As Booth explained, with silent film, "you could throw the film around in any way. When you got the sound track, you had to be careful that it was always in sync."[15] The other challenge was the new sound experts, mostly men, who interfered with the editing process. "[S]ound was their background, and they all knew everything," Booth declared with some bitterness years later. "And they didn't know a *damn* thing, but they 'knew everything.'"[16]

Booth quickly mastered sound, however, and during the 1930s was MGM's go-to editor for the studio's prestige releases such as *Dancing Lady* (1933) with Joan Crawford and Clark Gable, *The Barretts of Wimpole Street* (1934) with Norma Shearer and Frederic March, *Mutiny on the Bounty* (1935) with Gable and Charles Laughton, *Camille* (1936) with Greta Garbo, and *Romeo and Juliet* (1936) with Shearer and Leslie Howard. Although she was passed over for an Academy Award nomination for editing in 1934, the first year an editing award was given, she was nominated the following year for *Mutiny on the Bounty*. She lost out to Warner Brothers editor Ralph Dawson for his work on Warner's *A Midsummer Night's Dream*, which Booth considered "a terrible picture." In later years she found consolation in the fact that, while she initially didn't think that *Mutiny on the Bounty* was "very good," it is now considered a "classic."[17]

Shortly afterwards, another tragedy struck that, again ironically, launched Booth into a very different phase of her career. On the morning of September 14, 1937, her great colleague and for many the heart and soul of MGM, Irving Thalberg, died of pneumonia at age 37. Soon afterwards, Mayer, in an effort the shore up production in the midst of this enormous loss to the studio, named Booth to the post of MGM's supervising editor, a position she would hold for the next 30 years. For Mayer, who had an instinctive distrust of writers and directors, the move was an excellent political gambit. With Booth, he had a loyal ally and a true professional who could more than hold her own with anyone else at the studio, and, as long as he was at MGM, Booth reported directly to him.

While not as well-known as other, higher-profile MGM department heads such as Douglas Shearer (in sound) and Cedric Gibbons (in art direction and production design), Booth ran a tight ship committed to maintaining high standards of quality. Always conscious of staying current, she made sure her department adapted to the latest changes in technologies and styles. In addition to supervising the editing, she also offered comments to producers and directors that most considered quite helpful. When looking at the rushes of 1944's *Gaslight*, for example, she pointed out to director George Cukor that the film's star, Ingrid Bergman, was underacting. Agreeing, Cukor sought to get more from Bergman, and the result was both an excellent performance and her first Academy Award win for Best Actress.

Booth's main job, however, was supervising the editors under her, and, according to many of these editors, she took it very seriously. "[She] was a tough taskmaster and used to drag me over the coals every day—but I learned," said Ralph Winters who later won two Academy Awards for editing. And, Winters also noted, he was by no means alone. "Time and again, editors were sent back to their cutting rooms to adjust their work to her liking," he added. "But she was consistent and fair, and appreciated both good work and good effort."[18] Frank Urioste, another MGM editor who later received three Academy Award nominations for his work, was even more emphatic in his assessment. "Maggie was probably the toughest and most feared women at MGM," he once said. "I mean, people would shudder when they heard that she was on the phone or when she'd bust into the editing room. You'd get a call saying to come down to Room F, which was her room. You'd think: 'Oh God, what have I done now?'"[19]

Booth's power also extended well beyond MGM's editing department. "She had her own projection room and saw all the rushes and cuts for every MGM film," Winters said. "She was empowered to make changes and present the editing of sequences to various producers and directors as she saw fit."[20] Many people didn't like this arrangement, but, since Booth reported directly to Mayer, there was little anyone could do about it.

While Booth was always firm in exerting her power, she could also soften the sting of her criticism with a certain droll delivery. Once, when working with director George Roy Hill, she expressed her displeasure at something she saw by saying: "Mr. Hill, are you telling me you want *that* on a 60-foot screen?"

"I guess I don't, do I?" Hill said.

"No, you don't," she replied.[21]

It's virtually impossible to assess Booth's full impact in her three decades as MGM's supervising editor. If, as many people claim, she did have the final say over every film that MGM produced during that time, the number of features alone was well over a thousand. Add to that, there's the immense influence she had on the scores of editors who worked under her from the 1930s to the 1960s.

When Booth finally left MGM, she wasn't idle for long. She soon began working for independent producer Ray Stark and his company, Rastar, as a supervising editor and associate producer, and she stayed with him until her retirement in 1986 at the age of 88. Together, they churned out a steady stream of commercial and critical successes such as John Huston's *Fat City* (1972), Sidney Pollock's *The Way We Were* (1973), and Herb Ross' *Funny Lady* (1975) as well as several films based on Neil Simon plays, including *The Sunshine Boys* (1975), *The Goodbye Girl* (1977), *California Suite* (1978), and *Chapter Two* (1979).

"One doesn't 'hire' her, one is lucky to get her," Stark told film writer Ally Acker after Booth's retirement.[22] "[H]er instincts were remarkable even in her later years, when she saved many a film for me," he added shortly after Booth's death. "Margaret was a tough, unsentimental editor who read film like others read a book."[23]

When Booth was working with Stark, the industry honors—recognition that had long eluded her—finally began to come. In a 1977 *Film Comment* magazine poll that asked 100 editors to rank the top practitioners in their field, Booth was ranked number three. At the Academy Awards ceremonies the following year, she received—for her "exceptionally distinguished service to the motion picture industry"[24]—the first Lifetime Achievement Oscar ever given to an editor. Four years later she received the Crystal Award from the organization Women in Film, an honor for women who have helped expand the role of women within the entertainment industry. In 1990, she became one of the first recipients of the American Cinema Editors (ACE) Career Achievement Award. And, on the occasion of her 100th birthday in 1998, the Editors Guild presented her a special award commemorating her long and distinguished career. Other than that competitive Oscar she felt she deserved for her work on *Mutiny on the Bounty*, Booth couldn't have asked for much more.

Margaret Booth died in Los Angeles from complications following a stroke on October 28, 2002, at the time the longest living person ever to win an Academy Award. Among the many who commented on her passing was Roger Mayer (no relation to Louis B. Mayer) who was then president of Turner Entertainment, which owns all of MGM's films through 1986. Booth, he noted, "represented much of what was good about the studio system: the loyalty, the continuity, the knowledge of what went on at a particular studio."[25]

Booth left behind only one close blood relative, a cousin named Marie Cetner. But, she also left behind several generations of film industry producers, directors, and editors who enormously respected her talent, commitment to the editing art, and ability to teach. She could certainly make young editors cringe with fear. As she herself observed in an interview late in her life, "Boy, was I tough."[26] But, she could also inspire them and win their abiding admiration. As Ralph Winters noted: "[S]he was consistent and fair, and appreciated both good work and good effort.... She was not afraid to go to the mat with anyone, and producers and directors alike felt her wrath when she thought that they were going in the wrong direction. She fought hard for what she believed—and she was usually right. But she always protected her editors.... Eventually, I worked my way up to become one of her favorite editors and, more important to me, a close personal friend."[27]

~

Throughout her career, Booth always insisted that, rather than imposing a personal style on a film, an editor's job was to adapt to the style of the film's director. She did, however, develop a personal style that was a combination of several important influences as well her own aesthetic preferences. Then, practicing what she preached, she adapted it to accommodate different directors she worked with.

The major influences on her included Griffith, Stahl, and the German films of the 1920s. Griffith, for example, particularly impressed her with his ability to use editing to build and control the emotional tempo of a film and his practice of using a series of shots from various angles and distances to make scenes more interesting visually.[28] Along with various cutting techniques, Stahl taught her the value of prudence in editing. Fifty years after she had worked with him, for example, she still found it worthwhile to tell people how Stahl taught her to use close-ups sparingly, only when "you want to punctuate something."[29] Finally, she learned from the early German filmmakers the value of editing for smoother continuity, an artistic preference film writer Ronald Bergan finds "more significant" in Booth's development than what she learned from Griffith.[30]

Throughout her career, Booth believed that editing should seem seamless, virtually invisible, and that its main purpose was to advance the narrative. "She hated editing for editing's sake," Ralph Winters recalled, "but if you had to make a bad edit to advance the story, that was fine with her."[31] Frank Urioste also noted how she always put story first, recalling: "She used to say: 'If [you] feel there's a cut at an important spot—whether it matches or not—cut. And you cut for the emotion, and you can get away with so much by doing that."[32]

Although Booth believed that editing should not interfere with the narrative, she also felt that it could enhance the narrative in much the same way that good poetry can elevate language—by finding the right rhythms. "Rhythm counts so much," she said, "the pauses count so much. It's the same as when people speak or dance—you can tell right away when it's wrong. Everything has to be rhythmic."[33] If she were editing a comedy, for example, she sped up the tempo. If the film was a musical, she cut on the downbeats. "Otherwise, you get a jarring cut and it throws things off," she said. "You should not feel the breaks. It's like pauses and breaths that you take on the stage. It has its ups and downs and its pace."[34]

Although Booth could be very firm in her ideas about what constitutes good editing and maintained a fairly traditional style and philosophy throughout her career, she was also quite open to stylistic changes she saw as beneficial. In her 1965 interview with Kevin Brownlow, for example, she talked about one significant change that she very much liked. "They're doing away with fades and dissolves," she said. "I like this much better than the old technique of lap dissolves [when one scene gradually fades into another], which slowed down the pace. There was a time when we made eight- to ten-foot dissolves. We taught the audience for many years to recognize a time lapse through a lap dissolve. Now they're educating them to direct cuts—a new technique brought about by a new generation of directors who can't afford dissolves or fades. And I think that's very good."[35]

The Booth Touch at Work on Mutiny on the Bounty (1935)

When asked in her later years to name her favorite personal editing achievements, Booth immediately picked three from MGM in the 1930s. The first is director Victor Fleming's 1933 romantic comedy, *Bombshell*, which gave actress Jean Harlow her nickname, "the Blonde Bombshell." The third is George Cukor's 1936 romantic drama, *Camille*, starring Greta Garbo in one of her best roles. But, it's Booth's second pick that she will probably be best remembered for, director (and sometime actor) Frank Lloyd's 1935 version of the epic sea story, *Mutiny on the Bounty*.

Widely considered one of the great triumphs of mainstream Hollywood studio moviemaking in the 1930s, the film was also a labor of love for Lloyd, who was captivated by sea stories and who directed several sea films during his 40-year film career. A friend of writers Charles Nordhoff and James Norman Hall, who had published a fictionalized account of the story in 1932, Lloyd bought the rights to their book and pitched it to MGM. While Thalberg was enthusiastic about the project, Louis Mayer was hesitant, fearing that the absence of parts for any of MGM's popular female stars would hurt the film at the box office. But Thalberg countered, reportedly telling Mayer: "People are fascinated by cruelty, and that's why *Mutiny* will have appeal."[36]

For the time, when most films were made quickly and entirely at the studio, the scope of the production was quite impressive. Filming extended over several months and took place in numerous locations from the MGM studios in Culver City, to San Francisco, Monterey Bay, the Channel Islands, Tahiti, other sites in French Polynesia, and the open seas in the

Starring Clark Gable (third from left) and Charles Laughton (third from right), director Frank Lloyd's version of *Mutiny on the Bounty* (1935) is widely considered the best of several film adaptations of this famous tale of cruelty and mutiny on the high seas. Margaret Booth's contribution was masterly editing that has helped keep the film fresh and vital more than 80 years after its initial release (MGM/Photofest).

South Pacific. When in Tahiti, MGM hired more than 2500 locals to work as extras. And for the entire production, more than 3000 period costumes were made, including 600 British navy uniforms. Overall, the budget came to nearly $2 million, the most MGM had spent on a film since its 1925 epic *Ben-Hur*.

When production wrapped, more than 650,000 feet of film had been shot—a huge amount for a movie of this time when 100,000 feet was closer to the norm. Eventually, all this footage would have to be whittled away into the 12,000 feet that became the finished 132-minute film. Lloyd and Thalberg would be closely involved in the process. But the bulk of the work—and with it much of the responsibility for the film's ultimate success or failure—would fall squarely on the shoulders of Margaret Booth.

Looking at the finished film, it's impossible not to be impressed by its vitality and verve even more than 80 years after its release. At 132 minutes, it's much longer than the vast majority of films made at the time, but there's never the sense that it drags. Physical movement seems to be constant, but, since constant movement easily becomes monotonous, slower, quieter scenes are sprinkled through the proceedings with great care. The pacing, or "tempo," as Booth would say, has many of the elements of a rousing symphony with slower, change-of-pace interludes. The narrative movement, however, is constant throughout. Not one split second seems to be unnecessary to propelling the action—whether physical or psychological—forward.

In addition to providing the film with its near-perfect pacing, Booth uses editing throughout to suggest, reinforce, and sometimes enhance meaning in the story. One way she does this is in her ingenious use of reaction shots in numerous scenes. This is a common technique to cut to get the responses of other characters to a development in the story, of course. But Booth does this with excellent results repeatedly. In scene after scene, for example, we see the reactions of various characters to Bligh's various actions, and, as we do, we can sense the collective anger mounting and feel all the more that something's got to give.

As an example of Booth's work in individual scenes, especially to reinforce meaning, let's look closely at the first four scenes of the film. Together, they make up the film's first major unit, or sequence, and take up just 17 minutes. They also demonstrate Booth's ability to take Lloyd and cinematographer Arthur Edeson's mountain of raw footage and sculpt it into a finished work of art.

The film begins with movement. We see the figure of a man walking along a wet city street and stopping to say, "All's well." Instantly, he is upstaged by a group of men tromping past him with an emphatic sense of urgency. The men stop, and one of them peers through the window of a pub. Immediately, they are recognized as a "press gang," a group ordered essentially to kidnap ordinary Englishmen and force, or "press," them into naval service. Within seconds, six men are told that they are now in the navy, will be serving on a ship bound for the South Seas, and won't return for at least two years. The wife of one young man, Tommy Ellison (Eddie Quillan), pleads desperately for her husband to be spared, but of course he isn't. The lives of these six—as well as the lives of their loved ones—are upended, perhaps forever.

To modern audiences, the treatment of ordinary people here is cruel and shocking. But, the almost casual tone of the scene—reinforced by the fast-paced editing—suggests both the callousness of the system and the tenuous nature of these people's lives: In a split second a good, decent man can be separated from his loving wife and child and forced into virtual servitude for at least two years.

Rather than cutting to the next scene, the upper-class home of Midshipman Roger Byam (Franchot Tone) and his family, Booth employs a quick dissolve between the two scenes, suggesting a strong connection or juxtaposition between them. We get the point immediately. As opposed to young Tommy Ellison who is forcibly taken from his family, young Roger Byam enters in his new tailor-made uniform brimming over with romantic ideas of the sea and adventure. Well-born, well-educated, and well-connected, the exuberant Byam has signed on to go to Tahiti to compile a dictionary of the Tahitian language. For him so far, this has been nothing but dreams and joyous anticipation. As opposed to the first scene, there are fewer cuts here, suggesting a more relaxed, leisurely tone and, of course, less disruption.

Next, the action shifts to Portsmouth Harbor just before the *Bounty* sets sail. All is hustle and bustle, and this is reinforced in brisk cutting between short personal exchanges. Within moments we are introduced to the drunken ship's doctor with his peg leg, the nervous ship's cook, first officer Fletcher Christian (Clark Gable), and several of the other characters who will play key roles in the story. Then, Captain Bligh (Charles Laughton) comes on board and orders the decks cleared for the ship's departure. He also takes great pride in learning that the *Bounty* will participate in a "flogging of the fleet," a practice in which men from several ships administer lashes to a seaman for a serious offense. Then, when he hears that the seaman about to be flogged has already been whipped to death, he orders the flogging anyway. The men—we see in numerous reaction shots—are appalled. The young, naïve Byam even faints. After the flogging has been administered, Bligh gives the order to set sail.

During these initial parts of the scene, the pacing of the editing is usually fast, but it often slows when Bligh is in the action, which suggests a couple of things. First, it underscores Bligh's manner of always putting a damper on whatever is happening no matter how pleasant or harmless it is. And second, it tells us that, by nature, Bligh clashes with the natural rhythms of the lives of the other characters. Again, the editing subtly reinforces the central conflict in the story between Bligh and his crew.

Then, as soon as Bligh orders the ship to prepare to sail, we see one of the film's most dramatic editing flourishes. The next two and a half minutes consist of no fewer than 60 cuts, an average of one cut for every two and a half seconds, and including many, many cuts that are only a split second apart. In the action, the film cuts back and forth from officers giving orders to men pulling ropes, other men climbing the rigging and untying the sails, the sails unfurling and filling with wind, the men racing down the rigging. The film also cuts to shots of people reacting to the ship's departure such as Ellison's wife, who is hopeful of her husband's safe return, and Byam's wise uncle, who is visibly concerned. It's a magnificent statement, communicating through a stunning variety of visuals and rapid-fire tempo both the excitement and adventure an exotic sea voyage must have meant for people in the 18th century and the complex feelings of loved ones left behind. As the sails fill with wind, we in the audience share in the sense of uplift. Going against this rapid succession of exciting action images, however, is the longest single shot of the segment: a full 13 seconds in which a shocked and disillusioned Byam shares his horror about what he has just seen—Bligh's order to flog the dead sailor. Once again, an action of Bligh's undercuts an otherwise exuberant, life-affirming moment.

As soon as the *Bounty* sails majestically out of Portsmouth, the screen fades to black for just a moment, suggesting not only a passage of time but also that something ominous may lie ahead. Then from black it fades into the next scene in Bligh's cabin. In stark contrast to the busy crowd/action scene we have just watched, this is a simple conversation between two men, Bligh and Christian, which spells out their relationship. While Bligh has a high regard for Christian, Christian has little respect for Bligh. This infuriates Bligh, but Christian agrees to carry out his orders. Neither loses his temper or raises his voice during their exchange, but the issues that divide the two men have become crystal clear and the eventual battle lines are drawn. The editing is slower here, underscoring Bligh's power over the usually more jovial and good-natured Christian. As Christian leaves Bligh's cabin after the exchange, the film again fades to black, again to suggest—along with the passage of time—a continuing ominous mood.

Overall, these four scenes show excellent filmmaking on various levels. The writing is sharp and crisp, introducing numerous distinctive characters and setting up all the film's key conflicts with great clarity and economy. The actors, even those in small character roles, are all in full command of their characters. The shooting, especially during the scene on board the ship, is vivid and dynamic. And the editing follows suit—finding the right rhythms for this story and, whenever possible, cutting between shots and linking between scenes to support and enrich the narrative.

For much of the story, Booth follows a similar editing strategy, but when appropriate, she sometimes deviates dramatically and with great effect.

One example of this occurs about midway through the film. The *Bounty* has arrived in Tahiti, Christian and Byam have enjoyed a wonderful day with two Tahitian women, and Bligh has ordered Christian to return to the ship. At this point, Christian is passionately drawn not only to the Tahitian woman Maimiti (Mamo Clark), with whom he has spent the day, but also to the gentle, very humane, and extremely pleasant Tahitian community, way of life, and values—all of which stand in stark contrast to Bligh's constant cruelty. He knows he must return to the *Bounty* and Bligh, but he can't resist having a little more time to savor life on the island.

Here, Booth (no doubt with input from Lloyd and perhaps others) engineers another beautifully edited segment, this one slower in tempo than most of the rest of the film. It lasts about three and a half minutes, and, in a radical departure from this largely dialogue-driven film, we hear no dialogue the entire time.

Christian has just bid farewell to the Tahitian chieftain, Maimiti, and Byam, and heads back to a longboat waiting to take him back to the ship. Maimiti, not wanting to see him go, follows him. He nears the shore, sees men from the ship waiting for him in the longboat, and looks at this with dread. Then he notices nearby Tahitians dancing and singing, looks over, and smiles gently and perhaps even longingly. He also notices Maimiti. We see back-and-forth close-ups of the two. He goes to her and, as they kiss once, a shot of a cresting ocean wave is superimposed over them, suggesting perhaps that they are being swept up in an unstoppable natural force. They kiss again and the scene slowly dissolves to palm trees. The camera pans down the trees, and again we see the dancers. It is later now, and they are in shadow. Then the image dissolves to a sunset as Christian and Maimiti, now in silhouette, look at it. With utmost grace, she slips to the ground. He follows her. Again they kiss, and the image dissolves again to the dancers. They are dancing at night now, each holding a small torch and suggesting that Christian and Maimiti have indeed lit a fire of their own. The image dissolves back to Maimiti, who smiles and then caresses Christian's head in a moment of sexual afterglow. This image fades out and fades in to morning as the sun rises. The two lovers walk together to the shore, kiss, and then Christian starts swimming back to the ship. Without his knowing, Maimiti follows him, and, just as he reaches the ship, surprises him. They share one last kiss before he climbs aboard. Once on board, he sees her and waves at her as she swims back. She returns the wave.

Here, the film depends heavily on some editing resources that are not used (or used far more sparingly) in the rest of the film. Perhaps the most obvious are the symbols of the ocean wave and then the dancers holding fiery torches to represent the passion between Christian and Maimiti. Obviously, sex could only be implied in Hollywood films at the time, and symbols were often used. The challenge was in how to use them, and here it is done deftly, giving us just enough to communicate the point but not too much as to seem clichéd or heavy-handed. Another editing resource is the frequent use of dissolves and fades (a few quite long) between the various scenes and images. During the three and a half minutes, there are ten of them, many more than we see in any comparable time span in any other part of the film. In addition to indicating a passage of time, they also hint at—as one scene softly flows into the next—a gentleness of feeling and a sense of connectedness (perhaps communion) Christian feels both with Maimiti and with the people and life he has found on Tahiti. In all, it is a beautifully orchestrated interlude that stands out as one of the few happy times Christian has during the story, and throughout the editing has subtly and quite effectively reinforced and enriched its meaning.

An additional factoid that helps one to appreciate the accomplishment here of Booth and MGM's technical personnel all the more is that, while scenes from the film were shot in Tahiti, most of the film's actors, including Clark Gable, did not make the long trip there for filming. Doubles were used in long shots, and in many scenes existing footage of Tahiti was shown behind the actors using "rear-projection" techniques. For years, filmmakers, even in technically advanced Hollywood, routinely had problems making rear-projection look believable. Even in the 1960s, such masters as Alfred Hitchcock and John Ford had great difficulties with it, respectively, in 1963's *The Birds* and 1964's *Cheyenne Autumn*. In *Mutiny on the Bounty*'s Tahiti scenes, however, it's almost impossible to imagine—especially on a first viewing—that Clark Gable was not there. Making the illusion work depended both on MGM's cinematography and technical teams as well as on Booth's expert editing.

Released in November of 1935, *Mutiny on the Bounty* was an enormous commercial and critical hit. On its initial run, it made nearly $4.5 million, more than twice its production budget, and was the biggest Hollywood hit of the year. Heading into the Academy Awards in early 1936, it also received eight nominations, including one for editing, and ultimately won in the Best Picture category.

In the decades since *Mutiny*'s initial release, film writers have generally remained positive in their appraisals of the film. Pauline Kael has written, "[F]or the kind of big budget, studio-controlled romantic adventure that this is, it's very well done."[37] And Adrien Turner has called the film, "an exotic and gripping piece of Hollywood mythology, made with all the technical skill and gloss one associates with Irving Thalberg's MGM."[38]

A good deal of that "technical skill" of course came from Margaret Booth, whose pitch-perfect editing has played an essential role in keeping the film fresh and gripping today.

A Passion for Perfection

Filmmaking has come a long way since Margaret Booth worked with film legends such as Griffith and Thalberg, ruled MGM's editing department with her firm hand, and supervised films for Ray Stark, but her enormous influence remains. Although she could irritate producers, directors, and others with her curt manner, strong opinions, and insistence that they change films to suit her requirements, her "uncanny perceptiveness," as Kevin Brownlow called it, was rarely seriously challenged. She understood the complicated art of film editing as well as anyone, and, when it came to standing her ground, she was fearless. Instead of digging in and fighting with her, nearly everyone—sooner or later—resigned themselves to the fact that it was simply better to listen and learn from her. In addition to teaching editors and (often) directors, she instilled in many of them her own passion for perfection. She constantly drove people to delve more deeply into the editing process and, by doing so, produce better work and feel proud about doing it. In fact, when we consider the enormous number of films that had to go through Booth before they could be released and the scores of editors whose work had to meet her exacting standards before it was declared done, one fact of film industry life becomes abundantly clear—without Margaret Booth, American films today would, in all like-lihood, not be held to the same exacting standards that they are.

4

"Bobbie Says…"

Barbara McLean's Four Decades as Darryl Zanuck's "Right-Hand Woman"

In the summer of 1933, 30-year-old Darryl F. Zanuck was still far from being the Hollywood legend people remember today. An ambitious writer-producer at Warner Brothers during the late 1920s and early 1930s, he and company president Harry Warner had recently parted ways after a loud, bitter argument over business at the fabled film-biz haunt the Brown Derby Restaurant in Los Angeles. Now—along with producer Joseph Schenck and some investment dollars from Schenck's brother Nicholas and others—he was trying to start a new film company from scratch.

The name of the company was Twentieth Century, and, as assistant Sam Engel—who had suggested it to Zanuck—noted with a smile, this name would be good for another 67 years. But the more pressing issue for Zanuck and Schenck at the time was whether the fledgling company formed during the worst year of the Great Depression had only short-term viability. Without a stable of contract stars or directors, a network of theaters to show films, extensive in-house production facilities, and other resources the major studios had, they knew they were a David pitted against four Goliaths. A couple of poorly made films or market miscalculations could mean that—instead of 67 years—their Twentieth Century might only be good for another six or seven months.

The new company's first production was a rough-and-tumble drama set on the lower East Side of Manhattan in the early 1900s called *The Bowery*. Directed by the talented Raoul Walsh, starring reliable stars Wallace Beery and George Raft, and focusing on a rivalry between two long-time male friends (a favorite Zanuck storyline), the film appeared to have all the ingredients of a hit. During post-production, however, there was a strike and, along with other employees, the film's newly hired assistant editor walked off the job. When the strike was over, bad feelings remained and people at the studio didn't want to bring several of the strikers—including this assistant editor—back. But, the film's lead editor (who considered this loss nothing less than a catastrophe for the film) personally pleaded with Zanuck to rehire the assistant—someone Zanuck hadn't yet met and knew only as "Bobby."

"Get him back," Zanuck ordered, assuming that "Bobby" was one of the men who now dominated in Hollywood's editing ranks. "Get him back."[1]

Soon afterwards, however, Zanuck learned that "Bobby" was really "Bobbie," a 29-year-old cutting room veteran named Barbara McLean (1903–1996). A skilled and insightful film editor himself, he immediately recognized her contribution to *The Bowery* (which went on to become the studio's second biggest hit that year). Calling McLean "one of the best editors in town,"[2] he quickly made her a lead editor, and soon she was handling the studio's most prestigious productions. Two years later, when Zanuck and Schenck purchased the ailing Fox Film Corporation and created 20th Century–Fox, she—along with other new hires such as screenwriter Nunnally Johnson—went with them.

And she stayed for the next 34 years.

As an editor, McLean worked on more than 60 films for such directors as Henry King, Clarence Brown, John Ford, Elia Kazan, and Joseph L. Mankiewicz and was, during her time, the most honored member of her profession. Between 1936 and 1951, for example, she received an eye-popping seven Academy Award nominations for editing (winning an Oscar for her work on 1944's bio-pic *Wilson*), a record she held or shared until 2013 when editor Michael Kahn received his eighth editing nomination for his work on Steven Spielberg's *Lincoln*. And, even after her retirement, she remained one of the industry's most respected editors, receiving one of the first two Career Achievement Awards given by the American Cinema Editors (ACE) in 1988.

McLean's achievements as an editor were, however, only part of the story. In her years at 20th Century–Fox, she also became a valuable creative resource for several of the studio's directors, the head of the studio's editing department, and one of Zanuck's most trusted advisors and confidantes. She worked on 29 films, for example, with one of Zanuck's favorite directors, the very under-appreciated Henry King. In fact, as King frequently said, if he could always have his way, he'd have McLean with him on *all* his films. As well as editing, King asked McLean to participate in shooting, occasionally going with him and his crew on location to advise on how scenes were shot and the kinds of shots she would need to tell the story most effectively. In 1949, McLean moved into a supervisory role, heading 20th Century–Fox's editing department until her retirement in 1969. During this period, she exerted the kind of influence over the studio's total output that only Margaret Booth at MGM could match. And, throughout McLean's tenure, Zanuck relied heavily on her advice on all matters from re-cutting the work of other editors to wardrobe choices, to the casting of actors. When looking at screen tests of actors vying for the lead role in King's 1936 film *Lloyd's of London*, for example, McLean went against the consensus choice of the more established Don Ameche, arguing for a then unknown 22-year-old named Tyrone Power. Ultimately, Power got the part,

One of Darryl F. Zanuck's most valued confidants at 20th Century-Fox, Barbara McLean—who received seven Academy Award nominations between 1936 and 1951—was perhaps the most honored film editor of the studio era. Much of her best work was with director Henry King, who found McLean's contributions to his films indispensable (© 20th Century–Fox).

carried the picture, and became one of the studio's most popular stars. In fact, Zanuck grew to value McLean's opinion so much that, as studio lore went, any time he would begin a sentence with the words "Bobbie says…" those listening knew that the time for further discussion on the matter had passed—that McLean had spoken.

While not as well-known as other long-time Zanuck confidantes such as King or writer/producers Nunnally Johnson and Philip Dunne, the shy, reserved, and very private McLean was nevertheless one of the most creative and powerful voices at one of Hollywood's elite studios for nearly four decades. When film scholar George F. Custen, in his 1997 biography of Zanuck, referred to her as "the centerpiece of his professional world,"[3] he wasn't exaggerating but simply reaffirming what everyone well acquainted with that world already knew.

"[Y]ou worked like mad because you loved every minute of it."

In contrast to most of her editing peers who learned their craft as adults, McLean, who was born Barbara Pollut in Palisades Park, New Jersey, began as a girl in grade school. Her father, Charles, ran a local film laboratory, and during her breaks from school she would work there, patching together release prints of films for an adjacent studio run by silent film actor and director Edward Kline Lincoln. She also studied music, an experience she later claimed helped to give her a keenly attuned sense of the natural rhythms of film editing.

When she was in her early 20s, she married a movie projectionist named J. Gordon McLean and the two moved to Hollywood. Gordon later became a cameraman. The couple never had children and divorced in the late 1940s.

Once in Hollywood, Barbara found work as a negative cutter for Grant Whytock, the film editor for the highly regarded silent film director Rex Ingram, and assisted Whytock on such exotic, sophisticated Ingram efforts as *Mare Nostrum* (1926) and *The Garden of Allah* (1927), films which would serve as excellent preparation for many complex, challenging films she would later tackle at 20th Century–Fox. Then, after a brief stint at First National Studio, she went to work for silent screen superstar Mary Pickford at United Artists on the early talkie *Coquette* (1930), for which Pickford would win a Best Actress Oscar. Delighted to work with Pickford, whom she greatly admired, McLean was also thrilled that the experience at United Artists gave her the chance to learn about filmmaking from numerous perspectives. "My God, we did everything," she recalled. "I could get into every department.... You'd go on the scoring stage when they'd do the music, to see what [they] would be doing. You know, to know that everything was going to fit. [With] each thing you learned a little bit more."[4]

While at United Artists, McLean also worked with Samuel Goldwyn, whom she remembered and admired as "a perfectionist."[5] Then, in 1933, she got a job as an assistant editor on *The Bowery*, the first film produced by Darryl Zanuck and Joseph Schenck's brand new company Twentieth Century. And, after her brief departure during a strike and Zanuck's plea to "Get him back," this studio would be her professional home for the rest of her career.

Just as Zanuck, King, and others at 20th Century–Fox valued working with McLean, she appreciated the opportunity to work not only with them but also in the environment that many at the studio had a hand in creating. "It was like the whole family, so naturally you worked like mad because you loved every bit of it," McLean once said. "You loved them, and you wanted the picture to be great, and you didn't mind how hard you worked. And that's the faculty that Zanuck had."[6]

Recognizing what McLean could do, Zanuck quickly promoted her. She was the lead editor on Twentieth Century's fifth film, a woman's drama starring Ann Harding called *Gallant Lady* (1934). And soon afterwards, she was editing many of the studio's prestige pictures, such as the comedy *The Affairs of Cellini* (1934) with Constance Bennett and Frederic March, the historical drama *The House of Rothschild* (1934) with George Arliss, and another historical drama, *Clive of India* with Ronald Colman and Loretta Young.

During these early years, some of her most impressive work was in 1935 film version of Victor Hugo's classic novel *Les Miserables* with March and Charles Laughton.

One of the great challenges of watching 1930s film adaptations of classic novels today is, certainly by current standards, their relatively slow, plodding pace. To McLean's credit, however, this version of *Les Miserables* tells the story of this sprawling novel with great speed and economy. Throughout, too, her excellent sense of rhythm helps to underscore the points being made in the story. In one excellent montage early in the film, for example, she captures the experience of being a prisoner consigned to row day after day on a galley ship along with the repetitive, oppressive sound cadences that are central to this experience. The prisoners row to the beat of a gong, the film's cuts and dissolves follow accordingly, and, as we in the audience watch and listen, we absorb both the horror and the haunting musicality of the situation. It's an entrancing few moments.

McLean's work here as well as throughout *Les Miserables* made a powerful impression on her peers, earning her the first of her Best Editing Academy Award nominations after only two years as a lead editor. The film was also nominated in the Best Picture category, and, while it has several other assets, including Gregg Toland's gorgeous black-and-white cinematography and fine acting performances from March and Laughton, McLean's contribution was critical to its success.

When Zanuck and Schenck bought Fox in 1935, McLean's work life only got better. Reflecting his understanding of the importance of editors in the filmmaking process, Zanuck built a new three-story editing building with all the most advanced equipment and facilities. The first floor was for screenings, where producers (rather than directors) conferred with editors and made the final decisions on films. The third floor was for film storage. And the second floor was where the editors worked—and where no one else was allowed.

For an editor, especially one with McLean's talents, this was the equivalent of heaven on earth. While directors were deeply involved in the editing phase in the early years of the film industry, and while they are usually deeply involved today, they were more hands-off during the heyday of the studios. A major reason was the assembly-line model the industry had adopted. Once directors had finished the production phase for one film, they were usually off to direct another. The editing was left for the editors, and much of the critiquing was the job of producers, such as Zanuck. Although editors didn't have the benefits of a director's continuous input, they were also spared the headaches of a director's constant meddling and, as such, had greater autonomy to make the decisions they considered best for the film. As McLean later recalled, "I've always been pretty fortunate in being able to put the picture in the first cut as I saw fit."[7] In addition, she had the clout to tell directors to reshoot scenes or to shoot additional close-ups if she believed this would help the editing and ultimately improve the final product. With this kind of model, it's no wonder that, from the 1930s to the 1960s, 20th Century–Fox offered an extremely appealing work environment not only for McLean but also for such other major editing talents as Hugh Fowler, William Reynolds, Robert Simpson, and Dorothy Spencer—all of whom McLean mentored.

Once Twentieth Century had merged with Fox, McLean also began working with a director whose career would parallel hers for the next 20 years, Henry King. A true film pioneer, King had directed his first film in 1915 and quickly developed a reputation both for his versatility and for his straightforward, unpretentious visual style. After working as an independent producer-director and then a director for Samuel Goldwyn in the 1920s, he joined Fox Studios in 1930, became one of Darryl Zanuck's most trusted directors after the merger with Twentieth Century in 1935, stayed with the studio until 1961, and died in 1982 at the venerable age of 96. In his time at 20th Century–Fox, he directed 37 films, 29 of them with McLean.

Their first notable collaboration was the 1936 historical drama *Lloyd's of London*, the film for which McLean suggested that the studio cast the 22-year-old unknown Tyrone Power in the lead. Set in England before and during the Napoleonic Wars, the film is the story of the fictional Jonathan Blake, a boyhood friend of Lord Nelson, who goes to work for the firm Lloyd's of London and eventually uses chicanery to help his old friend keep his fleet intact and win the crucial Battle of Trafalgar in 1805. Again, McLean's instinct for cutting to the rhythms of the story with seemingly perfect timing is apparent. While the film's pacing never seems rushed, it also flows with great crispness: we never feel that even a second of unneeded film can be excised. Here, too, McLean shows a real talent for cutting between close-ups of key characters in crowd scenes to reinforce dramatic tensions. She does this quite well, for example, in one scene at a party when Blake realizes that the woman he has fallen for is married to a callous ne'er-do-well (played brilliantly, incidentally, by George Sanders in his first American film). In a brief succession of reaction shots, the complex relationship dynamics among the three characters are conveyed with great economy and skill. For her work on *Lloyd's of London*, McLean received another Academy Award nomination.

In addition to cutting dramas, McLean was adept at musicals, and one of her great triumphs during this period was 1938's *Alexander's Ragtime Band*. Directed by King and starring Power, Alice Faye, and Don Ameche, the film is story of a bandleader, his songwriter friend, and the woman they both love that runs from the early 1900s to the 1930s and features a veritable smorgasbord of Irving Berlin songs. Here, McLean's work is often stunning. In the film's many big-band numbers, for example, she mixes long, medium, and close shots with great aplomb not only to show the various performers at work but also to reinforce some of the story's romantic tensions. In the film, she also does an excellent job mixing actual footage of World War I with scenes shot to incorporate the film's characters into the conflict, making it difficult to distinguish between them. (This is a skill she would later perfect in 1949's *Twelve O'Clock High*.) An enormous hit, *Alexander's Ragtime Band* received six Academy Award nominations, including one for McLean.

In 1939, McLean tried her hand at a disaster film, Clarence Brown's *The Rains Came*. Set in the fictional Indian city of Ranchipur in the 1930s, the dramatic center of the story is a massive earthquake and flood that leads first to a great plague and ultimately to the people's resolve to rebuild the ravaged community. The film, which beat out *The Wizard of Oz* that year for the very first Oscar for Best Special Effects for its depiction of the earthquake and flooding, required a special effort from McLean to edit all the disaster shots together in a way that not only was credible, gripping, and terrifying, but that also kept the various human stories moving.

The result, a sequence that lasts about for three and a half minutes, is quite powerful. An initial tremor shakes up a party the major characters are attending. For a moment, this one minor quake seems to be it. Then additional quakes hit, several larger than the first. We see buildings collapse on people, the earth opening up and people falling in, and even a large dam bursting and the escaping water overwhelming the ant-like humans in its wake. In between such shots, we also see the various characters we've been following thus far in the story. A young Indian doctor and his nurse rush to the hospital and are covered by floodwater. We don't know if they will survive. An arrogant British aristocrat and his bitter servant argue pointlessly just before one of the later earthquakes crushes their house, instantly killing the two of them. Throughout the sequence, both the large-scale events and the intimate events involving the film's characters are juxtaposed with great skill. The experience is everything it should be: fast-paced, chaotic, dramatically riveting, and a clear object lesson relating to the story's more self-absorbed, self-important characters, pointing out that—in the face of nature's enormous power—we are ultimately small, fragile creatures with largely petty concerns.

In addition to winning the first Academy Award for Special Effects, *The Rains Came* was nominated for five more Oscars. One of these was for best film editing, McLean's fourth nomination in five years.

McLean's work during the 1940s was no less exceptional. She received a fifth Academy Award nomination for her work on 1943's religious film, *The Song of Bernadette*. Then, the following year, she finally won an Oscar for her work on *Wilson*, a film biography of President Woodrow Wilson, which focuses on the period from when he was president of Princeton University to his last days in office as U.S. president. Nothing less than an obsessive quest for Zanuck (who greatly admired the former president), the film—largely because of its uninspired and rambling script—received generally poor reviews, was a major failure at the box office, and is rarely seen today. But, owing to the mysteries of Academy Award voting, it somehow managed to receive 10 Oscar nominations and win five of the golden statuettes.

Wilson presented some major editing challenges for McLean, many related to the size and scope of the project as well as to the excessive amount of film used in shooting it. (At the time, it was the most expensive American film ever made after *Gone with the Wind*.) As McLean later recalled, "I can remember *Wilson*. Holy Mother.... I'll never forget the [Democratic] convention … when you had miles and miles of film. And all those bands. You sit down, 'Where do I start and what do I do?' You just sit down and figure it all out."[8]

It's unfortunate, however, that, if McLean were to win only one Oscar, it would be for this film. Not only had she already done superb work on numerous, more deserving films, but she would also continue to do superb work for another decade.

After *Wilson*, King and McLean teamed on an adaptation of John Hersey's Pulitzer Prize winning novel *A Bell for Adano*, the story of an Italian-American officer determined to restore a 700-year-old bell the Fascists have taken from the Sicilian town of Adano during World War II, a bell that had been tied closely to the town's identity. The film, starring John Hodiak and Gene Tierney, is mostly a solid, respectful adaptation of the book, but, in their discussion of McLean's work, Susan Ware and Stacy Lorraine Braukman write how, even in a fairly routine film, McLean's editing could still "dazzle." As they note, "[S]he took material director Henry King shot on the return of the Italian POWs to their village and put it together with such a pure sense of emotion that when she cut at exactly the right moment to King's overhead shot of the prisoners and villagers coming together in the square, the cut was more heart-stopping than conventional close-ups would have been."[9]

In 1947, McLean attempted something quite different for her at the time, a very dark film noir titled *Nightmare Alley*. Directed by Edmond Goulding, it tells the story of the rise and long, hard fall of an amoral con man that begins and ends in two seedy carnivals. Eager to expand beyond the swashbuckling action roles he was playing at the time, Tyrone Power had purchased the rights to the novel the film is based on with the intent to play the lead himself. Although the film wasn't successful on its initial release, it is widely considered one of Power's best performances and has since become a noir classic.

One of *Nightmare Alley's* great strengths is its ability to convey—in true noir fashion—life's nightmarish aspects, and McLean ably does her part to support the overall objective through editing. As the blogger "monstergirl" wrote in 2012, "In *Nightmare Alley*, Barbara McLean contributes to creating a landscape of a distorted reality alongside the darkly, clandestine, and arcane carnival atmosphere. The film is beautifully woven, as the seamless images flow into one another.... McLean's editing constructs much of the surreal and tormented movement of the film. It's what transports each scene of the film, making it every bit as if WE were inhabiting someone's nightmare."[10]

The years 1949 and 1950 represented yet another high-water mark for McLean with her work on King's powerful and grim World War II film *Twelve O'Clock High* (1949), King's pioneering psychological western *The Gunfighter* (1950), and Joseph L. Mankiewicz's masterpiece *All About Eve* (1950). Again, her editing enriches these films in various ways. In *Twelve O'Clock High*, for example, she once again shows her amazing talent for integrating actual war film footage with dramatized scenes to create a riveting air battle near the end of the film. In *The Gunfighter*, she turns the claustrophobic environment of the saloon the title character is confined to for much of the film into an asset, occasionally mixing close-ups of characters' faces with close-ups of a steadily ticking wall clock to intensify suspense and audience anxiety. And in *All About Eve*, she is pitch-perfect in editing to the rhythms of the witty lines the urbane characters constantly exchange, exhibiting the keen sense of timing of an accomplished stage actor. For her work on *Eve*, she received her seventh—and last—Academy Award nomination.

McLean would continue to edit films until 1955, but, after 1949, when she became head of 20th Century–Fox's editing department, her work focus became more supervisory in nature. One major achievement during this time, however, was her editing on the 1953 Biblical epic *The Robe*. Directed by Henry Koster, this was the very first film shot in CinemaScope, a new widescreen film process the studio had invested in—and was heavily promoting—to compete with television. Almost overnight, the wide screen would become the norm for the movies, but, as film writer Kevin Lewis has noted, "The challenges involved in determining editing cuts in the widescreen process for the first time certainly seemed to deserve a special award."[11] Yet, while the film received five Academy Award nominations with two wins (in Art Direction and Costume Design), the film's editing was passed over.

As well as taking a new direction in her career during the 1950s,

McLean also took a new direction in her personal life. Recently divorced after her marriage of more than 20 years to Gordon McLean, she began dating Robert Webb, a long-time assistant director to Henry King, after actress Susan Hayward had invited them both to dinner. They married in 1951 and became one of only a handful of Oscar-winning couples at the time. Webb had received his Oscar in the short-lived category of Best Assistant Director for his work on King's *In Old Chicago* in 1938, the last year that particular award was given. He would go on to direct about 20 films, including Elvis Presley's first feature, *Love Me Tender* (1956).

McLean also co-produced two of Webb's films, *Seven Cities of Gold* (1955) and *On the Threshold of Space* (1956). But from the mid–1950s until she retired in 1969 to look after Webb, who was then in poor health, she focused entirely on her supervisory duties.

In many respects, these were probably not McLean's happiest years at 20th Century–Fox, either. After more than 20 years of being the master of all he surveyed at the studio he effectively created, Zanuck, seeing that times were changing, stepped down as the company's studio head in 1956 and went to live in Europe and work as an independent producer. In 1962, he returned with his son Richard to run the studio but found that the adage "you can't go home again" applied even to him. In late 1970, Richard was asked to resign and then in May 1971 Zanuck himself was forced out.

By that time, of course, McLean had already left, her departure coinciding closely with Margaret Booth's retirement from MGM and within just a few years of the deaths of both Anne Bauchens and Viola Lawrence. A great era, to which these women had all made enormous contributions, had clearly come to an end.

McLean and Webb lived quietly in retirement until his death in 1990. One highlight during this time came in 1988 when she and editor Gene Milford, who had won Oscars for editing Frank Capra's *Lost Horizon* (1937) and Elia Kazan's *On the Waterfront* (1954), became the first-ever recipients of the American Cinema Editors Lifetime Achievement Award.

In 1996, McLean died in Newport Beach, California, where she had lived since her retirement, of complications from Alzheimer's disease. She was 92. People who had worked with her remembered her both as a dedicated editor and truly supportive supervisor and as a person who usually kept to herself, rarely socializing even in the studio commissary.[12]

As one would expect, assessments of McLean's overall contribution to the films she worked on vary widely. In his 1996 obituary of McLean, for example, Adrian Dannatt called her "a revered editor who perhaps single-handedly established women as vital creative figures in an otherwise patriarchal industry."[13] Yet, as film historian J.E. Smyth has written, "Film critics have often said her work with Zanuck at Fox was more a 'corporate signature' than personal style."[14]

McLean certainly was "a revered editor," as Dannatt contends. But to say that she was "single-handedly" responsible for keeping women at the forefront of film editing, especially during a period when they were being squeezed out of a male-dominated industry, may be a bit much. She did play a major role in doing this from the 1930s through the 1960s, but—as Margaret Booth, Anne Bauchens, Viola Lawrence, Dorothy Spencer, Adrienne Fazan, and others might have argued—she was by no means alone.

Like Booth, McLean resisted being cast as a feminist later in her life. But, when asked once why there have been so many good women editors, she fired back with a question of her own, "Why do *you* think that the film editors who are women, who have been in it since I've been in it, are the best in the business?" she said. "Why? Because you had to be good or you wouldn't get there."[15] While not making a feminist speech, she was clearly suggesting that—in the male-dominated world of Hollywood at the time— the only way a woman could survive was to be just that much better than the men she was competing against for opportunities.

Looking at the films McLean worked on, it also seems unfair to dismiss her contribution as merely part of the 20th Century–Fox "corporate signature." In fact, because Zanuck made it a policy to shield his editors from meddling directors—and because Henry King and other directors so completely trusted her instincts, insights, judgment, and, when called for, ability to "dazzle"—she likely had far more freedom to cut films in ways that satisfied her artistic preferences than most of the editors of her era. By her own account, she always made the first cut by herself, and, although there were always modifications, the final cuts almost always remained close to her original.

～

In 1977, the magazine *Film Comment* asked McLean to answer several questions about editing, and her answers were so terse that one wonders if she secretly harbored disdain for her questioners. But, her answer to one of the questions—"What is great film editing?"—is quite intriguing. "Great film editing," she said, "begins with great pictures."[16] Just as great cooking begins with the best ingredients, she seemed to be saying, the best editing begins with—and effectively depends upon—great moments on film. If they aren't there, then the film is probably doomed, no matter how much clever cutting an editor does on it.

This small revelation might help illuminate McLean's core beliefs and the editing approach that emerged from them. Unlike most editors who simply work with the raw footage a director and cinematographer give them, McLean often took a more activist role, pushing for directors to shoot additional footage if she felt more close-ups and additional perspectives could in some way help improve the storytelling. Combined with her great instinct for the rhythms of a particular story and her commitment to keep stories constantly moving, the result is a dynamic, often highly creative visual style. For example, the galley sequence in *Les Miserables* could have simply consisted of a scene showing the main character rowing with a look of despair on his face. Instead, McLean created a brief montage, combining timely cutting and the rhythmic pounding of a gong to capture the oppressive monotony of the situation aurally as well as visually. In essence, she devised a very imaginative solution to convey the experience in a richer, more multi-sensory way. Another classic McLean solution came when she worked on Elia Kazan's *Viva Zapata!* in 1952. Dissatisfied with the existing footage of one scene showing peasants beating rocks to warn of danger, she took shots Kazan had made, duplicated them, reversed many of them, and put all these pieces together to transform a simple, straightforward scene into a more complex and more dramatic sequence that suggested many more people and perspectives. In doing so, she constructed a cinematic moment that was ultimately far more effective than even this ambitious director had originally envisioned.

This level of dedication also suggests a quality few people mention when discussing McLean's work: her level of emotional investment. A good editor, she once said, "uses the scissors on a film ... with affection and understanding and tolerance."[17] After seeing many of the films McLean worked on, it's difficult *not* to see this as a striking aspect about her work. She cared deeply about each story she helped to tell with strips of film, and—whether we're seeing a fast-paced musical such as *Alexander's Ragtime Band*, a downbeat film noir such as *Nightmare Alley,* or a gritty psychological western such as *The Gunfighter*—her sizable emotional investment consistently shows through. A big part of why so many films Barbara McLean worked on remain fresh and vibrant today is Barbara McLean.

Like virtually all the Hollywood film editors of her era, McLean adhered to the classical conventions developed by D.W. Griffith and others in the 1910s. She was by no means a radical stylistic innovator. But, in film after film, she clearly pushed the limits of the classical style and, in doing so, certainly proved that editors could put their artistic stamp on films.

McLean's Work on All About Eve

All About Eve may be the most celebrated film Barbara McLean ever
worked on. On many peoples' short lists of American film masterpieces,
it received a record 14 Academy Award nominations in early 1951, was one
of the first 50 films added to the Library of Congress's National Film Reg-
istry in 1990, and, in 2007, placed number 28 on the American Film Institute's list of the best 100 U.S. films ever made.

When evaluating the film, most people have—and rightly so—
focused on its brilliant, acerbic script by writer-director Joseph L. Mankiewicz and several wonderful acting performances, especially Bette Davis'
tour-de-force as aging Broadway diva Margo Channing. But the film owes
its enormous success to numerous other contributors as well, and one of
them is Barbara McLean.

Bette Davis and Anne Baxter face off as Gary Merrill and George Sanders look
on in Joseph L. Mankiewicz's *All About Eve* (1950). The film, which hinges on
conversation and includes relatively little physical action, presented editor Barbara McLean with some daunting challenges (Photofest).

A film about the theater, *All About Eve* is far more theatrical than cinematic in nature. In some respects, we can rightfully call it "all about words." Physical action—the heart and soul of most films—is minimal here. Words are both omnipresent and omnipotent. Language reigns supreme. Even when characters aren't uttering words in scenes, we hear them in voiceovers from multiple narrators. And in place of guns or daggers, words often—and ably—serve as the weapons of choice.

Such a film presents special challenges for a film editor. Mostly, it's a very stagy experience, and the challenge is to make it seem less so.

A big part of McLean's strategy here was to vary textbook editing whenever possible to make the story more interesting visually and aurally. We first see this strategy at work in the film's opening scene, which consists almost entirely of well-dressed people sitting politely at an awards reception listening to a presenter drone on as we listen to a long expository voice-over by the character of Addison DeWitt (George Sanders). There doesn't seem to be a lot for an editor to work with here, but McLean does some very interesting things.

One—when two major characters, writer Lloyd Richards (Hugh Marlowe) and director Bill Sampson (Gary Merrill), are introduced together—is to delay an immediate (and logical) cut from Richards to Sampson. Instead, McLean allows the camera to linger on Richards for a few additional seconds, perhaps with the intent of arousing our curiosity about who this director character is. The delay is subtly jarring, but it also keeps us on our toes. Visually, we are challenged a bit.

Another wonderful touch is the use of a freeze frame near the end of the scene at the moment the award recipient Eve Harrington (Anne Baxter) is about to take her trophy in her hands. At this time freeze frames were not at all common in mainstream films, and the effect is akin to an exclamation point. We know that something significant is about to happen—a change of scene perhaps. But the change is more elaborate and elegant than we might expect. Instead of a straight dissolve or fade out from the freeze frame to another scene, the film goes from the freeze frame to a live action reaction shot of Addison continuing his voice over; back to the freeze frame; then to a live action reaction shot of another key character, Karen Richards (Celeste Holm), who now begins a voice-over narration of her own; and finally to a long (five-second) dissolve to the moment in the past when Karen first meets Eve. Taking less than a minute, this is both quite arresting and visually stimulating.

In the film's famous party scene, McLean adds more subtle touches that give big moments special impact. One of these is the way she helps to set up Margo Channing's memorable line: "Fasten your seatbelts. It's going to be a bumpy night." Margo is in a bad mood, and other characters fear that a volcano is about to erupt. As they talk, innocuous music is played on an unseen piano. Then Karen confronts Margo, saying: "We know you. We've seen you like this before. Is it over, or is it just beginning?" At this, the piano music changes to a much more raucous, "bumpier" tune. It plays as Margo—in her most theatrical manner—finishes her martini, crosses the room, steps up one stair, turns, and delivers the line. In the way she synchronizes this music with the dialogue and the cutting of the visuals as Margo crosses the room and positions herself to deliver the line, McLean does an especially good job of maximizing its impact. If the music were synchronized differently or the timing of the editing were off, even just a bit, this line—one of the most famous in all of American cinema—might not be nearly as well-known or admired.

Throughout the film, McLean also does a wonderful job of cutting to the rhythms of one of the film's central elements: conversation. The timing of cuts is so natural—so in the moment—that we really do feel that we are in the room with these people listening to real conversations as they are actually taking place—not watching hundreds of pieces of film all assembled together well after the fact. Important in all films, the ability to make the conversations seem so real and immediate is especially important in this film that not only hinges on conversation but also celebrates it. Here, McLean achieves the illusion of complete invisibility, something that nearly all editors aspire to but that few actually pull off as well as she does.

As she often did, McLean also made ample use of close-ups and other reaction shots to flesh out scenes in *All About Eve*, giving them more texture, depth, and dramatic complexity. In this film especially—with its complicated characters and the complicated dynamics that exist between them—doing this well was of critical importance. There is a lot going on with these people; it all had to be communicated; and, to her credit, McLean got it all across with amazing clarity and insight. There is not a reaction shot or interaction between characters that seems forced or out of place in the entire film. Again, her editing was totally in synch with the film's grand plan.

While the editing in a film such as *All About Eve* is not as much of an attention-getter as the editing in some other films McLean worked on such as *Alexander's Ragtime Band* or *The Rains Came*, it was no less challenging to pull off. In fact, the challenges, when there is so little physical action in the film, were perhaps even more daunting. But, as McLean usually did, she found ways—even with these constraints—to intrigue, amaze, and yes, to "dazzle."

The Top Hollywood Editor of Her Era?

Few editors have ever had as much power to shape the final versions of films they worked on as Barbara McLean did.

And few have ever capitalized on this opportunity as fully as she did.

McLean was fortunate early in her career to connect with Darryl Zanuck, who appreciated and valued the contribution of a good editor as much as anyone in filmdom. But, just as he could be supportive, Zanuck could also be demanding and tough. To gain his trust, McLean had to prove her value, and, to keep that trust, she had to consistently perform at the top of her game. A driven perfectionist who also put a great deal of her heart into each film she brought to fruition, this came naturally to her. And for decades at 20th Century–Fox, she thrived.

Her personal style was very different from her long-time counterpart at MGM, Margaret Booth, with whom she is often compared. While Booth could be prickly and authoritarian with subordinates and peers, McLean tended to be more nurturing and collaborative. While Booth was more attuned to studio and industry politics, McLean preferred to assume a less visible profile.

McLean, nevertheless, was no less powerful and her contribution no less substantial than Booth's. In fact, unlike Booth, who came to MGM when it was already a first-tier studio, McLean was both present at the creation of 20th Century–Fox in 1935 and instrumental in its becoming a formidable filmmaking force within just a few years. In her role, she was also key—along with Zanuck, Henry King, Nunnally Johnson, Phillip Dunne, John Ford, Joseph L. Mankiewicz, Elia Kazan, and others—in creating and cultivating the studio's distinctive, highly compelling storytelling style from the late 1930s until the mid–1950s, a style that has influenced filmmakers around the world ever since.

Was Barbara McLean—as her seven Academy Award nominations and unique position in Darryl Zanuck's brain trust suggest—the top Hollywood film editor of her era?

The answer would be highly speculative and totally subjective, of course. But it could very well be *yes*.

5

Cutting to the Chase

Dorothy Spencer's Action-Packed Half-Century in Hollywood

When veteran Hollywood filmmaker Mark Robson agreed to direct Universal's ambitious 1974 disaster epic, *Earthquake*, he knew that he'd have his hands full. Hopes were running high that the film, which followed on the enormous successes of other formula disaster-centered thrillers such as Universal's *Airport* (1970) and 20th Century–Fox's *The Poseidon Adventure* (1972), would be a huge hit as well. To add to the pressure, there would be stiff competition. Two other big-budget disaster films, Universal's *Airport '75* and *The Towering Inferno*—a production so expensive that Warners and 20th Century–Fox opted to co-produce it—were both in development and set to open in theaters about the same time as *Earthquake*. The scope of *Earthquake's* story was also a consideration. Instead of showing a jetliner in peril or the capsizing of a cruise ship as *Airport* and *Poseidon* had done, the intent of *Earthquake* was to convincingly depict nothing less than the destruction of the city of Los Angeles by an earthquake and flood. To complicate matters more, *Earthquake* would be the first film to use "Sensurround," a new audio process developed by sound speaker manufacturer Cerwin-Vega to replicate the sound and (to some extent) the vibrations a person feels when experiencing a real earthquake. Added to this, four cameras were needed to film most of the action sequences. This ultimately resulted in more than 200,000 feet of shot film footage, an enormous amount for a two-hour feature. Finally, there was the unique editing challenge of cutting film footage shot from cameras that were deliberately shaken to simulate the trembling of the earth during the quake. How could this be done so the editing wouldn't look awkward or the overall effect cheesy?

To assure that this disaster film would not itself become a disaster, Robson—a thoughtful, versatile craftsman with a couple of Academy Award nominations to his credit—took particular care in his choices for key behind-the-scenes assignments. And for the job of his chief film editor—the one who would assume the enormous task of whittling all this footage down and then integrating it with various visual and sound effects—he sought out a petite, soft-spoken 65-year-old woman who was then living in the country in semi-retirement.

Her name was Dorothy Spencer (1909–2002), and, while she may have struck a casual observer as an odd choice for his assignment, she was—Robson knew—the perfect choice.

Spencer's Hollywood career had begun more than 45 years earlier when she worked as an assistant editor on silent films for Frank Capra, Raoul Walsh, and others. She began to receive editing credits in 1929, and by 1974 she had edited more than 70 films both as a freelancer and as a long-time staff editor at 20th Century–Fox. Although she had worked on virtually every kind of film from urbane comedies to serious dramas, to westerns, to suspense thrillers, she had gradually found a niche for herself in action films. "For some reason, I always seem to get assigned to pictures that are very physical," she once wrote. "I don't know why. Pictures [that] had a lot of physical action—fighting and brawling and things like that.… [T]hat suited me fine, because I like working on action pictures very, very much. They're more flexible and I think you can do a lot more with them. I like dialogue pictures, too, but, still and all, you're locked down with dialogue."[1]

Action, after all, was what *Earthquake* was all about, and, for Robson, who had worked with Spencer in seven previous films, choosing this action specialist who was as adept as anyone at cutting to the chase made absolute sense.

In opting for Spencer once again, Robson was in good company. In addition to him, Capra, and Walsh, she had worked on multiple occasions for such respected directors as John Ford, Alfred Hitchcock, Ernst Lubitsch, Fred Zinnemann, Joseph L. Mankiewicz, Jean Negulesco, Anatole Litvak, Tay Garnett, Archie Mayo, Edward Dymtryk, and Henry Hathaway. And, along the way, she had picked up three editing Academy Award nominations for her work. These included her contributions to Ford's enormously influential *Stagecoach* (1939), Litvak's moving war drama *Decision Before Dawn* (1951), and Mankiewicz's overblown but technically impressive *Cleopatra* (1963).

Spencer did not disappoint Robson during the making of *Earthquake*,

From the 1930s until the 1970s, Dorothy Spencer (pictured here in the mid–1930s) was one of Hollywood's most respected and sought-after film editors, working on notable films ranging from John Ford's *Stagecoach* (1939) and *My Darling Clementine* (1946) to Alfred Hitchcock's *Lifeboat* (1944) and picking up four Academy Award nominations for her work (Photofest).

either. Relishing the various challenges, she often came up with ingenious solutions to difficult problems such as speeding up the film's final rescue sequence while still keeping it credible. And, while the film's human story is usually clichéd, the editing and special effects (certainly for that time before computer-generated images) were quite impressive. When Oscar time rolled around in 1975, *Earthquake* received four nominations mostly in technical categories, and among those nominated was Dorothy Spencer for her editing.

Spencer came out of retirement one last time five years later to edit another disaster film, *The Concorde…Airport '79*. But, *Earthquake* was

effectively a last Hollywood hurrah in a career that bridged both the classic
film era and the "New Hollywood" and was responsible for accentuating
hundreds of riveting moments in all kinds of films from the tightly edited
final gunfight in Ford's *My Darling Clementine* (1946) to the flooding of
Los Angeles near the end of *Earthquake*. Unlike her later editing contemporaries such as Dede Allen, who introduced a variety of new editing techniques into her work in the 1960s and 1970s, Spencer basically remained
a traditionalist, adhering to the classic rules of editing established by Griffith in the 1910s and championed by people such as Margaret Booth. But,
through it all, she also remained the consummate craftsperson—an editor
so many great directors turned to again and again simply because she was
that good.

"[C]utting is very creative": Spencer's 50-year Run

For someone as accomplished as Spencer, it's amazing how little is
known about her personal life. We know that she was born in Covington,
Kentucky, in 1909 and died in Encinitas, California in 2002, for example,
but sources differ on whether her actual birthday was February 2 or 3. We
also know that she had an older sister, Jeanne, who edited about a dozen
films in the late 1920s and who was married to a film editor named Frank
Ware. It's possible (but only conjecture) that these two could have been
helpful in giving the Dorothy her start in Hollywood in the 1920s.

We do know, however, that she began in the film business at a very
early age, perhaps as young as 15, when she did entry-level jobs at the
Consolidated-Aller Lab in 1924. After work as an uncredited assistant editor on several films for several directors, including Frank Capra and Raoul
Walsh, between 1926 and 1929, she joined Fox Studios in 1929, where she
received her first credits on low-budget musical and comedy efforts such
as *Married in Hollywood* and *Nix on Dames* (both 1929).

During most of the 1930s, she freelanced, eventually teaming with
veteran Otho Lovering to share editing credit on several films for United
Artists and independent producer Walter Wanger. Many of these, such as
the comedies *Stand-In* (1937), *Trade Winds* (1938), and *Eternally Yours*
(1939), were with Tay Garnett, a solid journeyman director, who is probably
best remembered today for his 1946 film version of the noir story, *The
Postman Always Rings Twice*. But, she and Lovering also worked with other
directors, and by far their most important collaboration during this time
was their contribution to John Ford's landmark western, *Stagecoach* (1939).

Stagecoach, which marked Ford's return to the western genre after 13 years and nearly three-dozen non-western films, is, for numerous reasons, one of the most influential Hollywood films of the 1930s. Famously called "the first adult western" because of its sharp writing, complex characterizations, and top-notch production values, it gave the then-lowly genre a level of respectability it had not had since the mid–1920s and, in the process, launched the "Golden Age" of the western that ran from the mid–1940s to the early 1960s. In addition, it served as a primer on good filmmaking for the young Orson Welles as he developed *Citizen Kane* (1941), arguably the most influential film ever made. According to numerous accounts, Welles and many of his Mercury Theater players watched *Stagecoach* some 40 times as part of their preparation for *Kane*.

Part of why *Stagecoach* captivated audiences in 1939 and remains surprisingly fresh today is the tight construction in every element from its script (by frequent Ford collaborator Dudley Nichols) to Spencer and Lovering's editing. When watching certain scenes and sequences over and over again, they seem just about perfect in their timing and rhythms—nothing is too leisurely or too rushed, nothing is extraneous, every frame matters.

The sequence that Spencer and Lovering are often praised for is the famous Apache attack on the stagecoach and ensuing chase over desert salt flats. Not only does it remain riveting more than three-quarters of a century later, but it has also fascinated film historians because it deliberately breaks the 180-degree rule—one of the cardinal precepts of traditional editing—and succeeds admirably.

The 180-degree rule is essentially a guideline for on-screen spatial relationships to help reduce possible confusion for audiences watching a scene. For example, two characters having a conversation are shot from roughly the same vantage point so that one is always looking to one side, say right, and the other is always looking to the other, say left. In an action scene such as a chase, when things are happening quickly, adherence to this rule is especially helpful in clarifying the action for viewers. There is much less disorientation and confusion.

In *Stagecoach*, Ford, Spencer, and Lovering's decision to break this rule and cut accordingly was—for a Hollywood film at the time—quite radical. The objective *was* to disorient, confuse, and heighten anxiety for viewers, and, by achieving this, the scene achieved a couple of intriguing results. First, by heightening viewer anxiety, it also heightened suspense, making the action all the more compelling. And second, by disorienting and confusing the audience, it created a closer bond between viewers and the characters in the stagecoach, who are themselves thoroughly disoriented and confused. So, rather than compromising the cinematic experience, this deliberate breaking of the 180-degree rule actually intensified it. After *Stagecoach*, it would be done with increasing frequency in commercial films.

To make the scene even more nerve-wracking, Spencer and Lovering also mixed in frequent (and quick) crosscuts between the passengers and the attacking Apaches. And the combined effect is startling: the camera placement is deliberately disorienting to convey the confusion and anxiety of the stagecoach passengers, while the crosscutting between shots of the passengers and shots the pursuing Apaches ratchets up the scene's tempo and intensity to even higher levels. The passengers have this sense of everything spinning out of control, and we in the audience share their experience more fully than if it had been presented in a more conventional, less imaginative way.

To increase the scene's suspense even more, Spencer and Lovering also interplayed sound in some fascinating ways that wouldn't become standard practice until decades later. One is the climactic moment when—fearing capture, torture, rape for the women, and death for all the white people—one male passenger chooses to shoot a very ladylike female passenger so she will not have to suffer "that fate worse than death." We see his gun pointed at the unknowing woman who is deep in prayer. Then we see his gun fall, suggesting that he has been killed. Then, as the woman continues to pray unaware of what has happened, we hear—just as the woman hears it—the sound of a bugle. Her face lights up: the sound means of course that the cavalry has come to the rescue. She and most of the other passengers will be saved. Again, a more conventional approach would be to cut to a cavalry bugler as he sounds the charge and then cut to the woman's reaction shot. But, the sound of the bugle, Spencer and Lovering knew, would be enough, and their choice would make this moment more exciting.

Although Ford was legendary for shooting just what he wanted to use and giving his editors little to work with, Spencer credited him later in her life with giving her a great deal of editorial freedom. "With most directors, you cut it exactly the way they want it, and there's no room for editorial creativity," she wrote. "[But] Ford never told me anything and he never looked at the picture until it was finished."[2]

Seven years later, Spencer was the sole editor of another great Ford western, *My Darling Clementine* (1946), and her touch is also apparent there in numerous scenes. One highlight is the film's climactic gunfight in the iconic OK Corral. It plays like some of the best edited scenes in *Stage-*

coach—nothing too leisurely or too rushed, nothing extraneous, every frame important, and all editorial choices combining to achieve a highly suspenseful result. In fact, writer Peter Flynn notes that, without significant mood music, the film actually "achieved its suspense ... in its editing, a tight, pared-down construction in which only the barest (and most pertinent) of information is conveyed."[3]

For their work on *Stagecoach*, Spencer and Lovering received an editing Academy Award nomination, a first for both. And, by 1941, Spencer was the sole editor on major films for major directors. Just a few of her credits during the 1940s include *Sundown* (1941) for Henry Hathaway, *To Be or Not To Be* (1942) and *Heaven Can Wait* (1943) both for Ernst Lubitsch, *Lifeboat* (1943) for Alfred Hitchcock, *A Royal Scandal* (1945) for Otto Preminger, *A Tree Grows in Brooklyn* (1945) for Elia Kazan, *The Ghost and Mrs. Muir* (1947) for Joseph L. Mankiewicz, and *The Snake Pit* (1948) for Anatole Litvak.

As these credits suggest, most of these films were made by 20th Century–Fox, where Spencer went to work as a staff editor in 1943 (and where she would remain until 1967). In addition to Ford, directors who made films for the studio during those years included Lubitsch, Preminger, Kazan, Mankiewicz, and Litvak—by any standard an impressive group. But, these directors all had an equally impressive group of in-house film editors to work with, including Barbara McLean, Robert Simpson, William Reynolds, and Hugh Fowler. And, while the editing supervisor often assigned editors to specific films, several of these directors repeatedly asked to work with Spencer.

Throughout the 1950s, Spencer continued to turn in good work on a wide variety of films. These ranged from Nunnally Johnson's thoughtful social drama, *The Man in the Gray Flannel Suit* (1955); to Fred Zinnemann's moving story of drug addiction, *A Hatful of Rain* (1957); to Edward Dmytryk's character-centered wartime drama, *The Young Lions* (1958).

Increasingly, however, her growing reputation for excelling in action films and large spectacles was leading her toward more of those kinds of assignments. A turning point may have been her work on Litvak's taut, stark World War II espionage thriller, *Decision Before Dawn* (1951). Her editing on that film received a great deal of praise and a second editing Academy Award nomination. After that, came assignments for more action-oriented films such as Delmer Daves' Biblical epic, *Demetrius and the Gladiators* (1954); Jean Negulesco's disaster epic, *The Rains of Ranchipur* (1955); and Henry Hathaway's knockabout western, *North to Alaska* (1960).

One of Spencer's greatest challenges came in 1963 when she edited Joseph L. Mankiewicz's *Cleopatra* with Elizabeth Taylor, Richard Burton, and Rex Harrison. Initially budgeted at $2 million, the film—constantly beset with production problems and cost overruns—eventually cost more than $31 million (before adding the marketing and promotion costs). Easily the most expensive film ever made at the time, *Cleopatra* also had the dubious distinction of being both the highest grossing film of the year and a money loser.

Mankiewicz, who was brought in to replace the film's original director, Rouben Mamoulian, when the film was already $5 million over budget, had a hair-raising experience throughout. In addition to countless problems with sets, logistics, and the weather, stars Taylor and Burton (both married to other people at the time) started an off-screen affair that brought the film much negative publicity (but eventually curious audiences). Then, Taylor became seriously ill, delaying production even longer and running costs up even higher. Add to this—Mankiewicz, unhappy with the script, was rewriting constantly throughout the entire shoot. At one point during the editing, he was fired, but he was soon rehired when the Fox's executives realized that the story was basically in his head and, like it or not, they needed him.

Working with Mankiewicz to turn what seemed like an inevitable train wreck into a respectable film was, according to film writer I.S. Mowis, "arguably the most difficult task of [Spencer's] lengthy career."[4] When the shooting was finally completed, Mankiewicz had amassed some 70,000 feet (or 13 hours of footage) that needed to be edited down. The cut that Mankiewicz first screened for 20th Century–Fox executives was six hours long. At the executives' request, Mankiewicz and Spencer cut the film down to four hours for its premiere. The executives—wanting to maximize the number of showings per day per theater—thought this was still too long. Again (and this time over Mankiewicz's objections), the film was cut to slightly more than three hours. Fortunately, the version available for the home market today closely resembles the Mankiewicz-approved version, running just over four hours.

Despite such difficult working conditions, the finished film received many more positive reviews than most jaundiced industry observers would have figured. The film industry magazine *Variety* said: "*Cleopatra* is not only a super colossal eye-filler (the unprecedented budget shows in the physical opulence throughout), but it is also a remarkably literate cinematic recreation of an historic epoch."[5] More recently, film writer Matt Thrift has noted: "*Cleopatra* remains an agreeably old-fashioned epic in the definitive sense. A camp melodrama if ever there was one, its opulent gaudiness and the unimpeachable craftsmanship of its production design now more than ever keep the eye enthralled through even the more plodding longueurs of its 243-minute running time."[6]

When the Academy Awards were announced in early 1965, *Cleopatra* received nine nominations, second only to the British import, *Tom Jones*, which had 10. Again, Spencer was singled out for her work, receiving another Best Editing nomination, but again she failed to win an Oscar.

Undeterred, Spencer continued to work regularly through the 1960s, and then more infrequently in the 1970s, before retiring for good in 1979 after working on *The Concorde: Airport '79*. Ten years later, in only the second year that the American Cinema Editors, perhaps the most prestigious society of film editing professionals, presented a Lifetime Achievement Award, she was one of the two recipients, making her one of the first four ever to receive this honor.

Late in her career, Spencer, in a rare public statement, shared some of her thoughts on what it takes to be a good film editor and, in doing so, also exhibited some of the intensity and passion that had served her so well during her half-century in Hollywood cutting rooms:

[W]hen young cinema students ask me—as they often do—what it takes to become a film editor, I always tell them that patience is the first requirement. For example, there was a situation on [*Earthquake*] where we wanted to delete a scene, but I didn't have enough material to cover the cut. [Director] Mark Robson told me that I wouldn't have the patience to solve the problem, but I said: "It's a challenge, and I'll lick it." I just insisted that there had to be a way of doing it. There's always a way. Well, I found a way and he liked it. He just walked away shaking his head, but I thought it was fun.

Besides patience, I think you have to be dedicated to become a film editor. That's always been more important to me than anything else. I guess my whole life has been made up of wanting to do the best I could. I enjoy editing, and I think that's necessary, because editing is not a watching-the-clock job. I've been on pictures where I never even knew it was lunchtime, or time to go home. You get so involved in what you're doing, in the challenge of creating—because I think cutting is very creative.[7]

Dorothy Spencer died at age 93 in 2002, just a few months before the passing of another grande dame of the cutting room, Margaret Booth.

〜

While Spencer certainly broke new ground as an editor in films such as *Stagecoach*, she remained largely a practitioner of classical editing technique throughout her career. This includes the 1960s and 1970s, when Dede Allen, Verna Fields, and others were shaking up mainstream editing practice and philosophy in films such as *Bonnie and Clyde* and *Jaws*. And this adherence to the "old school" might be a major reason why Spencer is not as well known today as Allen, Fields, or other contemporaries.

Within the classical editing tradition, however, Spencer did wonders. On one hand, she was a minimalist adept at cutting every extraneous frame to give a scene maximum dramatic impact. On the other hand, she was a master of pacing and rhythms. While action scenes moved quickly, they never moved too quickly. There was always just enough time for the audience to absorb what was happening not just visually but also emotionally. The final gunfight in Ford's *My Darling Clementine* is an excellent example of this. The sequence is bristling with energy generated largely from the dynamic cutting. It moves quickly, but it is never rushed. It runs without music to amp up the drama because, quite simply, it doesn't need it; the editing does the job.

In addition, Spencer was a pragmatic problem solver. She loved to look for more ways to add suspense and generate more action in stories and usually found them. One example she once shared was from *Earthquake* involves a scene that features actor Richard Roundtree as a daredevil motorcyclist. During one take, a stunt double for Roundtree took a spectacular fall. Luckily for the double, he wasn't hurt badly, just shaken up a bit. And luckily for the production, Spencer saved the take and, with the help of a little reshooting, was able to use it in the film, adding to the excitement of the scene.

Spencer's Work on Alfred Hitchcock's Lifeboat

Lifeboat was the second film Spencer edited for Alfred Hitchcock, and, sadly, it was also her last. After *Lifeboat*, Hitchcock, displeased by the lack of support studio head Darryl Zanuck had given the film, left 20th Century–Fox and never returned. Meanwhile, Spencer remained on staff. It would be interesting to imagine the possibilities, though, if the two had continued to work together. Like John Ford, Hitchcock, edited— to use the saying—"in his head," shooting exactly what he wanted and little more and giving editors a minimal number of choices to work with. But, just as she could tirelessly whittle away at miles of footage when editing enormous films such as *Cleopatra* and *Earthquake*, Spencer was also adept at fine tuning the very limited amounts of film she received from people such as Ford and Hitchcock. In other words, she could also start with a film that was already pretty much edited in a great director's head and then take it up a few notches. In *Lifeboat*, she did precisely that.

Although *Lifeboat* is not one of Hitchcock's best-known films, it is still a wonderful example of his work. The project began when the U.S. Maritime Commission asked Darryl Zanuck of 20th Century–Fox to make a film that dramatized the dangers of German U-boats in the North Atlantic during World War II. Zanuck then contracted with David O. Selznick for the services of Hitchcock, who was still under a long-term (and increasingly irksome) contract with the producer. The technical challenges of setting a film almost entirely in a confined space, such as a lifeboat, had long appealed to the director, who apparently had once considered setting an entire film inside a telephone booth. (After *Lifeboat*, of course, Hitchcock would experiment with this idea even more in 1948's *Rope* and 1954's *Dial M for Murder* and *Rear Window*.) And the project was a "go."

The film—based on a story by John Steinbeck and involving numerous writers including Hitchcock and his wife Alma—centers on eight survivors

Attempting to replicate the experience of being stranded in a lifeboat on the Atlantic Ocean but shot mostly on the 20th Century-Fox studio lot, Alfred Hitchcock's *Lifeboat* (1944) presented major technical challenges for everyone involved with the production, including its editor, Dorothy Spencer. Pictured here is most of the film's cast: (from left to right) John Hodiak (back to camera), Walter Slezak, Hume Cronyn, Tallulah Bankhead, Heather Angel, Mary Anderson, Henry Hull, and Canada Lee (back to camera) (20th Century–Fox/Photofest).

of an Allied ship sunk by a U-boat and one survivor (the captain) of the U-boat, which was also sunk in the attack. All come from different walks of life and different social classes, and, of course, one is a German—the enemy. After the opening credits, which are filled with images suggesting the shipwreck, all the action takes place on the boat with the characters— among other things—working together, squabbling, learning bits and pieces of personal history about each other, grieving for a dead baby, operating on one character's gangrene-infected leg, wondering which direction they should sail, and ultimately trying to determine how to deal with the German—kill him, keep him as a prisoner, or allow him to use his skills and captain the boat.

To compensate for the confined setting, Hitchcock focused on several areas. First, he (and others who wrote various versions of the script) developed several complex, nuanced, genuinely interesting characters. Then he cast actors excellently suited for these roles. Three of the standouts are Tallulah Bankhead's Connie Porter, a self-absorbed socialite/journalist with a biting wit who learns to become more sensitive to the suffering of others; William Bendix's Gus Smith, a tough, working class man who must accept the fact that he must lose his leg; and Walter Slezak's mysterious German, Willi, who constantly lies but eventually gets some of the others to trust his thinking and eventually his leadership. Second, even though the film was shot in the studio, Hitchcock and his technical people did a fine job of giving viewers the sense of what it might actually be like to be on a lifeboat in the middle of the ocean. For people who get seasick, the endless rocking of the boat on the big screen, can—and has—produced headaches and even nausea. Also, to reinforce the film's sense of place, Hitchcock made the very conscious—and for the time daring—decision, not to use music, except during the opening credits.

These and other choices consequently led to another challenge: they put more pressure on the film's editor. There was no music to mask subpar edits. The editing of the rocking boat had to be constantly checked so that the "knocked-about" experience remained credible to audiences. And, with so much riding on the interaction between characters, every bit of blocking, every line of dialogue, and every reaction shot had to be handled just right. In many films an editor can use the tricks of the trade to hide various problems, but in *Lifeboat* Hitchcock and Spencer had no such luxury. The editing had to be perfect, or the experience would appear false.

Throughout the film, one of the impressive characteristics of the editing is how it captures the rhythms, the ebbs and flows, of being at sea for an extended period with long stretches of boredom punctuated by fleeting moments of humor, drama, and conflict. Often, the editing mirrors this experience with lengthy shots, sometimes going for a minute or more. These are immediately followed by quick reaction shots to heighten the intended mood, be it humorous or dramatic. Then, these are followed by longer shots, underscoring that the moment has passed and we are back to the boredom.

One scene that's particularly well handled comes toward the end of the film. It's preceded by a comic bit in which one character is about to show his winning hand and the wind blows away the cards; a darkly comic bit in which it begins to rain and then, seconds later, stops; and a poignant moment when the weakening, increasingly delusional Gus finally succumbs to drinking salt water from the ocean.

After Gus sips the water, there is a long (about six seconds) fade to black and fade in on Willi, alone, rowing. As we watch Willi, we hear Gus talking alternately about his thirst and his girlfriend. (Everyone else at this point is asleep at the other end of the boat.) As he listens and gently advises, Willi seems patient and understanding, but he can also be disguising his disgust at Gus's vulnerability. After a brief interchange in which Gus shifts between delusion and lucidity, Willi—seeming quite kindly—matter-of-factly pushes him off the boat. Gus's calls for help eventually wake the others, but, by the time, they are fully awake, Gus has gone under.

Here, the editing, which has been fairly leisurely, picks up. Shots cut more quickly between Willi on the front end of the boat and the others, all grouped together against him, on the back end. As the others learn what Willi has done (not only killing Gus but also secretly hoarding water), the cutting quickens, hinting that the main conflict in the story is coming to a climax. (In the next four minutes, there are more than 30 cuts of various lengths, averaging about eight cuts per minute or seven and a half seconds between cuts.) Then—as if to suggest a release of all the built-up anger the others feel—the quick cuts stop and we see one very lengthy shot in which five of the six characters rush Willi, overwhelm him with everything from fists to a block of wood, throw him overboard, and, with the help of Gus's old shoe, finish killing him in the water. At a minute and 15 seconds, this is easily the longest single shot in the scene. It's also fairly gruesome, showing both how ugly a real killing can be and how almost anyone, even the kind nurse Alice (Mary Anderson), is capable of participating.

As a final touch, the film cuts to a close-up of Gus's shoe, the murder weapon, in the hand of Rittenhouse (Henry Hull) and then follows the shoe as he releases it and lets it fall to his feet.

From here, we slowly dissolve to the next scene. Again, it is the bow of the boat, but a little time has passed. The remaining six characters sit around each other, all spent, subdued, in a bit of shock, and trying to absorb what has just happened and how they came to do it. The cutting returns to the pace it has been for most of the story.

From the fade in until the dissolve out, this scene runs about nine and quarter minutes, consists of about 60 separate shots, and is a masterpiece of pacing and cutting. The cutting between shots begins slowly, picks up as Willi prepares to and eventually does push Gus overboard, and quickens as the other characters learn about Gus's death and Willi's hoarding of water, building to a moment of climax. Then, there's the release—the long and very disturbing single shot in which the others gang up on Willi and kill him. Finally, there's even a mini-denouement—a last, relatively brief shot showing Gus's shoe falling from Rittenhouse's hand to the deck of the boat, a subtle suggestion that the civilized people who thought they were above murder have also fallen.

Altogether, this scene is a highlight in a film that's superbly crafted throughout. And, while Hitchcock was clearly at the helm of this production, Spencer's great sense of knowing exactly where to cut for maximum effect clearly had an impact. Without her, neither this scene nor this film would have been quite the same.

A Special Stamp

Calling Spencer "a consummate studio craftsperson," writer Peter Flynn has noted that "her competence in the field, her success within the industry, and her devotion to her craft remain uncontested."[8]

Looking at films Spencer worked on 40, 60, and 80 years ago, it is totally understandable that so many great directors wanted to work with her. Even supremely confident people such as Ford, Hitchcock, Lubitsch, and Mankiewicz sought her out because—as they knew as well as anyone else—her editing choices often gave their films a special truth and vitality. And they appreciated that. While not a great innovator who changed the art of editing, she nevertheless had a special stamp that she put on each film she collaborated on. And, if it is true that films really are made or destroyed in the editing room, her impact on U.S. film history really has been immense.

6

The Revolutionary

Dede Allen Upends American Film Editing in the 1960s and 1970s

"If I have to get up and pee," Hollywood mogul Jack Warner told director Arthur Penn before seeing Penn's *Bonnie and Clyde* at a private screening prior to the film's 1967 release, "I'll know it's a lousy movie."[1]

As Penn reported many years later, not only did the crusty 75-year-old studio head get up before the end of the film's first reel but he was also up several more times before the film had finished. "He didn't like it, didn't understand it, didn't get it," Penn said. "It was the beginning of a dark time, because it was clear that, if he didn't like it, it was going to get dumped.[2]

Among his many complaints with *Bonnie and Clyde*, Warner had a special disdain for the film's editing. From the very first live-motion shot, when viewers see only a young woman's painted red lips in extreme close-up, the experience seemed alien, confusing, and probably very amateurish to him. "Why begin there?" he must have been wondering. "Lips don't tell the viewer anything about where or when this is supposed to be."

Warner's displeasure was certainly understandable. For more than half a century, he (and nearly everyone else) had watched films that told the story in a very particular, and usually very literal, way, the classical Hollywood editing style. Developed by D.W. Griffith and others in the 1910s, this style called for editors to follow certain conventions when cutting films, conventions that soon became hard and fast rules the entire industry adhered to: gospel. Individual scenes, for example, should begin with establishing shots, usually long shots that identified the setting for viewers, and then progress to a mix of medium and close shots. Any change to another time or place should be signaled by a dissolve or fade.

Sound from one scene should never overlap into another. And so on. Although these conventions often slowed the pace of a film, people continued to use them because they assumed that viewers needed these visual cues to sufficiently understand the film's action.

Now, as he watched *Bonnie and Clyde*, Warner saw these and countless other "rules" repeatedly—and almost defiantly—broken. There was even talk that, if the project were to continue at all, the editor should be fired and the film re-cut.

Penn and *Bonnie and Clyde*'s producer/star, Warren Beatty, were adamant in their opposition to compromising their vision for the film, however, and eventually prevailed. The two were also so impressed with the film's editing (which they considered brilliant and highly innovative) that—in recognition of this contribution—they lobbied hard to assure that the editor received a separate title card in the opening credits. Again, they prevailed, and, for first time ever in a Hollywood feature film, an editor—the person who for decades had shared semi-anonymity on a group title card with other contributors ranging from a film's costumer to its make-up specialist—had been so honored.

The person at the center of this post-production firestorm was 43-year-old Dede Allen (1923–2010), a 20-year film industry veteran, who, after a long apprenticeship in such jobs as a production "messenger girl," editing assistant, sound editor, and editor of television commercials and industrial shorts, had edited only a handful of feature films. Her big break had come in 1959 when director Robert Wise asked her to cut his gritty film noir *Odds Against Tomorrow*. She then followed up with highly praised work on Robert Rossen's *The Hustler* (1961) and Elia Kazan's *America America* (1963). And, while these films—*The Hustler*, in particular—showed signs that Allen was not only a fine editor but also a major new editorial stylist, many people were simply not ready for her breakthrough in *Bonnie and Clyde*.

Her work on that film was—without exaggeration—revolutionary. It integrated numerous aspects of the French New Wave movement and other innovative foreign films, her own work in sound editing and television commercial editing, and traditional feature film editing techniques to create something groundbreaking and—for millions of enthusiastic film viewers—breathtaking. Gone were many of the time-honored literal conventions of the classical Hollywood editing style. And in their place were a plethora of different (and often non-literal) storytelling techniques from the use of slow motion mixed with regular action (to distort time or emphasize critical moments) to "pre-lapping" sound (the introduction of sound from a film's next scene into the last moments of the current scene in order to speed action), rapid-fire cutting within scenes (to intensify action and build drama), to "shock" cuts (abrupt, jarring, and unexpected changes between scenes that are intended to jolt the viewer). In addition to drawing upon new storytelling techniques, Allen, as she had done in her previous films, used editing whenever she could to bring more nuance and depth to characters. To do this, she often retrieved previously overlooked or discarded bits of film—an actress's insecure glance or an

Drawing upon numerous influences ranging from French New Wave films to 1950s American television commercials, Dede Allen helped transform and revitalize American film editing in the 1960s and 1970s. Some of her most respected work is in films such as *The Hustler* **(1961),** *Bonnie and Clyde* **(1967),** *Dog Day Afternoon* **(1975), and** *Reds* **(1981) (Photofest).**

actor's surprised reaction—that provided just a bit more information to enrich the cinematic moment. As film scholar Hope Anderson has written, "*Bonnie and Clyde* features superb acting, directing and cinematography, but the editing makes it a masterpiece."[3]

Almost immediately, others began to imitate the film and its editing style. Soon, in technique as well as sensibility, American films became very different from what they had been just a few short years before. And, as film editors began to enjoy new creative freedoms and revel in the prospects of expanded possibilities, they also received enhanced status. As film writer Claudia Luther has noted, "[In *Bonnie and Clyde*], Allen raised the level of her craft to an art form that was as seriously discussed as cinematography or even directing."[4]

For the next two decades, Allen continued to push the limits of her art in films not only for Penn (1970's *Little Big Man*, 1975's *Night Moves*, and three other films) but also for other auteur directors such as Sidney Lumet (1973's *Serpico* and 1975's *Dog Day Afternoon*) and George Roy Hill (1972's *Slaughterhouse-Five* and 1977's *Slap Shot*). In addition, she worked on major films for some of the industry's most respected actor/directors such as Paul Newman (1968's *Rachel, Rachel*), Warren Beatty (1981's *Reds*), and Robert Redford (1988's *The Milagro Beanfield War*).

After an executive stint as head of post-production for Warner Brothers for most of the 1990s, Allen returned to editing, working on Curtis Hanson's *Wonder Boys* (2000) and several other films until she was well into her 80s. In all, she edited or co-edited about 30 films over nearly a half century. And along the way she received numerous honors for her work, including the prestigious Crystal Award from Women in Film in 1982 and the Career Achievement Award from American Cinema Editors in 1994.

Although Allen received Academy Award nominations for her editing work in *Dog Day Afternoon*, *Reds*, and *Wonder Boys*, she never won an Oscar. In fact, she wasn't even nominated for her work on *The Hustler* or on *Bonnie and Clyde*, perhaps her two most impressive and influential achievements. She often attributed this to what she saw as the Hollywood community's prejudice against filmmakers on the East Coast, where she was often based. But this lack of Oscar appreciation could also be due to the nature of much of her earlier work, which was so radically new that it took many people time to understand and appreciate its power and value.

Coming into her own professionally during the 1960s, a decade of enormous upheaval for American films, Allen was a true editing revolutionary: a person who literally transformed her art by integrating her own sensibilities and experiences deeply into her editing process, by innovating relentlessly, by helping to break down the strict adherence to the more literal classical editing style, by freeing other editors to think differently and explore the storytelling possibilities of their art more fully, and by inspiring the next generation of superstar editors from Walter Murch to Michael Kahn, to Thelma Schoonmaker. She was—and remains—one of the all-time editorial greats.

"I wouldn't let it go if I thought I could make it better."

"I think I developed my interest in film because my mother had been an actress," Allen observed late in her life. "[She] took me to the movies a lot because she loved them. When I lived with her—which was not that often—we would go all the time."[5]

In those three short sentences, Allen revealed much about an unusual childhood that shaped her adult life in numerous ways.

Born Dorothea Carothers Allen on December 3, 1923, in Cincinnati, she was named after her mother, a theater actress who had quit the stage under pressure when she married Dede's father, a Union Carbide executive named Thomas H.C. Allen III. The marriage was both unhappy and short-lived. When Dede was just three, her mother traveled to Europe (without Thomas), settled in Paris, and placed Dede and her sister, Manette, in a boarding school in the Swiss Alps. A year later, Thomas was killed in an automobile accident, and Dorothea stayed in Paris, keeping her daughters in the boarding school for another six years. Although young Dede loved her life at the school, she eventually realized that she had—for all intents and purposes—been "orphaned."[6]

After these years and until she went to college, Dede lived with her mother for short periods of time, but more often than not other relatives took care of her. "My mother was like a Gypsy," Allen once said. "She loved to move on. She loved to travel and she wasn't very much into raising kids."[7] During those times when she stayed with her mother, however, one experience both enjoyed sharing was the movies. "In Tryon, North Carolina, they changed the movie almost every day," Allen recalled. "We were down there for a winter and I went to the movies every day."[8]

Back in Cincinnati during her teens, Allen attended College Preparatory School, where she met a teacher named Ruthie Jones. According to Allen, Jones, who became a kind of surrogate mother during these years, had a "tremendous effect" on her and what eventually became her very liberal political thinking.[9]

After graduating from College Preparatory School, Allen went to Scripps College in Claremont, California. There she took a basic liberal arts curriculum, focusing on architecture and taking courses in subjects such as weaving and pottery.

During these years, Allen's interest in films remained passionate, and in 1943, when she had finished at Scripps, she persuaded her grandfather to call in a favor from a family friend, a director at Columbia Pictures named Elliot Nugent. Happy to help, Nugent had her hired as a part-time "messenger girl" at the studio, a job that Allen greatly appreciated in later years because it gave her access to virtually all the studio's many departments and turned into an extremely valuable learning experience. Soon, she moved into the sound department, where she worked as an assistant, recalling that—as preparation for her work as a film editor—this was "the best thing that ever happened to me."[10]

In 1945, however, Allen took a break from her film career when she married filmmaker Stephen Fleischman and, in 1946, the two moved to Europe for his work. During this time, Allen (who remained "Allen" after her marriage) worked as a translator.

In 1951, Allen and Fleischman returned to the U.S., Stephen went to work as a producer for CBS-TV in New York, and their son Thomas was born. (They also had a daughter, Ramey.) During the next few years, Allen worked at a variety of jobs around New York, mainly as a sound editor for television commercials and industrial films. Part of what impressed her about this work, especially the commercials, was their staccato pace and startling sound and visual shifts. In commercials, a great deal of information usually had to be crammed into a very small amount of time, and people putting them together were employing techniques that were strikingly different from standard 1950s filmmaking. This experience would prove hugely influential in her later work.

Meanwhile, Allen's work had also impressed a sound editor named Dick Vorisek, who recommended her for a job that would prove to be her big break: as film editor on *Odds Against Tomorrow*, a noir crime drama director Robert Wise was making in New York. The prospect of working with Wise—who had risen to fame 18 years earlier when he edited Orson Welles' *Citizen Kane* and soon gone on to become a highly respected director in his own right—was at first quite intimidating for the first-time feature film editor. "I was terrified," Allen said. "But we had a wonderful relationship. I adored Bob; he was a wonderful man."[11] Part of what Allen admired about Wise was his enthusiasm for her risk taking, something that made her "juices flow."[12] The fast pace of her cutting (something she had learned from her work on commercials) had greatly impressed him, and he encouraged her to continue to experiment.

Considering that she was just beginning as a film editor, Allen's work on *Odds Against Tomorrow* is quite confident and distinctive. One contribution she made to this film that would soon became a signature technique is the pre-lapping of sound over visuals: just a split second before the scene changes we hear a significant sound from the next scene. As well as speeding the action just a bit, this pre-lapping also served to ease some of the transitions while also heightening the contrasts between others. One of numerous examples of the latter is the cut between a quiet shot of a front door to a boisterous merry-go-round at the park, with just a split second of merry-go-round noise over the front door. Another contribution was Allen's fast cutting in certain scenes to increase tension and intensify drama. One scene when this is especially effective is the first time the three main characters (played by Robert Ryan, Harry Belafonte, and Ed Begley, Sr.) meet to discuss the robbery they are planning. Here, the rapid cutting between the characters both emphasizes the hostility between Ryan's racist character and Belafonte's African-American and the anxiety

Begley's character feels, knowing, that for their robbery to succeed, he needs these two men to get along. Still another contribution is the deliberately slow pacing as the three men wait for the appointed time of the robbery. All essentially sit around, waiting, waiting. As viewers, we feel their growing tension acutely. We want this waiting to be over almost as much as they do.

As these scenes suggest, *Odds Against Tomorrow* also gives us a very early glimpse of another of Allen's editorial strengths: an ability to draw something extra out of actors' performances by the timing and ordering of cutting. She was a master at this. "I love actors," she once said. "I think it helped having come from a theatre background, because of my mother.... I am very much an actor's editor and a director's editor. And it takes a lot of patience. You go through the stuff and find these little jewels and gems and then you put them together in a certain way and it becomes something else. It takes perseverance. I wouldn't let it go if I thought I could make it better."[13]

On another occasion, Allen took this subject even further, revealing some intriguing aspects of her work process. "When I start cutting a movie, I always cut with ambivalence," she observed, continuing:

> I have a definite intention, a definite starting point: the thematic function of the scene, the psychology of the characters, etc. But, when I become absorbed in the material, I suddenly see all the possibilities the material contains—the unexpected, intended, and unintended possibilities. I can't help wandering into the material. I milk the material for all the small possibilities I see in it—a look, a smile I see after the director has said "Cut," an unintentional juxtaposition of two images. Afterwards, I form a general view again. But it is in the ambivalence, in the collision between the general strategy and the pleasant abstractions along the way that constitutes editing as art.[14]

～

In addition to the attention she gave both her family and her work in the late 1950s and early 1960s, Allen began to pay more attention to the growing number of fresh, innovative foreign films flowing into the U.S. during this period. For her—as well as many other Americans attracted to new and different filmmaking styles and sensibilities—these were thrilling times. From the U.K., for example, came films of stark realism such as Tony Richardson's *Look Back in Anger* (1959) and *The Loneliness of the Long Distance Runner* (1962). From France, there were the "New Wave" films such as Jean Luc Godard's *Breathless*, which—in their efforts to open up the possibilities of visual storytelling—broke many of the seemingly sacred rules of traditional editing. From Sweden, came Ingmar Bergman's films of existential angst. From Italy, there were Federico Fellini's idiosyncratic blends of bizarre fantasy, baroque images, and earthy humor. And from Japan came Akira Kurosawa's stylish, highly distinctive tales that often evoked mythical pasts.

As they did for many other Americans, these and other foreign films both energized Allen, giving her a better sense of the medium's enormous untapped potential, and dampened her enthusiasm for conventional Hollywood efforts, which increasingly seemed old fashioned and out of touch. Looking back to many of the major U.S. releases at this time, it's difficult to disagree. They were largely a mix of tired westerns, bloated historical epics, even more bloated musicals, and strangely regressive sex comedies often starring Doris Day and Rock Hudson. If filmmaking around the world is changing so radically, Allen must have thought, it can happen here as well.

It would, however, be a couple of years until she could follow through on turning this wish into a reality. After *Odds Against Tomorrow*, Allen had to go back to commercials and industrial films. Then, in 1961, veteran director Robert Rossen hired her to edit his edgy, craftily subversive drama, *The Hustler*.

Allen's work on *The Hustler*, a similarly dark but otherwise very different kind of film from *Odds Against Tomorrow*, was—especially when we take her relative lack of film editing experience into account—quite notable. In addition to her use of pre-lapping sound to bridge many key scene transitions, she also created several amazing montages highlighted by long, lingering dissolves between scenes to convey the seemingly endless days and nights the film's characters spend in dark, claustrophobic pool halls. As viewers, we feel that we're right there with these people, experiencing the long, long sessions. Film writer Kevin Lewis has called this "a remarkable feat" considering that the film was shot in wide screen Cinema-Scope, which he added was "no friend to intimate moments."[15] Allen was also excellent at fleshing out the film's two main characters played by Paul Newman and Piper Laurie, showing in wordless reaction shots the many sides of this sad, vulnerable, highly insecure couple as well as the fragility of their tender but doomed relationship.

In commenting on Allen's work on *The Hustler*, film scholar Greg S. Faller has also cited both the new British films such as *Look Back in Anger* as well as the French New Wave films such as *Breathless* as key influences. "The realism of the British school and the radical editing of the French school made strong impressions..." he has written. "*The Hustler* employs a [style derived from both]: lengthy two-shots, unexpected shot/reverse-shot patterns, and strategically placed 'jump cuts....' The combination of these two schools and the focus on character over a seamless narrative flow gives *The Hustler* its unique quality of realism and modernism."[16]

Allen must have impressed Paul Newman as well, because seven years later the actor asked her to edit his first directorial effort, 1968's *Rachel, Rachel*. Here, Allen again does a wonderful job of mixing sound—particularly atmospheric sound—with the visuals, minimal music, and strategic silences to create the sad and empty world of the main character, a lonely school teacher named Rachel (beautifully portrayed by Joanne Woodward). Interesting here is Allen's respect for silence as well as sound as a critical storytelling component in film. "Sound and silence are so important in a film," she has noted. Coming out of sound "helped me become a better picture editor."[17] In addition, Allen's sensitive cutting also gives resonance to the periodic flashbacks that let viewers in on key events in Rachel's life.

In addition to working on several more projects for Arthur Penn after *Bonnie and Clyde* (which we'll look at in some depth later in this chapter), Allen spent the 1970s working with great success with other directors such as George Roy Hill and Sidney Lumet. Among these collaborations, two of the three films she edited for Lumet are clearly standouts.

The first is 1973's *Serpico*, the story of real-life New York undercover policeman Frank Serpico. As film writer Hope Anderson has noted, the Allen imprint is unmistakable here from the opening credits when we hear blaring sirens, a rhythmic beating sound, and the sound of someone struggling to breathe; see a close-up of Al Pacino's bleeding face; and then realize that the rhythmic sound (which reminds us of a heartbeat) is actually the sound of the windshield wipers of the car taking his injured character to the hospital. "Plunging headlong into the story's emotional center was Dede Allen's signature," Anderson wrote. "Though the decision to open the film with the immediate aftermath of the shooting was probably in the script, the heart-pounding elements—pre-lapping sound and rapid cutting—were purely editorial."[18]

While her work on *Serpico* certainly reinforced Allen's standing as a bold innovator, her work on her next Lumet project, *Dog Day Afternoon*, was in many respects even more significant. Here, as Faller observes, she "continued to refine her editorial signature (audio shifts, shock cutting, and montage) ... especially the temporal and spatial shifts."[19] One striking example of her work in action is the film's famous "Attica" moment, when Al Pacino's bank robber protagonist incites a crowd by referring to an episode of law enforcement brutality that had recently taken place at New York's Attica prison. Coming after the film's fairly subdued opening, this scene—a few moments of great energy and chaos—explodes on the screen. To reinforce the fragility of this situation, the mounting tension, and the potential for violence, Allen overlaps audio and cuts rapidly—and often disruptively—between various people (both outside and indoors) and even to a helicopter flying overhead. Even 40 years after the film's initial release, this scene remains very strong stuff.

While it's irresistible to focus on Allen's bold stylistic touches in *Dog Day Afternoon*, it's important to not overlook—especially in the early and mid-1970s, an era known for its self-conscious filmmaking flourishes—that she never sacrificed character to style. And, in *Dog Day Afternoon*—despite its often dramatic editing—her focus throughout is on character. Both Pacino's Sonny and his fellow bank robber Sal (John Cazale), the film's two main roles, are handled beautifully, Allen's editing often revealing additional facets to their already multi-dimensional characters. She is particularly good, for example, at bringing out Sonny's incredible frustration with various developments as shown in Pacino's body language and Sal's naïve, deeply troubled, dysfunctional personality as shown in Cazale's. She also does a wonderful job of showing both the deep feeling in—and the impossibility of—the relationship between Sonny and his gender-conflicted "wife" Leon (Chris Sarandon) in the one interaction, a telephone conversation, they have in the film. Faller also notes how Allen's sometimes unconventional editorial choices in this scene "intensified their performances."[20]

For her work on *Dog Day Afternoon*, Allen—at age 52—finally received an Academy Award nomination. Unfortunately, though, she was up against some stiff competition that year, including Verna Fields' work on Steven Spielberg's *Jaws*, which ultimately won.

For the rest of the 1970s, Allen continued to work with familiar directors such as Penn (1975's *Night Moves* and 1976's *The Missouri Breaks*), Hill (1977's *Slap Shot*), and Lumet (1978's *The Wiz*), bringing her distinctive style to the western, sports, and musical genres.

Then, at the end of the decade, Allen tackled a film epic that would prove to be an epic experience for her as well. As had happened with actor Paul Newman after she had worked with him on *The Hustler*, Warren Beatty, the star of *Bonnie and Clyde*, asked her to edit a major film he planned to direct—a love story set against the 1917 Russian Revolution, 1981's *Reds*. Partnering with (and effectively mentoring) a younger editor named Craig McKay, Allen, from a logistical standpoint, was taking on her biggest challenge ever. Overseeing a team of more than 60 assistants, Allen and McKay edited six or seven days a week for two years—a huge undertaking even by the standards of big three- and four-hour-long Hollywood epics.

In addition to the immense size of their task, Allen and McKay had an additional and quite unusual challenge with *Reds*: to successfully interweave interviews with elderly survivors of the era (often people who had actually known the story's characters) with the dramatic narrative. This was a risky venture, and the result could have been choppy and pretentious. But Allen and McKay managed to pull it off, introducing these "witnesses" at the very beginning of the film and incorporating their memories and observations, often commenting on characters or developments in the story, at just the right times. It's a very complex undertaking that ultimately appears seamless.

Allen and McKay also had all the challenges people normally have with epics—foremost among these to make sure that the large historical events depicted in the film don't overwhelm the intimate personal story. The pair managed this delicate balance as well. The love story between Beatty's John Reed and Diane Keaton's Louise Bryant has real complexity and more than holds its own in the larger story. The editing of Keaton's not-always-likable character is especially sensitive as well, helping to give the portrayal added depth and poignancy.

For their work on *Reds* Allen and McKay were nominated for both an editing Academy Award and the American Cinema Editors (ACE) Eddie Award for best editing on a feature film. Again, she lost, this time to Michael Kahn, who won both awards that year for his work on Steven Spielberg's *Raiders of the Lost Ark*.

During the 1980s and early 1990s, Allen stayed busy editing a variety of films for directors as diverse as John Hughes, Robert Redford, Philip Kaufman, and Barry Sonnenfeld. While she continued to deliver polished work in her distinctive style, her work increasingly seemed less radical because, simply put, so many other editors were imitating her. Her style had become the norm. She continued to experiment, however. In Kaufman's *Henry and June* (1990), for example, she played with fades and partial fades in quite interesting ways to distort time and point of view.[21]

In 1992, Allen made a major career shift, moving from editing to an executive post as head of post-production for Warner Brothers. By the late 1990s, however, the creative challenges of editing lured her back to the editor's suite, and she worked on five more films between 2000 and 2008. Of these, perhaps the most notable was her contribution to Curtis Hanson's quirky drama *Wonder Boys* (2000). While not as groundbreaking as her earlier work, the film's editing still "works beautifully," according to Hope Anderson. "[B]eginning with the opening frame, [we see] a blur of colors over which bells and murmuring voices can be heard," Anderson wrote. "As the scene comes into focus, we see an academic quadrangle through rain-speckled glass and hear Michael Douglas's voiceover, which begins as the reading of a short story and veers into witty commentary. In *Wonder Boys* the story begins just before our arrival; the fact that we're immediately in the thick of it says everything about her [Allen's] genius."[22]

For her work on *Wonder Boys*, Allen received her third and final Academy Award nomination. Once again, though, Oscar eluded her. That year she lost to Stephen Mirrione for his work on Steven Soderbergh's *Traffic*.

~

With the focus usually on Allen's innovative technique, emphasis on character, and contributions to transforming the way American films are edited, many people overlook another important facet of her work: her long history of mentoring talented young editors. In addition to Craig McKay, who partnered with her on *Reds*, these have included several editors, such as Steven Rotter, Jim Miller, and Robert Brakey, who have gone on to successful careers.

When once asked about this practice, Allen responded with a story from her early years in the business. "I remember I was working as an assistant to a man who shall remain nameless, trying to anticipate what he might need next," she said. "I remember him turning around and saying, 'Young lady, would you mind *never ever* looking over my shoulder...! It's taken me a great many years to learn this craft, and I don't intend to have young people like you come in and think you can learn it overnight.'" Allen continued, adding: "I believe whatever I've learned, I've learned from someone else, and it's up to me to pass it on—because we're here, and we're gone. I have a loyalty. People work very hard for you."[23]

In evaluating his experience with Allen, McKay confirmed that this indeed was the person he knew. "When I worked with Dede," he said, "she was willing—and wanted—to hear what I had to say and what I could contribute; I think that was the case for most of the people she worked with.... She helped create a lot of very successful careers."[24]

~

Just as Allen learned from bad professional experiences, she followed a similar path in her personal life. Disturbed by the pressure put on her mother to give up her acting career for marriage, her parents' unhappy relationship, and her mother's lack of interest in her and her sister when they were children, Allen mapped out a very different course for herself. She and her husband remained a two-career couple throughout most of their happy 65-year marriage, balancing jobs with parental responsibilities. And she cultivated very close relationships with her two children, both of whom—no doubt inspired by Allen and their father—became involved with film business. Daughter Ramey Ward became a producer, writer, and production coordinator. And son Tom Fleischman became a sound editor. Tom, who has done sound work on such highly regarded films as *Goodfellas* (1990), *Silence of the Lambs* (1991) and *The Departed* (2006), even surpassed his mother in one respect: In 2012, for his sound work on Martin Scorsese's *Hugo*, he won an Academy Award.

In addition to leading the kind of life she wanted for herself, Allen— believing that forthright talk can lead to increased awareness and change— was never hesitant to talk about the difficulties women typically faced in the film business. "I came out of a period that you just didn't take a job from a man," she once remarked. "You just didn't. It was a sin."[25]

Once employed as a "messenger girl" at Columbia, however, Allen wasn't shy about seeking advancement and soon set her sights on opportunities in editing. "When I finally pestered my way into the cutting room, I carried more film cans and swore more than anyone else," she recalled. "That way I proved myself. I felt the men accepted me." And, she added, "[A]s a woman, I can tell you I had to work harder to prove I was equal."[26]

When asked in her mid-80s if she felt she had inspired younger woman with her example, Allen (no doubt with her tongue in her cheek) shared an anecdote. In the 1970s, when she was in her 50s and solidly established in the industry, she gave a seminar at Ohio State University. "It was just when women's liberation was happening. There were two young women sitting in the front with their feet on the rail, kind of defiant," she said, perhaps sensing that these women might be viewing her as a dinosaur. "One of them said to me, 'What do you know about women's lib?' I laughed and said, 'I beg your pardon. I *am* women's lib.'"[27]

∼

Despite her Oscar disappointments, Allen nevertheless received numerous awards and recognitions for her work. Just a few of the honors include a Crystal Award from Women in Film for helping "to expand the role of women within the entertainment industry"[28] in 1982, an ACE Lifetime Achievement Award in 1994, a Hollywood Film Festival award in 1999, and a Las Vegas Film Critics Association Career Achievement Award

in 2000. The Crystal Award, which is given each year to women throughout the film industry, has to date honored only three other film editors,
Margaret Booth, Verna Fields, and Anne V. Coates.

Continuing to work until she was 84, Allen suffered a stroke on April
14, 2010, and died at her home in Los Angeles on April 17. She was 86. Her
husband of 65 years, Stephen, and her two children, Tom and Ramey, survived her.

Hearing of her death, her long-time friend and six-time filmmaking
partner, Arthur Penn said: "She was just an extraordinary collaborator....
Indeed, she wasn't an editor, she was a constructionist."[29]

"Constructionist" was perhaps an odd term to choose. But Allen apparently didn't like the term "auteur" when applied to her, and Penn very
possibly was trying to call her an auteur without actually calling her one.
In any case, she was much more than an editor in the traditional sense.
Her work—especially in the 1960s and 1970s—was radically different from
what had come before in American films, often electric in its immediacy,
and enormously influential. She was in the truest sense an editor's editor.

Allen Puts Her Signature on Bonnie and Clyde

"The movie opened like a slap in the face," wrote film critic Roger
Ebert in 1998, recalling his initial experience seeing the film 31 years earlier. "American filmgoers had never seen anything like it."[30]

Ebert was of course writing about *Bonnie and Clyde*, the film many
critics have called the first modern American movie and one of those rare
examples of cinema—like *Birth of a Nation*, *Citizen Kane*, and perhaps
Psycho—that literally changed the way people think about and make films.
Reviled by most critics at the time for its graphic violence and what seemed
to be its bizarre shifts in tone from slapstick comedy to harsh, often brutal
reality, it nevertheless thrilled audiences and is now considered one of the
most innovative and influential American feature films ever made.

The story of how the film finally came together could also make for
an entire book in itself, one filled with all kinds of burning aspirations,
gut-wrenching setbacks, strange plot twists, and much more. Many times
the project was on the verge of being scrapped, and many times people
tampering with the unfinished product could have done it irreparable
harm. But, largely due to the persistence and toughness of its two prime
movers, producer/star Warren Beatty and director Arthur Penn, it managed—somehow—to be released intact and go on to become the stuff of
film industry legend.

Part of the great thrill of seeing *Bonnie and Clyde*, especially for a person seeing it in 1967 or 1968, was, as Ebert suggested, this striking newness. Americans had flocked to films about outlaws since the first decade of the 20th century, even films with very similar plotlines, characters, and themes such as Joseph L. Lewis' fine noir *Gun Crazy* (1950). But they had never seen anything quite like this. Some Americans had also seen films from the French New Wave such as *Breathless* and *Jules and Jim* that both explored subjects such as life on the run and doomed love and experimented with startling new editing techniques. But again, they had never seen anything like this that was also so fundamentally American. Americans had seen plenty of chase scenes, too. But they had never seen any that incorporated such a strange mix of slapstick comedy and explicit, sometimes horrific violence. In addition, Beatty and Penn consciously sought out new faces and cast many of the roles with stage actors new to film. Ironically, the stunning nature of their debuts made instant film stars of Faye Dunaway and Gene Hackman and launched film careers in character roles for Michael J. Pollard and Estelle Parsons.

In fact, in every creative contribution from the writing and directing to the acting and cinematography, there is a new dynamic at work here. But, it is in the film's bold and highly innovative editing that everything comes together.

When discussing the editing in *Bonnie and Clyde*, almost everyone focuses on the film's ending: the scene when Bonnie and Clyde are ambushed in a barrage of bullets after they've stopped by the road to help Malcolm Moss (Dub Taylor). And it is an amazing moment. Consisting of about 50 cuts and lasting a little more than a minute, the scene, shocking for audiences in 1967, retains nearly all of its impact today. Critic Pauline Kael, who, along with Roger Ebert, was one of the few critics to give the film a positive review upon its initial release, made a special point to praise the way this was handled. Calling it "brilliant," she referred to the moments as we watch Bonnie's body jerking back and forth as bullets enter it in rapid fire, naming it the "rag-doll dance of death." Continuing, Kael noted that the horror in the scene "seems to go on for eternity, and yet it doesn't last a second beyond what it should."[31]

In addition to the rapid cutting to portray a horrific event, which clearly owes a debt to Sergei Eisenstein's famous use of montage in the "Odessa Steps" sequence in his 1925 film *Battleship Potemkin*, Allen gives this scene richness and dimension in a number of ways.[32]

One is in how it ambushes viewers in the audience similarly to how the law officers ambush the film's two protagonists. The scenes leading up

Bonnie and Clyde's notorious Barrow Gang poses for the camera. From left to right: Buck (Gene Hackman), Blanche (Estelle Parsons) Clyde (Warren Beatty), Bonnie (Faye Dunaway), and C.W. Moss (Michael J. Pollard). Considered radical for its time, Dede Allen's editing on this film has been hugely influential and widely imitated (Warner Brothers/Seven Arts/Photofest).

to it are quiet, under control, happy. There is a bit of concern when Clyde sees some law officers in town, but he and Bonnie manage to quietly slip away. He is even munching on an apple, relaxed, happy. The two have finally consummated their relationship, achieving a new level of harmony with each other as well. At first, as Malcolm waves at them to stop, they are happy to help. Then, as they see a flock of birds bolt out of nearby trees, they seem confused, concerned. Immediately, Malcolm jumps under his truck, and they are a bit more confused. Even so, they each have one more look at each other, and we see the contentment in both their faces. Then, of course, all hell breaks loose, and the contrast is stunning.

Another is the artfulness of the actual killing scene. The cutting back and forth between the two bullet-ridden bodies is perfectly timed to keep us simultaneously shocked and mesmerized. In addition to Bonnie's "rag-doll dance of death," we see slow motion shots woven in to accentuate certain moments—Clyde's body rolling over on the ground, Bonnie's body falling down beside her seat with her limp arm also falling and simply dangling in the air.

Yet another is the absolute silence and stillness after the fact. Everything stops for a moment until the law officers and Malcolm come in to assess the scene. Much like us in the audience, they are all still in a state of shock and absorbing what has just happened. Again, the timing seems just right. And again, as in other films, Allen uses silence to punctuate a critical moment. We all have a few seconds to digest and perhaps begin to process what we have seen. Then the film ends. Bookended by this scene and the calm, peaceful scenes before it, the moment of stunning, bloody violence becomes all the more horrific—and beautifully balletic.

The influence of this scene on American and some international films has been profound. Sam Peckinpah, Quentin Tarantino, Hong Kong's John Woo, and countless other directors have used key elements in it from the fast cutting to graphic violence, to slow-motion punctuation over and over again in work seen by hundreds of millions (perhaps even billions) of viewers worldwide.

The editing of many of *Bonnie and Clyde*'s chase scenes is also discussed frequently. Combined with the famous Flatt and Scruggs guitar and banjo tunes we hear over the chases, the fast-paced comic style gives these scenes a slapstick quality that was new, strange, and, certainly for some viewers, off-putting. These are people who, after all, have just committed armed robberies, yet their escapes are portrayed as broad comedy. What is ultimately so compelling about these scenes, however, is how they mirror the states of mind of Bonnie, Clyde, Buck, and C.W. These are all virtual children who see their bank robbing as a naughty, thrilling game and these chases as part of that game. Initially, they are all only vaguely aware of what they are really doing and ultimately what the consequences will be. Everything is a big joke. Only as they continue on their course do they see that this will only end in violent deaths for most of them. As the story proceeds, of course, the chases become far less whimsical and more violent, now mirroring their growing understanding of the real situation they are in.

We see some characteristic Allen touches in the film's first scene as well. As mentioned earlier, it opens—not with a traditional establishing shot—but with a signature "shock cut" on a tight, sensual close-up of a woman's painted lips. In a succession of fast, hard cuts, we then see that she is naked, assume that the temperature is probably hot, and that she is clearly in need of a man. Then, outside her window, she notices a young man trying to steal her mother's car. He sees her looking down from the

window. There is another quick succession of shots, suggesting an immediate, shared attraction. The two have already begun to bond.

Here, the film's very first live-action shot of a woman's lips takes us
instantly to the heart of the story—this lonely, sexually charged young
woman is in need of a man and adventure. The handsome but shifty young
man she meets is someone who quite possibly can supply her with both.
With great economy and artfulness, the story has been launched. We don't
need an establishing shot to tell us where and when this story is taking
place. All that is apparent almost immediately, anyway.

Although Allen's touch is particularly evident in specific scenes, film
writer Mark Harris, in his excellent 2008 book, *Pictures at a Revolution:
Five Movies and the Birth of the New Hollywood*, offers a very insightful
analysis of Allen's overall contribution to *Bonnie and Clyde*—one that goes
well beyond the construction of a string of showcase scenes:

> [Allen] was almost peerless in her ability to focus on "character, character, character."
> She had visited the set for a few days to get a sense of what Penn and his cast were
> trying to accomplish and returned to her Moviola with a sense of what to bring forth
> in each actor. Allen knew just how long she could hold a shot of Beatty to reveal the
> insecurity beneath Clyde's preening; she seemed to grasp instinctively that sudden
> cuts to Dunaway in motion would underscore the jagged, jumpy spirit of Bonnie
> Parker and that slow shots of Michael J. Pollard's C.W. Moss would mimic his two-
> steps-behind mental processes. And Allen cut *Bonnie and Clyde* with an eye and ear
> for the accelerating pace of the story, making the building of its panicky momentum
> her priority.
>
> Allen and Penn shared an admiration for the suggestive, almost sensual editing of
> French New Wave movies: The sequence in which Bonnie first sees Clyde's pistol—
> the series of disembodied shots of her moist lips and flashing eyes, his gun at his
> waist, her lips parting in excitement as her mouth plays over the rim of a Coca-Cola
> bottle, her hand tentatively reaching over to fondle his gun, and a couple of close-
> ups of his distracted, detached expression—conveys Bonnie's charged, troubled sexual
> appetites and Clyde's uneasy relationship to his own body purely through the rhythm
> of shot selection and cutting. Beyond that, Allen proved instrumental in shaping the
> performances of a group of actors who, aside from Beatty, were largely new to film
> and whose work could vary widely from take to take and within single takes as well.
> "Dede is enormously sensitive to a good, well-acted moment," says Penn. "A lot of
> actors owe a great deal to her."[33]

Although signs of the distinctive Allen style are evident in earlier films
such as *Odds Against Tomorrow* and *The Hustler*, this style came into full
bloom in *Bonnie and Clyde*. From her Hollywood roots, she brought both
her respect for the primacy of character and story and her abiding belief
that, rather than drawing attention to itself, editing should always be done
in service to these elements. From her work on television commercials,
she brought unusual, arresting shot combinations and rapid-fire cutting.
From her exposure to British Neo-Realism and French New Wave films,

she brought a host of new editing techniques such as shock cuts that gave films rough, threatening qualities and heightened audience anxiety. And, with help from Arthur Penn, she integrated it all into a harmonious whole. "What we essentially were doing," Penn once said, "was developing a rhythm for the film so that it has the complexity of music."[34] And judging from the continuous praise *Bonnie and Clyde* has received over that last half-century, the two succeeded admirably.

An Influence on Feature Films ... and Beyond Them

When Dede Allen first came on the scene, feature film editing in the U.S. had become very staid and traditional. The editorial style of Griffith and others, which began to dominate in the 1910s, had, by the late 1950s, become a set of hard and fast rules that editors were usually forced to follow.

But the world was changing, and films and film editing were bound to change with it. In the classic sense, Allen was the right person at the right time—a major artist who brought a new way of seeing to her art, a way that was very much in sync with the turbulent times in which she was working. In directors such as Robert Wise, Robert Rossen, and Arthur Penn—and later Sidney Lumet, Warren Beatty, and others—she found collaborators who saw her special talents and encouraged her to cultivate them. And she responded, delivering in a big way. Influenced by experiences from her work on television commercials to her exposure to innovative European films, she literally created a new style of American feature film editing—one that spoke more directly to the film audiences of the 1960s and 1970s and that remains fresh and vibrant decades later. In the process, she raised the stature of editing as a film art and made editing more a part of the ongoing discussion of cinema.

In addition, her influence—because it of its enormity—has gone well beyond the making of feature films. Today, we see bits and pieces of her distinctive style in virtually every kind of video form including television drama and comedy series, television commercials, animation and children's television, and especially music videos, which almost entirely depend on fast cutting, shock cuts, and other signature Allen techniques.

Much more than just innovative film editing, Allen's way of seeing—because it was (and remains) so right for the times—has also been woven into the larger tapestry of our culture. Even if we haven't seen one of her films for a while, she is with us every day.

7

"Mother Cutter"

Verna Fields Mentors a
New Generation of Film
Directors in the 1970s

When Steven Spielberg began work on the film version of Peter Benchley's 1974 novel *Jaws*, just about everything seemed to be going right in his young career. At only 26, he had already earned a reputation as a "comer" among Hollywood's emerging directing talents. He had received his first professional directing assignment at just 22, helming part of the premiere installment of Rod Serling's *Night Gallery* television series, a chilling half-hour story called "Eyes" and starring screen legend Joan Crawford. From there he went to other TV directing assignments on popular shows such as *The Name of the Game* and *Columbo*, to the highly praised made-for-TV movie *Duel* (1971) to his first feature film, the well-received neo-noir *The Sugarland Express* (1974)

Once immersed in *Jaws*, however, Spielberg seemed to be drowning in a sea of production problems and delays that seriously tested his mettle and led him to wonder if—after this—he might even have a directing career at all. All totaled, these problems, which inspired disgruntled members of the crew to nickname the film "*Flaws*,"[1] caused the production to take more than 100 days longer than was originally scheduled (159 days instead of 55) and drive the budget up from about $4 million to about $9 million. "I thought my career as a filmmaker was over," Spielberg later recalled. "I heard rumors that I would never work again because no one had ever taken a film 100 days over schedule."[2]

Among these problems, perhaps the most frustrating was a notoriously undependable mechanical shark—actually several sharks—named Bruce (after Spielberg's lawyer, Bruce Raimer). As the director has many times recalled, instead of working as planned, Bruce often just lay in the water like a "great white floating turd."[3]

As a solution, the resourceful Spielberg opted for another approach. Since he couldn't rely on his mechanical sharks to achieve the frightening effects he desired, he would shoot many scenes that suggested the shark without showing it in its entirety. Sometimes, for example, the shooting is from the shark's point of view. Other times, yellow barrels the shark drags around are all that indicate its presence. Still other times, all we see is the shark's dorsal fin.

The suggestions of the shark, of course, likely proved to be more effective than actual shark shots. "The film went from a Japanese Saturday matinee horror flick to more of a Hitchcock the-less-you-see-the-more-you-get thriller," Spielberg later said.[4] Another compensation the director made for the absence of a shark was to focus on getting more realistic performances from the actors. "The more fake the shark looked in the water," he observed, "the more my anxiety told me to heighten the naturalism of the performances."[5]

While some of the big problems were solved in production, many others remained. One was the musical score, which Spielberg's long-time collaborator, composer John Williams, addressed with his now-iconic music to indicate the approaching shark. And another, perhaps the most daunting of all, was the challenge of putting all the thousands and thousands of film fragments together in a way that would truly surprise and frighten theater audiences.

That task—the editing—fell to a warm, maternal Jewish woman in her mid–50s who preferred to keep all things casual; worked independently from the pool house in the backyard of her home in Encino, California; and, at the time, was mentoring not only Spielberg but also other rising filmmakers such as George Lucas and Peter Bogdanovich. Her name was Verna Fields (1918–1982), and the young filmmakers who worked with her affectionately called her their "mother cutter."

Unlike many of her fellow female editors who began to learn their craft at a young age and worked primarily in-house at studios, Fields started later, worked freelance most of her career, and took a much more circuitous route to the top of her profession, working—among numerous jobs—as a sound editor for television, a producer of U.S. Government documentaries, and a film teacher. She did not have a long stay at the top, either. In fact, the work she is most famous for took place between the late 1960s and the mid–1970s, just six or seven years. In that time, though,

Nicknamed the "mother cutter" by the young filmmakers she worked with—a group that included Peter Bogdanovich, George Lucas, and Steven Spielberg—Verna Fields was a key figure in the birth of the "New Hollywood" in the 1970s. Here, she is conferring with Spielberg on the set of *Jaws* (1975), the film that brought her an Oscar (Universal Pictures/Photofest).

she played a key role in changing how studio feature films were edited and what the finished products ultimately became. And, in the process, she helped to create the "New Hollywood" that emerged in the 1970s.

Perhaps Fields' crowning achievement was her contribution to *Jaws*, a film that went—largely because of her contributions—from potential fiasco to critical and box-office hit and (before *Star Wars* surpassed it a few years later) the highest grossing film of all time. While Spielberg, John Williams, the film's writers and actors, and many, many others have all been widely and enthusiastically praised for their work on the film, the adulation for Fields never seems to cease. The year after *Jaws* premiered, she received both a Best Editing Academy Award and an Eddie Award from the America Cinema Editors (ACE), the film editors' professional society for her work on the film. More than 25 years later, critic Leonard Maltin was still calling her work "sensational."[6] And a full 37 years afterwards, writer Ian Freer proclaimed, "*Jaws* remains a highpoint in film editing."[7]

Since so much of the initial popular discussion of *Jaws* focused on the effectiveness of Fields' editing, she was asked to join Spielberg, the film's producers, and others on the film's extensive promotional tour—something unprecedented for an editor. In the process, she became a celebrity in her own right, film editing's first "rock star." But, more important, she also served as an articulate ambassador for her profession, helping to make "the invisible art" much more visible to millions of people and, by doing so, to raise its stature considerably.

"About as famous 'overnight' as an editor ever gets."

In his 1980 interview with Fields, film writer Gerald Peary noted—no doubt with tongue in cheek—that *Jaws* had made her "about as famous 'overnight' as an editor ever gets."[8] The tip-off that Peary was having a bit of fun here of course is the use of quotation marks around the word "overnight." *Jaws* had indeed made Fields a celebrity, but her rise had been anything but instantaneous. In fact, it had been more than 30 years in the making.

Born Verna Hellman in St. Louis, Missouri, on March 21, 1918, she was the daughter of Selma Schwartz Hellman and Samuel (Sam) Hellman, then a journalist for both the *St. Louis Post-Dispatch* and the *Saturday Evening Post*.

Later, after Sam had become the managing editor for the *Post-Dispatch*, he moved his family to Hollywood to fulfill an ambition of his own to write for the movies. And, between the 1920s and the late 1940s, he wrote either the scenarios or screenplays for more than 40 films, including 1939's *Stanley and Livingstone* with Spencer Tracy, 1946's *My Darling Clementine* with Henry Fonda, and numerous Shirley Temple and Jack Benny vehicles.

Sam also had big plans for Verna, sending her to a fancy Parisian secondary school at the College Feminin de Bouffemont. After graduating, she attended USC, where she earned a bachelor's degree in journalism.

Verna's first brush with the film industry came during World War II when she met a young assistant editor named Sam Fields and would hang around the studio to be with him. Seeing this young woman with time on her hands, director Fritz Lang hired her as an apprentice sound editor to work on his 1944 film noir *The Woman in the Window*, and eventually she joined the editor's union.

In the meantime, she married Sam Fields, quit work, had two sons, and focused on raising them. She might have continued in this role indefinitely, but, in 1954 at the age of 38, Sam died suddenly of a heart attack, leaving Verna with the two young sons to support.

Hearing that sound editing jobs on television shows were available, she began to work on such series as *Death Valley Days* and the Saturday morning children's series, *Sky King* and *Fury*. "I'd tell the kids I was the Queen of Saturday Morning," she once quipped.[9]

But, being a single parent working in a demanding industry also brought with it great challenges. "I made special arrangements to be able to come home in the afternoon [of each work day] and make dinner for my kids," she recalled. "When they went to bed, I'd keep on. I built a cutting room in back of the house and I'd stay there until 2:00 a.m."[10]

In 1960, Fields met a man who would, perhaps more than anyone else, serve as her professional mentor, a film director, cinematographer, and editor named Irving Lerner. As she noted years later: "Lerner's trust really helped me. He taught me the right way to approach film."[11]

Perhaps best known today as the director of the low-budget cult noir *Murder by Contract* (1959), Lerner asked Fields to edit an upcoming project for him, a slimmed-down low-budget film version of James T. Farrell's fiction trilogy *Studs Lonigan*. With this experience, Peary observed, "Fields had found her calling."[12]

During the 1960s, Fields—now in her 40s—worked on a wide variety of projects ranging from independent films to major studio films, to television, to U.S. Government documentaries, to teaching. In 1960, she did the sound editing for *The Savage Eye*, a film that has since become a classic of the *cinéma vérité* movement of the 1950s and 1960s. The following year, she worked as the sound editor on Anthony Mann's epic *El Cid*, winning the Motion Pictures Sound Editors' Golden Reel Award for her efforts. With an interest in using film for social reform, she went to work in 1965 for the U.S. Government and President Lyndon Johnson's Great Society, making films for the U.S. Information Agency; the Department of Health, Education, and Welfare; and the Office of Economic Opportunity. In 1967, she returned to television, editing the feature-length *The Legend of the Boy and Eagle* for the series, *Walt Disney's Wonderful World of Color*. Then, in the late 1960s, she returned to USC, this time to teach editing. In her classes, she met several students who would later become major Hollywood players and valuable professional connections. One of them was John Milius, the future film producer and director as well as the prolific screenwriter who would receive an Academy Award nomination for his work on the screenplay for Francis Ford Coppola's *Apocalypse Now* (1979). Two others were film editor Marcia Griffin and the man who for the next decade would be both Marcia's close professional collaborator and her husband, George Lucas.

In 1968, Fields made still another contact that would be of great importance to her later on. In one of her last sound editing assignments, she worked for a young director named Peter Bogdanovich on one of his first film efforts, a low-budget thriller about a deranged sniper called *Targets*. The film, which still has an enthusiastic cult following, is skillful in many respects from its crisp writing to its imaginative camera work. But, according to film historian Bill Warren, even amid so many other good elements, the film's sound editing clearly stands out. Describing the scene in which the sniper, Bobby, starts shooting randomly at freeway drivers from the top of an oil storage tank, Warren writes: "The sound is mono, and brilliantly mixed—the entire sequence of Bobby shooting from the tanks was shot without sound. Verna Fields, then a sound editor, added all the sound effects. The result is seamlessly realistic, from the scrape of the guns on the metal of the tanks, to the crack of the rifles, to the little gasps Bobby makes just before firing."[13]

While pleased with her contribution to *Targets*, however, Fields was increasingly drawn to film editing and, for the next seven years, concentrated on it almost exclusively.

One of her first projects after *Targets* was Haskell Wexler's *Medium Cool*, a disturbing *cinéma vérité* piece that explores the social and political unrest during the 1968 Democratic Convention in Chicago. At the time, the film packed a real punch. Calling it "technically brilliant" and praising its "tremendous visual impact," *New York Times* critic Vincent Canby went on to describe it as "a kind of cinematic *Guernica*,[14] a picture of America in the process of exploding into fragmented bits of hostility, suspicion, fear, and violence."[15] Equally impressed, Roger Ebert ranked *Medium Cool* second on his Ten Best Films of 1969 list and called it "important," "absorbing," and "an almost perfect example of the new movie."[16]

Seen decades later, the film's impact is still quite powerful, and one of the main reasons is Fields' strong, confident, and fearless editing that captures those "fragmented bits of hostility, suspicion, fear, and violence" with great skill. We don't simply see the chaos and conflict, we actually feel caught up in it—tossed about, if you will—the editing often jerking our focus from one line of dialogue, action, or scene to another abruptly, unexpectedly, and sometimes harshly. Fields' work represents a major contribution to the overall impact of Wexler's film.

After *Medium Cool*, Fields began perhaps the most fruitful part of her career, working as the "mother cutter" on six films for three of the "young Turks" of a new generation of Hollywood directors: Peter Bogdanovich, George Lucas, and Steven Spielberg.

For Bogdanovich, she edited three films: the popular screwball comedy *What's Up, Doc?* (1972) and the highly praised Depression-era road picture *Paper Moon* (1973) as well as the less critically and commercially successful adaptation of the Henry James novella *Daisy Miller* (1974). With the success of *What's Up, Doc?*, Fields—at age 54—had finally established herself as a go-to editor of feature films for a major studio.

Of the three films she did with Bogdanovich, her work on *Paper Moon* remains the most impressive today. While not especially groundbreaking, it does show her mastery of craft. The timing of her cuts, for example, is especially effective. While the film never seems rushed, the story flows quickly and expeditiously. We never feel that there is a wasted moment. One technique she often uses to move us from one scene to the next is to cut just a few frames before where a more traditional editor might cut. This could be in the middle instead of at the end of an action or just as a line of dialogue is concluding rather than right afterwards. The effect—in addition to keeping things moving briskly—is to give greater flow and unity to what is essentially a fragmented, episodic story. Fields was also wonderful at cutting to reaction shots to show us what characters are feeling (sometimes very complex, conflicting emotions) without dwelling on the actors' faces. A striking example is how her cutting captures young Addie's (Tatum O'Neal) conflicted feelings when she knows she has successfully broken up Moze and Trixie's (Ryan O'Neal and Madeline Kahn) relationship. "Verna was always in favor of making less to be more," Spielberg once said.[17] And in *Paper Moon*, we definitely see how effective this "less-is-more" editing philosophy can be.

Fields' professional relationship with George Lucas had actually begun well before the 1970s—in 1967 to be exact—when he was her student at USC. She had hired him and another student, Marcia Griffin (who would marry Lucas in 1969), to help her on a documentary she was making for the United States Information Agency. In 1972, their paths crossed again when Lucas was directing his nostalgic look at small-town America in 1962, *American Graffiti*, and Universal asked him to add Fields to the editing team. For the first 10 weeks of post-production, Fields worked with the Lucases as well as sound editor Walter Murch to put together a 165-minute version of the film. After this, Fields left to fulfill another business commitment, and Marcia Lucas spent several months more whittling the film down to

110 minutes. For their efforts, both Fields and Marcia Lucas received a shared Best Editing Academy Award nomination.

While it is always difficult (and frequently impossible) to assess who contributed what to the finished film when several people are involved, Fields' experience both as a sound editor and as an editor in *cinéma vérité* films clearly had an impact on *American Graffiti*. From the first moments of the film, there is something electric about how the visuals and the over-laid rock-and-roll music complement each other, how the cuts between scenes sometimes pop from one visual image to the next, and how the action seems to drive as relentlessly as a Buddy Holly song. Much imitated since its release, there was something new, fresh, and vibrant about *American Graffiti*, and the Fields touch—the same touch she would soon bring to *Jaws*—played a key role in giving the film this freshness and energy. As Gerald Peary has noted, between them, Fields and Marcia Lucas "set the style of cutting for the rest of the 1970s."[18]

In late 1973 and early 1974, Fields worked with yet another young director, Steven Spielberg, co-editing (with Edward M. Abroms) his first major feature film, a darkly humorous and ultimately downbeat piece based on a real-life hostage drama in Texas called *The Sugarland Express*. While a hit with critics and often praised for its taut editing, the film was not a hit with audiences, which, as Spielberg later acknowledged, were now less receptive to downbeat stories than they had been in the late 1960s to films such as *Bonnie and Clyde* (1967) and *Easy Rider* (1969).

Despite his disappointment with *The Sugarland Express*'s box-office performance, Spielberg had been greatly impressed with Fields and was happy to work with her again in his next project, an action-horror film named *Jaws*. The rest, as they say, is film history. For four decades, the editing of *Jaws* has constantly been studied and analyzed. And the film is widely considered to be—along with *Citizen Kane, Raging Bull, Bonnie and Clyde*, and a handful of other classics—one of the best-edited films of all time.

Ironically, though, *Jaws* would also be the last film Fields ever edited. In 1976, she received an offer to become the vice president for feature production at Universal Studios—a position that, at the time, made her one of the most powerful women in Hollywood—and she accepted. Serving in this role for the next six years, she remained—in an industry where people can quickly turn against each other—highly and widely respected. As producer-director Joel Schumacher said of her work at Universal for a July 1982 *Los Angeles Times* newspaper article: "In the record business, you have Berry Gordy and Ahmet Ertegun. They're executives who actually made records. In the movie business, as an executive who's worked with film, you have only Verna. She saves Universal a fortune every day."[19]

This praise came on the heels of another recognition Fields received the previous year from the organization Women in Film. It was the prestigious Crystal Award, which is presented to "outstanding women who, through their endurance and the excellence of their work, have helped to expand the role of women within the entertainment industry."[20] To date, Fields is—along with Margaret Booth, Dede Allen, and Anne V. Coates— one of only four film editors to receive this award.

Fields doubtlessly would have continued at Universal, but in 1982 she discovered that she had cancer, and she died on November 30 of that year in Encino. She was survived by her two sons, one of whom, Richard, had followed her and her husband, Sam, into the film editing profession.

In appreciation of her contributions to both Universal and the film industry, the studio posthumously accorded Fields another rare honor. It named a major company facility the Verna Fields Building. Today, it stands on the Universal lot just across from another building named for a film industry luminary—Alfred Hitchcock.

Like many of her fellow female film editors, Fields tended to shy away from criticizing the film industry for the lack of opportunity women had in the editing, directing, producing, and executive ranks during her career. Instead, she preferred to lead by example. When asked to comment on the success of *Jaws* late in her life, she simply suggested how tickled she was when "people discovered that it was a woman who edited *Jaws*."[21] The implication of course is that, if a woman could do such a fine job of editing an action-horror film such as *Jaws*, then other women could certainly do well editing similar films. She took a similar approach once she became that rare creature for 1976, a female film industry executive. Instead of complaining about the lack of women in comparable positions, she focused on proving that, if this woman deserved such a job, then others did, too.

"A near-matchless legacy"—Fields' Work on Jaws

In the editing profession Fields was a true original, the rare person who thought differently and soon changed the way other people thought about and approached their art.

In many respects, she was a creature of her time and the sum of her experiences. She came of age as a film editor in the 1960s when younger editors actively challenged the rules of the classical Hollywood editing style established back in the 1910s. The edgy new kind of cutting she saw in the French New Wave films of the late 1950s and 1960s doubtlessly influenced her. And her years of experience first as a sound editor and then as a film editor on *cinéma vérité* films such as *The Savage Eye* and *Medium Cool* affected her future work as well.

But there was also—and perhaps primarily—her witty, iconoclastic, and ultimately radical personality. While she respected the primacy of the director in all filmmaking matters, she saw her role as adding "out-of-the-box" creative value in the editing phase (and sometimes in the production phase) of the director's film. In this process of thinking differently to better tell the story, she broke traditional rules. We see frequent examples of this practice in Fields' later work from her abrupt, often harsh and unsettling cutting in *Medium Cool* to her exuberant cutting and juxtaposition of sound and visuals in *American Graffiti*, to her numerous contributions to *Jaws*. By doing this, she brought additional freshness and vitality to these films, and she helped extend and enrich the editor's art.

～

Of Fields' achievements, the one that's discussed and praised most often of course is her work on *Jaws*.

Over the years, numerous people have even gone so far as credit her with saving the film and perhaps even the young Spielberg's career. While intriguing, such claims are also highly speculative. Spielberg, as we have seen during his long and storied career, has repeatedly found ingenious solutions to major script, production, and editing problems. The script, which the film's writers revised and revised throughout the production, and John Williams' simple, brilliant musical theme were critical as well. And undoubtedly many others helped in both large and small ways.

But, while it may be overreaching to say that Fields singlehandedly saved the film, she did make an indispensable contribution that led to the film's powerful initial impact and lasting appeal. Without her, the film might still have been a success, but it probably would not have been as special as it is.

Specifically, how did Fields help enrich the finished product? Let's look at several of her key contributions.

First, there was the unusual timing of her edits.

Typically, editors will cut to a rhythm or flow in order to give a film a certain pace, usually one that feels right and natural to them. Ever the iconoclast, however, Fields toyed with this tried-and-true editing practice. As she told her audience at a lecture she gave at the American Film Institute in 1975: "There's a feeling of movement in telling a story and there is a

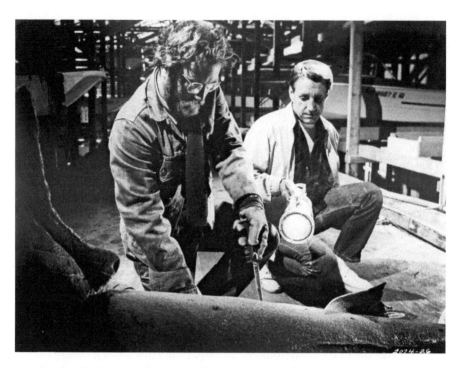

Hooper (Richard Dreyfuss) and Chief Brody (Roy Scheider) inspect the insides of a dead shark to prove that another shark—the one that has been terrorizing the coastal town of Amity—is still alive, well, and out there in 1975's *Jaws*. Many people, including director Steven Spielberg, consider Fields' editing on *Jaws* as critical to the film's success (Universal Pictures/Photofest).

flow. A cut that is off-rhythm will be disturbing and you will feel it, unless you want it to be like that. On *Jaws*, each time I wanted to cut I didn't, so that it would have an anticipatory feeling—and it worked."[22] In other words, by cutting "off-rhythm," as Fields put it, she helped to ratchet up suspense and audience anxiety, two key storytelling objectives.

Film writer Craig Bloomfield also believes that this off-rhythm cutting did quite a bit more. "[Fields] gave [*Jaws*] rhythm, shape, mystery," he noted. "The prolonged tension was her doing. Her cuts helped sculpt the narrative for greater emotional resonance, giving extra urgency to the characters' motivations."[23]

Second, Fields did a masterly job of structuring specific scenes to give them a distinctiveness and resonance usually lacking in action or horror films.

Of these, one of the most riveting is the film's first sequence, which mixes dark humor with horror to transform a potentially cliché-filled episode into something that explores multiple perspectives in a fresh and unique way. This actually begins when we see the Universal logo and we hear, of all things, underwater sounds (definitely a bit of dark humor). Then, as the credits are first shown over black we hear the first ominous notes of John Williams' "shark" theme. This continues as we next see underwater "roaming" shots, presumably the shark's point of view, as more credits are shown. Then, as we see the editor's credit, the film abruptly cuts to a beach at night. Just as the shark is roaming beneath the water's surface, the camera's eye roams leisurely across a group of young people— perhaps college students—around a bonfire, talking, listening to music, drinking, smoking cigarettes and pot, and making out. The camera stops for a second to show a young man in a medium-close shot with a cigarette and a beer. He is in a roaming mood, too, and his eyes have now spotted a young woman, Chrissie (Susan Backlinie), sitting a few feet away from the group. They make eye contact, and the pursuit is on. Chrissie runs along the beach and then into the ocean, taking her clothes off one piece at a time. He follows but is too drunk and ultimately hapless. As she enjoys the water, he fumbles around on the beach. Now, the film cuts back to the kind of underwater shots we saw earlier accompanied by the ominous shark music. The scenes then cut back and forth between Chrissie on the surface and the point of view from underwater as the shark closes in on her. On the surface (at her eye level), we see her reaction to first contact with the shark—disbelief, fear, and horror. At one point she clings to a buoy for dear life and pleads with God to spare her. Then, in the middle of her flailing and screaming, the film cuts back briefly to her other pursuer, the drunken young man who now lies unconscious on the safe, peaceful beach just before sunrise. Quickly, the action returns to the attack, Chrissie screaming and going down for the last time. Another cut back to the young man asleep on the beach. Then a final cut to the buoy calmly floating in the now utterly peaceful pre-dawn sea.

This sequence, just five minutes from beginning to end (including credits), is laid out with great skill and care. Certainly, the pairing of the Universal logo with underwater sounds is a clever, funny, and very fitting initial touch. Next, the abrupt cut between the first underwater point-of-view shots and the young people around the beach bonfire hints at a strong connection between the two, which, of course, we will soon see in some very careful crosscutting. Seconds later, a new juxtaposition emerges— one between the young man and Chrissie. Once she is in the water, still another juxtaposition emerges—one between Chrissie and the shark. Meanwhile, while it is no longer as prominent, the juxtaposition between

Chrissie and the young man continues. In fact, one of the most effective cuts in the sequence is between Chrissie flailing and screaming in horror and the young man sleeping peacefully on the beach. Not only does this shift in point of view give us a short but necessary break from the killing that's in progress, but it also, as writer Ian Freer has noted, "intensifies the attack when we return to it."[24] Finally, we see the final juxtaposition between the young man, who sleeps peacefully on the beach, and the ocean beside him, now as serene as he is. In the end, this young man whose attraction to her had inspired Chrissie to go into the water has—ironically—been saved by his own drunken ineptitude. Overall, this is a wonderful sequence, one that sets up both the story and the mixed tone of horror and dark humor that will be prominent throughout the film.

Third, Fields made brilliant use of new editing techniques to increase suspense and keep audiences on edge.

One of the most famous is the use of a late-1960s innovation Fields herself named the "wipe by cut," which can be employed when a character is filmed from a distance using a telephoto lens. The effect is to hide a cut by showing a shot of a figure that passes between the camera and a character, creating the impression of an old-time movie "wipe" to hide a cut, be less distracting for a viewer, and give a scene greater continuity.

The scene when Fields and Spielberg use this to great effect is before the second shark attack (Alex Kintner's death) as Chief Brody (Roy Scheider) sits in the crowd on the beach looking out for any potential danger. Here, as various people go by him, the "wipe by cuts" block Brody's (and our) view of the water and anything that might be going on in it. As audience members sharing Brody's point of view in this scene, we experience both his frustration at having his views blocked and his anxiety that he (and we) might also be missing something important. Again, it's a superbly orchestrated scene, one that keeps viewers on edge throughout.

Fourth, Fields did something that at first seems impossible: although we don't even see the shark in all its glory until well into the film, she nevertheless managed made it a well-rounded character throughout.

As film writer Susan Korda has noted: "What is fascinating in *Jaws* is that the shark has a personality, the shark has an intelligence, indeed sometimes I think the shark has a sense of humor, morbid as it might be. And that was all achieved in the first two acts of the film before you see the shark. So the cutting was very essential for that."[25] Again, John Williams' music and Steven Spielberg's decision to shoot more from the shark's point of view helped fill out this characterization. Yet, it was Fields' cutting that brought this well-rounded (but often invisible) character to life.

Fifth, Fields managed to surprise us constantly in ways that never seem to grow old.

Certainly one of the biggest stunners in the film is when we first see the shark in all its glory, prompting Brody to utter his famous line: "We're going to need a bigger boat." Until this moment, we have repeatedly been set up for a shark interaction by the point-of-view underwater shots accompanied by the shark's theme music. Rather than doing this again before the shark's big entrance, Fields does the opposite—employing no visual or musical build-up at all. Brody is simply doing the unpleasant job of throwing smelly bait out to sea to lure the shark, and with absolutely no warning it appears—enormous, ferocious, terrifying. As Brody jumps back in shock, so do we—every time we see the film.

Another much-talked-moment is when Hooper (Richard Dreyfuss), diving down to the wreckage of Ben Gardner's boat, sees Ben's disembodied head pop up right in front of him. The scene was Spielberg's brainstorm. "Yet," as Freer notes, "it is the editorial skill that garners the scare. The length the shot is held before the head jumps out. The slow build of John Williams' music ... fools us.... And the literal scream ... forms part of the soundtrack. Still you can know all that, know that it is coming, and it still gets you every time."[26]

In summing up Fields' contribution to the film, Bloomfield wrote, "*Jaws*' visceral impact was of course due to the strength and toil of its collaboration, but Fields' judicious cutting was instrumental in maintaining its flow.... Her work on *Jaws* holds its own today and leaves a near-matchless legacy."[27]

Even for those who find the film over-rated, it's almost impossible to disagree with this last statement. *Jaws* may not be one of the most profound films ever made, but it could very well be one of the best edited. Fields did fine work on a number of films, but her work on this one clearly puts her in the company of the film industry's greatest editors.

A "Mother Cutter" for Editors, Too

While every notable female film editor who began her career in the silent or classical eras was a positive role model to all (particularly the women) who've followed in the profession, Fields holds a special place among them. Barbara McLean was enormously creative at working within constraints and solving specific problems. Margaret Booth was a skilled and powerful executive. Dede Allen was an editing innovator who literally changed the way people approached and made films. And Fields was all of the above. In addition, she was that rarest of editors, male or female: a household name who brings attention and recognition to a profession that has always been under-appreciated—the editing "rock star." Today, the only editors who even come close in this category are Thelma Schoonmaker (mostly for her work with Martin Scorsese) and Michael Kahn (mostly for his work with Steven Spielberg).

Viewed in this light, Fields was not only the "mother cutter" to a trio of emerging film directors in the early 1970s but also a "mother cutter" to all those, male as well as female, who followed—and continue to follow—her into the editing profession. In her work with Peter Bogdanovich, George Lucas, and Steven Spielberg, she helped to forge a dominant new editing style that led to the revitalization of U.S. studio filmmaking in the 1970s and the emergence of the "New Hollywood." Her influence has been pervasive and lasting, and, while most of today's film editors might be hesitant to call Fields their "mother cutter," a bit of her professional DNA resides somewhere within each of them.

8

Making the Most
of Her Moments

The Ever-Adaptable and Always
Adventurous Anne V. Coates

There is a moment early on in David Lean's great film *Lawrence of Arabia* (1962) that gives nearly every first-time viewer a tremendous jolt. The main character, T. E. Lawrence (Peter O'Toole), is chatting in a stately government room in Cairo with a world-weary British diplomat named Dryden (Claude Rains). Lawrence, a young British Army officer, has just been assigned to go to Arabia and make contact with an important Arab leader, Prince Faisal. He is excited and talks about the "fun" he will have on this adventure. Dryden cautions him, saying that the desert is a hostile "furnace" where only Bedouins and gods have fun and that Lawrence is neither. As they talk, Dryden selects a cigar and puts it in his mouth. Lawrence strikes a match, lights the cigar for Dryden, and then—as the picture cuts to a close shot on the match—lets it burn down a bit as he watches in fascination. After a long, curious pause, he blows it out. Then—from this intimate shot—the image suddenly (almost shockingly) cuts to another light: the sun beginning to rise amid the vast, starkly beautiful expanse of the Arabian Desert.

When seen in a theater on a 70-millimeter screen, the experience is nothing less than mesmerizing. It is one of those moments that nearly everyone, even decades after seeing the film, remembers. Steven Spielberg has said that the moment "blew me away."[1] And film writer Ian Jefferys has called it both "the most famous of edits" and "one of the most recognizable and celebrated cuts in the history of cinema."[2]

Ironically, this "most famous of edits" wasn't supposed to be a cut.

139

As Anne V. Coates (1925–), then a young editor working with Lean on the film, later recalled: "It was in the script as a dissolve, but we saw it cut together before we had the optical delivered. We looked at the job and said, 'My God, it worked fantastic…!' I literally took two frames off of the outgoing scene and that's the way it is today."[3]

Although Coates, with characteristic modesty, has also praised Lean's astuteness, others have given her much—if not most—of the credit for this "Eureka" moment. At the time, the traditional editing techniques to show major changes of time and place were either dissolves or fades. Since the earliest days of the movies, this was the visual grammar that audiences understood. But, starting in the late 1950s, younger filmmakers such as the French New Wave directors began to change all of this. One of their strategies was to employ new, more jolting editing techniques, which at the time seemed quite radical. And one of these techniques was to substitute strong, sudden, emphatic cuts in places where fades or dissolves would traditionally have gone. The intent was to startle audiences, put them on edge, shake them out of their complacency. By 1962, Coates, then a big fan of New Wave films, was clearly aware of the power of these techniques. Seeing the sharp, sudden cut between the extinguished match and the desert sunrise, she immediately recognized its value. In its place, a dissolve would have been slower, less emphatic, and ultimately weaker. It would still have been dramatic, but it would have lacked a cut's sharp, sudden, unexpected impact. If Steven Spielberg had seen a dissolve instead, he might have still been impressed, but the transition probably wouldn't—to paraphrase his words—have blown his mind.

Seeing and then seizing opportunities in moments such as this—opportunities others might easily overlook—has been a behavior that has served Anne Coates well throughout her long and extremely productive career as a film editor first in her native England and then in the U.S.

Throughout her work, examples abound. In addition to "the cut," *Lawrence of Arabia* alone is filled with great cinematic moments made better by Coates' excellent sense of rhythm and composition: the motorcycle ride that begins the film, the scene when Lawrence says "No prisoners" and then proceeds to slaughter a small group of opposing fighters, the attack on the city of Aqaba. The very moving 1980 drama *The Elephant Man* includes a scene when the title character goes to the theater and we see, through his eyes, a beautifully conceived, dreamlike montage of dancers. The 1993 thriller *In the Line of Fire* features a series of brilliantly crafted "cat-and-mouse" phone conversations between John Malkovich's would-be presidential assassin and Clint Eastwood's anxious Secret Service agent.

The off-beat 1998 romance/caper film *Out of Sight* shows the now-famous succession of romantic shots between George Clooney's charming thief and Jennifer Lopez' FBI agent in a hotel room as we hear snippets from a conversation they have just had in the hotel bar. And the 2002 drama *Unfaithful* includes a series of shots in which Diane Lane's adulterous wife—returning home on a subway train from an intense sexual encounter with a man she barely knows—relives the encounter (and runs the gamut of emotions) in a series of short, sharp flashbacks.

The list of such unforgettable moments in the more than 50 films Coates has edited since her first in 1952—films that also include 1964's *Becket*, 1992's *Chaplin*, and 2000's *Erin Brockovich*— is long and quite impressive. They have led to much recognition and many awards including five Academy Award nominations over 36 years, one Oscar win (for *Lawrence*), an American Cinema Editors (ACE) Lifetime Achievement Award in 1995, a Woman in Film Crystal Award in 1997, numerous editing nominations and wins from the British Academy of Film and Television Arts (BAFTA), BAFTA's prestigious Academy Fellowship Award in 2007, and much more.

Beginning her editing career in the late 1940s as an assistant on British films, Anne V. Coates moved to Hollywood permanently in the 1980s. Over her long career in both the U.K. and the U.S., she has received five Oscar nominations, winning in 1963 for her work on director David Lean's classic film, *Lawrence of Arabia* (Photofest).

In addition, Coates—insistent about a film career since she was a teenager—has always found ways to make things happen in her life: getting into the film business despite family objections and lack of a union membership; being a woman in a field that by the 1950s men had come to dominate; working regularly while raising three children (all of whom would become filmmakers); leaving the U.K. to live permanently in Hollywood, where she could be more at the heart of the action; working with numerous (and increasingly younger) directors and consistently urging them to "stretch" her as an editor; and constantly adapting to, and mastering, new digital editing tools and techniques. Still active in the film business in her 90s, she has never stopped looking toward that next horizon.

In her work, Coates prefers to call herself hands-on and intuitive rather than a theorist or an intellectual, admitting that she once tried to read a book about the rules of editing and soon realized that she regularly broke most of them. For her, what seems to matter far more is having a "feeling for a film," a phrase she frequently uses.

Personally, she has a gracious, unassuming, down-to-earth manner that is spiced with a dry, sometimes self-deprecating British wit. When asked why she moved from the U.K. to Hollywood, for example, she has often said that one of the main reasons was valet parking.[4]

Putting all this together, she has been one of the most respected film editors in the business for more than 50 years—a consummate pro who has never stopped believing that her own best can always be better and then seeking out new ways to improve in her art.

"You have to be a little pushy": A Career on Both Sides of the Atlantic

As Coates often confesses, film was not her first love. Born in Reigate, a suburb of London, on December 12, 1925, she was enthralled with horses as a young girl and had aspirations of being a racehorse trainer.

This changed, however, when she was a teen in boarding school. Teachers at the school would take students to see movies such as 1939's *Wuthering Heights*, and Coates was entranced. What particularly impressed her was how filmmakers could bring dusty old novels to such vibrant life on a theater screen. "When I saw *Wuthering Heights* I was in another world," she recalls. "I was swept away by it and Laurence Olivier. It suddenly made me realize that would be quite an interesting job to be able to take a book like *Wuthering Heights* and make it something magical on the screen. It had a profound influence on my life."[5]

From then on, Coates wanted to be a filmmaker. First, though, she needed to finish her schooling, and, with World War II raging in Europe, she then chose to serve in the war effort, working as a nurse at Sir Archibald McIndoe's pioneering plastic surgery hospital in East Grinstead in Sussex.

When the war ended, Coates' dreams of becoming a filmmaker remained as strong as ever. Her family, however, was not enthusiastic, and one of the most outspoken among her family members was her uncle—a man who also happened to be one of the most powerful film studio owners and film distributors in England—J. Arthur Rank. A devout Methodist who taught Sunday school for years, Rank took his Christian values seriously and, even though he was involved, felt that the filmmaking was an unsavory business that was unsuitable for his impressionable young niece. In addition, the various film unions were strong and difficult to get into. Anne continued to lobby her cause, though, and Rank finally relented, getting her an entry-level job in a small non-union company he owned that specialized in religious films. There wasn't much glamor there, Rank figured, and, if glamor was what young Anne was seeking, he felt she would quickly tire of the business. At the company, Coates did sound recording, projection, and various odd jobs for a short time, and then, to her delight, the union came to the company to sign people up. She eagerly filled out the papers, and soon (as a freshly minted union member) she was applying for jobs at one of England's most prestigious film houses, Pinewood Studios. "I heard about this job at Pinewood; they were looking for a second assistant in the cutting room," she said. "I applied and got an interview. I didn't speak the exact truth because I had not worked in a cutting room." But she sought out help from some friends, quickly got up to speed, and was soon working as an assistant to the highly respected editor Reggie Mills on the 1948 Michael Powell and Emeric Pressberger film *The Red Shoes*. "There I was," Coates said, "working with one of the top editors in the world on my first picture."[6]

For the next four years, Coates assisted different editors at Pinewood. One she credits with having an enormous influence on her was John Seabourne, a veteran who had been editing British films since the 1930s. "He was very old and very experienced, and I worked closely with him," Coates recalled in the 1990s:

> He was also slightly deaf, so often he didn't hear the notes the director gave him and I would tell him what to do. He frequently went home about 4:00 to tend his gardens and he'd say, "Finish that sequence," which was a great experience. He taught me the most of anybody, I think. He taught me to be ruthless, not to fiddle around with matching and such things, but to go for the heart of the scene, for the drama, and always keep your mind on telling the story through the pictures.[7]

Then, when one editor she was assisting passed on the chance to edit a film of Charles Dickens' *The Pickwick Papers* in 1952, Coates eagerly sought the opportunity. As she recalls:

> I went off and met with the director [Noel Langley]. I didn't feel like I said anything particularly bright, but apparently I impressed him. I got the job with the proviso that if I didn't work out in the first two or three weeks they would change me or bring

in someone over me. My friends said, "You must be mad working with Noel Langley, a known misogynist." I said, "He was very nice to me." He was a very good writer but not an experienced director; he was making a lot of mistakes and it was difficult to cut. I was doing my best, but I know they were not totally happy. Then they did a courtroom sequence, which I apparently did a really good edit of, and everything went smoothly after that. They put me under contract, and I did another picture for them. You have to take the breaks when they come.[8]

During the 1950s, Coates worked as an editor on a variety of Pinewood films. Averaging about one per year, they ranged from crime thrillers to comedies. Among these, two of the best known today are the comedy *The Horse's Mouth* (1958) and the drama *Tunes of Glory* (1960), both directed by Ronald Neame and both starring Alec Guinness. The positive response to the two films helped to give Coates more visibility in the British film industry, but they could hardly have prepared her for what lay straight ahead.

As Coates tells the story, she and her husband, film director Douglas Hickox, were shopping at London's Harrods department store one Saturday morning when they bumped into an assistant director named Jerry O'Hara, who was working on pre-production for director (and former editor) David Lean's upcoming film, *Lawrence of Arabia*. O'Hara was doing a test of actor Albert Finney, then being considered for the title role, and, half-jokingly, Coates asked if they had found anyone to cut the piece. O'Hara didn't think they had, so she asked for the number of a person to call to see about it. "Luck is very often a good factor," Coates recalled. "But it's not only luck. You have to be a little pushy and follow up on things."[9] The call to a production supervisor led to the chance to cut the test, two scenes with Finney.

While Coates was thrilled with the chance to work with the highly respected David Lean, she also suddenly felt way over her head and quite nervous. She remembers being "terrified" as she brought the edited scenes into the room to screen for Lean and others involved with the film. "I was so frightened, I didn't see one cut," she said. "At the end David got up and said to the whole unit, 'That's the first piece of film I've ever seen cut exactly the way I would have done it!'"[10]

Although flattered, Coates felt that Lean and the film's producer, Sam Spiegel, would opt for another, more experienced, editor to work on the entire film. But, two days later, Spiegel invited her to come to London with him and Lean in his Rolls Royce, and she was offered the job.

Cutting *Lawrence* was a major turning point for Coates, then in her 30s. First, the experience proved that she could edit a film of its massive scale and scope. She has noted that about 31 miles of film footage was shot, all of which had to be edited down to a running time of nearly four hours—about twice the length of a typical film. Second, it proved that she could also work very quickly. In this case, time was of the essence. Spiegel had already arranged a special screening for England's Queen Elizabeth, and this was one deadline that had to be met. "We took 13 months to shoot the film and four months to cut it!" Coates recalled. "We just cut phenomenally, when you think about it. Seven days a week until about 11:00 o'clock at night. I now look back and wish we had a little more time to finesse some of the scenes."[11]

She and Lean did eventually get that chance when they both worked on a restoration of the film in the late 1980s that added about six minutes of footage to the story. "It's a much better film now," Coates notes. "So much meaning was taken out of it. I was extremely lucky to be available to do the restoration."[12]

Despite her concerns that the film initially needed more editing "finesse," *Lawrence* was immediately hailed as classic and remains so more than a half-century after its release. In 1963, the film received 10 Academy Award nominations, winning seven, including Best Editing for Coates. It also swept the BAFTA and the Golden Globe awards that year. More recently, *Lawrence* placed seventh in the American Film Industry's 2007 list of the top 100 American films and in the top 100 in the 2012 international critics poll taken by the British Film Institute's *Sight and Sound Magazine* of the greatest films of all time.

In addition to taking her career to a new level, Coates often speaks of the experience of working with Lean on *Lawrence* as a great education. "David Lean," she once noted, "always used to say, 'Have the courage of your conviction, tell the story your way. I'll respect what you did, although in certain instances I may want things another way.' He would hold these shots of the desert, and I'd say, 'David, you can't hold them that long.' However, he said, 'Wait until the music's on, wait until the whole rhythm is together.' And he was right."[13]

Coates' success on *Lawrence* immediately led to a job on 1964's *Becket*, directed by Peter Glenville. Based on a stage play by Jean Anouilh and much more dialogue-dependent than *Lawrence*, *Becket* presented different challenges for her. Again, she faced them in her characteristically bold, forthright manner. For example, there's one scene in *Becket* when the two main characters, Thomas Becket and England's King Henry II, have been estranged and the king decides to go see Becket. Instead of dissolving, Coates made a direct cut to Becket's coming in the door. "A lovely cut, nothing very complicated," she noted. "Hal Wallis (the film's producer) said to me, 'You can't do a direct cut. You've got to do a dissolve in there. He's 50 miles away.' I said, 'So what? It's a great cut and very dramatic, and goes right to the heart of the scene.' He never mentioned it again, and it stayed like it was.... That's what I mean by the fact that I never work with formulas or rules."[14]

Coates' instincts paid off again, and, for *Becket*, she received her second Academy Award nomination.

Soon after finishing *Becket*, Coates had the opportunity to work with another legendary director and, in characteristic form, went for it wholeheartedly. The film was *Young Cassidy*, a biographical drama based on the life of Irish playwright Sean O'Casey, and the director was John Ford. "Ford interviewed me and said, 'If she's good enough for David Lean, she's good enough for me,'" Coates recalled. "I never got to know him because I was in England, and he was shooting in Ireland."[15] Soon after starting to shoot the film, however, Ford had health problems and had to leave the film. While she enjoyed working with Ford's replacement, Jack Cardiff, Coates was also disappointed that she didn't get the chance to complete the film with Ford.

Another film Coates speaks of with great affection is David Lynch's 1980 film version of the play *The Elephant Man*, with John Hurt, Anthony Hopkins, and Anne Bancroft. As with *Becket*, some of the challenges she faced here involved adapting a stage play to the screen. One in particular was a sequence when the Elephant Man goes to a theater and sees pantomimes onstage. Originally, it had been shot as a straight sequence, but she and Lynch felt that it was "extremely flat." So, the two came up with the idea of turning the scene into a montage. "We had the music before we had the montage, so we worked from the music and made up this quite entrancing little montage where we superimposed the floor with twinkling silver over the dancing," she recalled. "You got completely what you wanted from the Elephant Man's reactions. It took on a dreamlike quality, which it wouldn't have had the other way."[16]

Her work on *The Elephant Man* led to more honors, including a third Academy Award nomination in 1981.

Receiving more and more work on American-produced films, Coates pulled up stakes in the U.K. in 1986 and moved to Los Angeles, where she felt more of the filmmaking action was. Soon afterwards, her three children—Anthony, Emma, and James—now educated, came to Southern California as well. All three, incidentally, followed in the family tradition and became filmmakers. Coates' two sons, Anthony and James, became directors, and her daughter, Emma, became an editor. (Emma has since moved back to London.)

Based mainly in Los Angeles since 1986, Coates has continued to work regularly and thrive on variety—both in terms of the projects she has worked on and the directors she has worked with. The films have ranged from thrillers to comedies, to fantasies, to serious dramas. And the directors have ranged from John Milius (1989's *Farewell to the King*) to Richard Attenborough (1992's *Chaplin*), to Wolfgang Petersen (1993's *In the Line of Fire*), to Steven Soderbergh (1998's *Out of Sight* and 2000's *Erin Brockovich*), to Adrian Lyne (2002's *Unfaithful*), to Chris Weitz (2007's *The Golden Compass*), to Tom Vaughn (2010's *Extraordinary Measures*), to Sam Taylor-Johnson (2015's *Fifty Shades of Grey*). The 2004 mystery/thriller *Taking Lives*, directed by D.J. Caruso, was a personal milestone—her fiftieth film credit as an editor. And, in addition to other honors, her work on *In the Line of Fire* and *Out of Sight* led to her fourth and fifth Academy Award nominations.

While she likes working with all kinds of directors, Coates has increasingly gravitated toward younger ones, feeling that, by working together, both she and a new generation of directors can benefit. Directors Weitz and Vaughn, for example, are both more than 40 years younger than Coates, and Caruso is 39 years younger. And she has often mentioned how she encouraged the adventurous young Steven Soderbergh to "stretch" her when they worked on *Out of Sight*. "He does a lot of flash cutting," she says. "He does a lot of nonlinear cutting, which is quite fun to do, and he kind of challenges you."[17]

Coates has noted that she also likes to work with directors who, in addition to being talented, are pleasant to work with. The script is a large factor as well. "I never cut ultra-violent films," she says.[18] She also confesses that she can't resist choosing films for the location, adding: "I love exotic places!"[19]

One additional challenge for Coates has been moving from traditional editing tools such as the Moviola (which she had been using for more than 40 years) to the newer, digital tools and techniques. The first film she and her team did digitally was the 1995 action/adventure *Congo*. "We had private teachers," she said shortly afterwards, "but we were really the blind leading the blind, and it was an extremely difficult picture. So I ran screaming and kicking into digital."[20] But, in an interview five years later, her attitude had clearly changed. "I used to think I would like to go back [to the older editing tools], but I wouldn't go back … now," she acknowledged. "I think we've moved on. My mind's moved on."[21]

Normally, Coates doesn't make much about being in a field that for many years was a difficult place for women. "There were some wonderful women editors who helped inspire me to go into editing in England," she has said. "I've never looked at myself as a woman in the business. I've just looked at myself as an editor. I mean, I'm sure I've been turned down because I'm a woman, but then other times I've been used because they wanted a woman editor. I just think, 'I'm an editor,' and I never expected to get paid less because I was a woman. I grew up with three brothers, and I never thought I would get paid less for anything than they did."[22]

She has, however, still been intrigued by the editing profession's gender-related evolution. "While it was just a background job, they let the women do it," she says,

> But when people realized how interesting and creative editing could be, then the men elbowed the women out of the way and kind of took over.... When I first came into the industry in England, there were quite a lot of women editors. And then slowly they fell by the wayside. They didn't seem to have the ambition, which I always thought was strange. When I left in 1986, I think there was only one other woman doing big features in England. There were quite a few doing television and commercials and things, but I can't put my finger on why that was.[23]

As of this writing, Coates, now in her 90s, continues to live in Los Angeles, work, consult on films, and speak about film editing and her career.

~

More often than she would like, Coates has been asked questions about her editing style, and, as a charming way to sidestep the subject, she sometimes answers with an anecdote. "I feel that I don't have a style of editing," she said in 2010. "I didn't think I did, but my daughter, who was studying [film] at university, asked me, 'What's your style, mum?' And I said, 'Oh, Emma, I don't have a style,' and she said, 'Oh, yes you do—we're studying it in class.' So, whatever my style was, they discussed it—but I never discussed it. I was so surprised that I had one."[24]

In an earlier interview, she told another story. A scene from one of her films was run for a production unit. After seeing it, an eager young associate producer asked her, "What was your psychology behind cutting that scene?" Coates responded, "Well, I don't really have any psychology. I just mark the film, cut it, and hope for the best." The rest of the crew, Coates recalled, "nearly died with laughter because they heard me and they knew [that] I'm more a doer than a talker."[25]

While she dislikes analyzing herself and her work, Coates has over the years revealed quite a bit about how she works and how her own personality is reflected in her work.

One very curious observation came from an extended interview she made in the 1990s. "I remember," she said, "one of the best compliments

I ever had paid to me was by the British director Carol Reed, who said, 'I've had some great editors work for me, but I've never had anyone with so much heart as you.' I've always treasured that remark."[26]

Certainly in terms of how she approaches her work, that word "heart" has a great deal to do with what she ultimately delivers. Intuitive and instinctive rather than intellectual and analytical, "feeling" strongly about a film is extremely important to her. Initially, this takes the form of a feeling for the story and its characters. She has noted time and time again that, whether serious or comic, she is most attracted to films that delve deeply into character. Then, when she is immersed in the editing process, this feeling takes the form of confidence in her work. Again, she has often noted that, when starting a new film, she usually feels lost—until at some point there is an internal "click" when something—perhaps a sense of clarity in the direction of the film and how it should be edited—takes place and she feels that she has found her way.

Over the years, this personal process has led to many different triumphs executed in both a traditional editing style and, increasingly, in a blending of both traditional and more contemporary editing styles. Just as she learned from Reggie Mills and David Lean, she has learned from David Lynch and Steven Soderbergh. A film such as *Out of Sight*, for example, is probably one of her most adventurous undertakings, mixing traditional editing techniques she has been using since the 1950s with more contemporary techniques such as freeze frames, shock cutting back and forth in time, shock cutting back and forth between dreams and reality, and overlaying dialogue from one scene onto another.

In a way, Coates is a chameleon, drawing from a full bag of editing tricks and techniques in each film she does for each director she works with both to serve the story and to reflect as fully as she can the essence of the director's intent. Her style changes from film to film and in each case is constantly calibrated to, above all else, serving and enriching meaning. What remains consistent throughout her work is her instinct for achieving this result—the abilities to cut at just the right time to just the right rhythm; to visually compose scenes so that what's being shown is always absolutely clear to the viewer; and to make edgy, highly stylized editing choices that rarely seem forced or overly self-conscious.

In Sync with Out of Sight

Most people would probably select *Lawrence of Arabia* as the supreme example of Coates' work. Virtually no one disputes that this is one of the world's great films. But it is also a relatively early example of Coates' work—work that has continued for another five decades after *Lawrence* and reflects both her continued professional growth and the ever-changing filmmaking landscape during her long career. With this thought in mind, it might make more sense here to look at her work in a more recent film that better reflects these changes, and certainly one of the fine examples from this group is Steven Soderbergh's brilliant 1998 adaptation of writer Elmore Leonard's novel *Out of Sight*.

In the mid- and late 1990s, film adaptations of the crime novels of Elmore Leonard were all the rage. *Out of Sight* followed in a series that included *Get Shorty* (1995), *Touch* (1997), and *Jackie Brown* (1997) as well as two made-for-television movies, *Pronto* (1997) and *Gold Coast* (1997). All of these, in turn, were partially inspired by the enormous success of Quentin Tarantino's *Pulp Fiction* (1994), which was itself hugely influenced by Leonard's writing.

While *Pulp Fiction* might be the most groundbreaking and influential of all these films, *Out of Sight* might be the most thoughtfully and elegantly rendered. Without being any less hip or stylish than the rest, it steers clear of the in-jokes and other self-conscious cuteness of *Pulp Fiction*, *Get Shorty*, and *Jackie Brown*. There is plenty of humor, but the film never descends into broad farce. The characters, too, are mostly multi-faceted and nuanced. Even the supporting hoodlum roles such as Ving Rhames' Buddy, Steve Zahn's Glenn, and Don Cheadle's Snoopy—the kinds of roles that in lesser films are almost always one-dimensional—are given unusual depth and complexity. Like *Pulp Fiction*, the film's story often moves back and forth in time. But here, the time traveling seems far more natural and less forced or self-conscious. We sense that it is employed because it is simply a good way to tell this story.

Many people made significant contributions to *Out of Sight*. The praise starts with Leonard, who wrote the quirky, consistently engaging novel, and Soderbergh, who improved upon the story in several ways (e.g. the inspired pairing of George Clooney and Jennifer Lopez in the lead roles) when translating it to the screen. Praise should also go to writer Scott Frank, whose script here is a couple of notches above his previous Leonard adaptation, *Get Shorty*, three years before, and to cinematographer Elliot Davis, who beautifully captures the "worlds" of the film from the loud, bright colors of Miami to the subdued grays of a cold winter in Detroit.

Then, of course, there is Coates' editing. Working closely with Soderbergh, she helped to give the film its unique and very stylish pace, tone, and feel. Watching it, we sense that, while we have seen similar films, we have never experienced anything quite like this.

Among the triumphs in the storytelling are the ways Coates and Soderbergh suggest rather than show certain violent and sexual moments. Not only is their approach more artful and economical than most other approaches, but it also amplifies the humanity in each of the situations.

One excellent example takes place about halfway through the film. The evil Snoopy tells Glenn, a sensitive but not-too-bright pothead, that he wants him to prove himself by killing a double-crossing drug dealer. In the audience, we prepare for some heavy-duty violence. Then, rather than showing the bloody massacre in all its gory detail, Coates and Soderbergh simply show a 32-second wordless montage with some disturbing sounds on the track that focuses on Glenn's face as he commits the murder and his sense of shame and horror at his own actions. The final touch is an image of Snoopy covering the scene with red spray paint. It's a riveting half-minute that suggests every-

Starring **George Clooney and Jennifer Lopez**, the romantic caper *Out of Sight* (1998) has received wide praise for Anne V. Coates' stylish and creative editing. Not only did Coates receive her fifth Oscar nomination for her work here, but in 2012 the Editors Guild ranked the film number 53 on its list, "The 75 Best Edited Films of All Time" (Photofest).

thing we need to know, gets us into Glenn's head, and affects us far more deeply than a more conventionally filmed shoot-out would. Writing about this scene in his initial review of the film, critic Mick LaSalle said that it "almost qualifies as a miracle," adding, "The miracle is that we come away not only with the event of the massacre but with a sense of its moral horror as well."[27]

Another example is perhaps the most frequently discussed scene (or confluence of two scenes) in the film. At this point, Karen (Jennifer Lopez) a U.S. marshal who's attracted to a handsome, charming thief, Jack Foley (George Clooney), meets up with him in a hotel bar in Detroit. Drawn to dangerous men, she fancies sleeping with him before she arrests him. Drawn to this smart, determined, and beautiful women, he fancies sleeping with her before he pulls off a big heist and escapes. They share a drink and talk about how much they've each been thinking about the other and about how they would both like to have a "time-out" before they must again face the other realities of their situation. Then, as the gentle, flirty conversation in the bar continues, we see visuals of the two, now in her hotel room. Many of the visual images from the bar are here, too—the snow falling outside, the drinks in their hands, the way they touch each other's hands and arms. As the bar conversation continues, we next see them take off items of clothing. Now, too, there is an occasional (and very brief) freeze frame to heighten the eroticism of the moment. It is exhilarating how these two scenes—the bar and the hotel room—flow together.

In her account, Coates describes how the initial plan called for the scene to go from the bar to the bedroom with the bar conversation overlaid, but that it had seemed flat. So, she and Soderbergh got the idea to intercut. "We just tried one or two things and it started to jell," she recalled in 2004. "Flashing back. Sometimes we'd flash forward.... It was really exciting.... [The scene is] very emotional. It's very sexual, I think, without really showing much.... It's really good and very good storytelling."[28]

Equally impressed was Roger Ebert, who singled out this scene in his 1998 review of the film. "[N]othing quite matches up," he wrote, "and yet everything fits, so that the scene is like a demonstration of the whole movie's visual and time style."[29]

Sharing Ebert's enthusiasm about the scene was Mick LaSalle. "This strategy is not just economical and not just a drawn-out tease," he wrote. "It has psychological truth. As the two are talking, the sex hovers over the moment. That's what they're thinking about, and that's all the audience is thinking about, too."[30]

Another of *Out of Sight*'s triumphs (and a departure from the novel) is the way the film moves back and forth in time with such skill and grace. The purpose is always to provide backstory, and we seem to get it in the same deft way that shipping services provide just-in-time delivery. For example, the film begins with Foley robbing a bank and getting caught. We see his hands up in one of the first of the film's periodic freeze frames and then we watch the freeze dissolve into a shot of the Glades Correctional Institution in Florida, where the main action of the film begins—a jailbreak during which he will meet Karen and eventually head to Detroit to rob multi-millionaire Richard Ripley (Albert Brooks). During the story, the action occasionally flashes back to another prison in Lompoc, California, where Foley originally meets Ripley, Glenn, Snoopy, and other characters who figure prominently in upcoming events and to Ripley's office.

In these flashbacks, we learn why Foley robbed the bank in the first scene of the film, why he has a special interest in robbing Ripley at his home near Detroit, and much more. It is all marvelously done, and, while much of the credit for this must go to scriptwriter Scott Frank, Coates' skill at orchestrating all this non-linear action while keeping the pacing and the tone of the film so consistent is remarkable.

Another challenge for an editor working on a film based on an Elmore Leonard story is working with his very distinctive and carefully crafted dialogue, and Coates does a fine job here as well. Leonard's dialogue often has the rhythms of poetry in it, and in some films based on his work, such as 1997's *Touch*, the editing doesn't sync up with his language as well as it should. With her excellent sense of pacing, Coates' editing sparkles in many dialogue scenes. For example, the timing between cuts in the (mostly dialogue) scene when Foley and Karen are both locked in the automobile trunk is superb, enhancing both the instant attraction each feels for the other and their shared sense of humor about the absurd situation they find themselves in.

In addition to LaSalle and Ebert, most of the critical response to *Out of Sight*, and especially to the artful way in which it was put together by Coates and others, was quite positive. As Kenneth Turan of the *Los Angeles Times* noted, "As always with the best of Leonard, it's the journey, not the destination, that counts, and director Soderbergh has let it unfold with dry wit and great skill. Making adroit use of complex flashbacks, freeze frames, and other stylistic flourishes, he's managed to put his personal stamp on the film while staying faithful to the irreplaceable spirit of the original."[31]

Out of Sight also received recognition from the various awards bodies, including two Academy Award nominations—one for its adapted screenplay and one for Coates' editing. More recently, too, the film was ranked number 53 on the Editors Guild's 2012 list of the "75 Best Edited Films of All Time."

For the 73-year-old Coates, who had received her first Academy Award nomination more than 35 years earlier, the fifth nomination was certainly evidence of continuous professional growth as well as staying power. After a half-century in the business, she was still at the top of her game.

A Life of Living (a Little) Dangerously

Describing the experience early in her working life of applying at Pinewood Studios with only the slightest wisp of a resume, Coates once remarked: "I've always believed you should take a risk and hope for the best."[32]

This is certainly an understandable attitude to have when one is young, has little if anything to lose, and imagines many more opportunities ahead. But one of Coates' most remarkable traits is that—despite more than 65 years in the business, editing credits on more than 50 films, numerous honors that include five Academy Award nominations, and an almost mythic status among her fellow film editors—she has never stopped taking risks in her choices of projects, the directors she works with, and the editing decisions she makes. In fact, judging from her various interviews over the years, she even seems to have a slight disdain for playing it safe and for those who do it too often. For her, risk-taking and personal/professional growth seem both intimately intertwined and key components of a fully lived life. In any case, her enthusiasm for risk-taking and growth has been indispensable to an amazing career in which she has not only survived but also consistently adapted and flourished. Along the way, she has had many moments. And she has made the most of them.

9

"The most modest of living legends"

Thelma Schoonmaker and Her Lifelong Artistic Partnership with Martin Scorsese

"It's about a sense of trust," Thelma Schoonmaker said in an interview in 2014.

> From the very first moment I worked with Marty, I think he realized I was someone who would do what was right for his films, and major egos would not be a problem.... He gradually over the years began to appreciate that and rely on that much more, and, as I became more experienced, he was able to rely on my judgment much more.... When we work together, it's just the most amazing time. We talk about *everything* in the editing room, in addition to the editing we're doing. It's a very rich collaboration. Wonderful. I'm a very lucky person.[1]

The "Marty" Schoonmaker refers to is of course Martin Scorsese, one of the most respected film directors working today. And she is of course the film editor who first teamed up with him in 1963 and, since *Raging Bull* (1980), has worked closely with him on all his projects ranging from about 20 feature films to several documentaries and even television programs. In addition to being Scorsese's trusted collaborator, Schoonmaker is one of most celebrated members of the film editing profession. With seven Academy Award nominations for Best Film Editing (that date back to her work on the 1970 documentary *Woodstock* for director Michael Wadleigh), she has tied Barbara McLean for most editing nominations by a woman. And with three editing Oscar wins, she has also tied Michael Kahn, Daniel Mandell, and Ralph Dawson for the most wins by any editor. This is in addition to more than a dozen nominations and wins for awards from the American Cinema Editors (ACE) and the British Academy of Film and Television Arts (BAFTA) as well as a Golden Lion Lifetime Achievement award from the Venice Film Festival in 2014. Finally, she is one of only a handful of editors—that includes people such as Dede Allen and Verna Fields—who, at least among film buffs, has become a household name. This is in part because of all the accolades she has received over the decades and in part because of Scorsese's immense respect for her and her work. Repeatedly, he has called her his "closest collaborator."[2] And repeatedly, he has backed up his supportive words with the appropriate symbolic actions. Whenever he promotes a new film, for example, she is often either sitting or standing in a place editors hardly ever get to be: right there next to the director.

Another testament to Schoonmaker's ability is the number of actors—a group often critical of editors for being insensitive to their best work in films—who have nothing but praise for her. "I trust her completely," says Robert De Niro, who has worked on numerous Scorsese-Schoonmaker projects, including *Raging Bull, Goodfellas* (1990), *Cape Fear* (1991) and *Casino* (1995).[3] "I've gotten killed in some films, and it wasn't my fault," adds Joe Pesci, who won an Academy Award for his role in *Goodfellas*. "That stuff never happens with Thelma. I don't have to think about it—she always chooses the best take."[4]

Just what makes Schoonmaker so special?

Many people have weighed in on the subject. Actor Ben Kingsley, who had roles in Scorsese's *Shutter Island* (2010) and *Hugo* (2011), has noted Schoonmaker's "intuitive deep grasp of each individual's narrative journey of the film."[5] Actress Juliette Lewis, who was in 1991's *Cape Fear*, has said that Schoonmaker's style "has such grace, but she knows when to buck convention, when to make it rough, when to make it seamless. She can nail it all."[6]

Since 1980, Thelma Schoonmaker has edited every film director Martin Scorsese has made and is widely considered one of his key collaborators. One of the most honored film editors ever, she has been nominated for seven Academy Awards, winning Oscars for *Raging Bull* (1980), *The Aviator* (2004), and *The Departed* (2006) (Photofest).

And Scorsese himself has said many times that, in addition to her technical mastery, he relies on her to make sure that the emotional heart of each of his films is maintained.

Perhaps Lewis' "she can nail it all" comment comes closest to being a good characterization. As opposed to some editors who strive to make editing invisible all the time and others who get caught up in effect-for-the-sake-of-effect gimmickry, the Schoonmaker style seems to be one that uses all the tools at the editor's disposal but only when appropriate and always to clarify and/or enrich the narrative. Sometimes—as in the famous airplane crash scene over Beverly Hills in *The Aviator* (2004)—the cutting is fast and flamboyant. Other times—as in *Raging Bull*—the use of slow motion often serves to give us insights into the mind of the film's main character. Still other times, as in *The Departed* (2006), the cutting is carefully designed to give us numerous non-verbal clues about the inner workings (and often anxieties) of the main characters. In other words, depending on what Scorsese needs, Schoonmaker can do just about anything.

In addition to doing what's right for Scorsese's films, the calm, charming, and unassuming Schoonmaker has been a long-time and highly valued friend of the director. According to De Niro, she has brought to her relationship with the intense and often moody Scorsese "a certain steadiness, sturdiness, and nurturing which I think is very important."[7] The director has reciprocated in many ways, too, including introducing Schoonmaker to her future husband, the legendary British director Michael Powell, in the early 1980s. Together, the two are also passionate champions of film restoration, and one of their major initiatives in recent decades has been restoring the films and furthering the legacy of Powell.

Now, in her 70s, Schoonmaker—who once inspired film writer Hamish Anderson to dub her "the most modest of living legends"[8]—shows no signs of slowing down and wants to work for Scorsese as long as possible. As she said in 2014: "I just hope we can go on until we drop."[9]

"There is so little understanding of what really great editing is"

A descendant of an old New York Dutch political family, Schoonmaker was born to Bertrand and Thelma Schoonmaker in Algiers, French Algeria, on January 3, 1940. Bertrand worked abroad for Standard Oil, and, until the time young Thelma was 15, the family lived in several countries and territories that, in addition to French Algeria, included Portugal and the island of Aruba in the Caribbean.

All this international exposure inspired young Thelma to be a diplomat, and, after moving to the U.S., she entered Cornell University in 1957, where she majored in political science, studied Russian, and took literature classes taught by Russian-American novelist Vladimir Nabokov. Then, after graduating from Cornell, she took a series of tests with the U.S. State Department as part of the application process for government diplomatic jobs, but, as she later recalled, "they said I was too liberal in my thinking."[10] Apparently, she had been quite strident in her opposition to the South African policy of racial segregation, or apartheid, a stance that caused some discomfort to those administering the tests. Realizing that diplomacy might not be her true calling, she immediately began studying primitive art.

Soon afterwards, Schoonmaker saw an ad in *The New York Times* to train as an assistant film editor. "It was [to work for] a terrible old hack who was butchering Fellini and Rossellini films for late night television," she said years later.[11] Although she hated doing this kind of work, she quickly learned many of the fundamentals of film editing and was curious enough to enroll in a six-week summer course on the subject at New York University.

It was there in 1963 that she met another student, a 20-year-old undergraduate who desperately needed help re-cutting a student film that had been poorly edited, a short-subject comedy titled *What's a Nice Girl Like You Doing in a Place Like This?*. The student's name was Martin Scorsese.

Impressed with each other's talents, the two were soon working on other projects together. One was Scorsese's feature-length directorial debut, 1967's *Who's That Knocking at My Door?*, a drama that also marked the film debut of actor Harvey Keitel. The film went on to win the grand prize at the Chicago Film Festival in 1968. Another was director Michael Wadleigh's concert documentary *Woodstock* in 1970, which both Schoonmaker and Scorsese helped edit. Enthusiastically received by critics and audiences alike, *Woodstock* is considered a milestone for concert films for effects ranging from its split screens to its psychedelic look. Critic Roger Ebert even wrote that it "may be the best documentary ever made in America."[12] And, at the 1971 Academy Awards, it received several Oscar nominations, winning for Best Documentary Feature. Among the nominations was one that the Academy hardly ever gives for documentary films, a nod for Best Film Editing, which went to Schoonmaker.

Although Schoonmaker and Scorsese wanted to work together during the 1970s, Schoonmaker first had to overcome a major professional obstacle: she had never become a member of the Motion Picture Editors Guild—something she needed to do in order to work with Scorsese after he had moved on to mainstream feature films. Already quite accomplished at this point, she felt that it would be silly and needless to put herself through the long preparatory process (which involved working for five years as an apprentice and then for three more years as an assistant) normally required to get in.

As a result, she spent much of the 1970s working on a potpourri of independent projects ranging from a concert film for Paul McCartney and his band *Wings* to an experimental film based on James Joyce's challenging novel *Finnegans Wake*. "I loved being a maverick," she said about her work at this time. "It meant that I could work on things I cared about.... Money didn't mean anything to me, but working with people who cared deeply ... about their films is very seductive—you never want to work any other way."[13]

After collaborating with several other editors on his films during the 1970s, Scorsese asked Schoonmaker in 1979 to cut his upcoming film, a bio-pic about former World Middleweight Boxing Champion Jake LaMotta called *Raging Bull*. She was excited about the prospect but declined because she still wasn't a member of the Editors Guild. Then, something unusual happened. A powerful person in the film industry intervened on her behalf, the guild's rules were waived, and she became a union member. Schoonmaker believes that this person may have been actor Al Pacino, but, to this day, she doesn't know precisely how all this occurred.

～

This development marked the beginning of two new chapters in Schoonmaker's life. The first, of course, was her reunion with Scorsese and the restoration of the close professional partnership that has now thrived for more than 35 years. The second was her marriage to British filmmaker Michael Powell and her ongoing work to restore and promote Powell's films.

Back with Scorsese, the two tackled the long and exacting editing process that resulted in *Raging Bull* (which will be discussed in more detail later in this chapter). The story of middleweight boxer Jake LaMotta, who battled fierce opponents inside the ring while battling inner demons elsewhere in his life, the film is now widely considered Scorsese and Schoonmaker's masterpiece as well as one of the finest films ever made. In 2007, for example, it placed fourth on the American Film Institute's list of the

100 greatest American films of all time just behind *Citizen Kane*, *The God-father*, and *Casablanca*. And, in 2012, the Motion Pictures Editors Guild named it the Best Edited Film of All Time, edging out such classics as *Citizen Kane*, *Apocalypse Now*, and *Bonnie and Clyde*.

The entire undertaking of *Raging Bull* was enormously ambitious. And the specific editing challenges—from presenting the expressionistic fight scenes that mirror the inside of LaMotta's mind to harnessing and pruning the miles of film footage used in the film's many improvised scenes (especially those between actors Robert De Niro as LaMotta and Joe Pesci as his brother, Joey)—could often be enormous. But Scorsese and Schoonmaker worked closely for months to achieve the results they wanted.

In the process, they established a working process that has served them both well since then. Unlike other editors who visit the set during production, Schoonmaker deliberately stays away, not wanting to be influenced by what occurs there and preferring to watch the dailies, follow detailed notes Scorsese writes as the filming takes place, and cut scenes to suit his and her preferences.

Then, when production concludes, he joins her and the process continues for several more months. "He's a great editor," Schoonmaker has said about Scorsese. "I knew nothing about editing when I met him. But he was born an editor.... He has this profound sense of the importance of editing. I don't think any director can become a great director without having a deep sense of editing. He thinks like an editor when he's conceiving of a film, when he's co-writing it, and when he's shooting it. And that's 50 percent of my job, y'know? He gives me footage that *works*. I don't think a lot of directors these days have that sense or knowledge of the importance of editing."[14]

When asked if she is being too humble about her contribution to Scorsese's films, Schoonmaker is quick to clarify. "You would have to be here to see what an incredible collaboration it is," she once stressed. "People think I'm always being too modest but I'm not. I know what I bring. You needn't worry about that." Looking for an example, she noted: "He [Scorsese] claims I pull the humanity out of his movies in the way I edit." Then, tipping her hat to him, she added, "but he puts it in there."[15] Elsewhere she has also said: "You get to contribute so significantly in the editing room because you shape the movie and the performances. You help the director bring all the hard work of those who made the film to fruition. You give their work rhythm and pace and sometimes adjust the structure to make the film work—to make it start to flow up there on the screen."[16]

After *Raging Bull*, Scorsese and Schoonmaker tackled a very different kind of film, a dark comedy titled *The King of Comedy* (1983) starring De Niro and Jerry Lewis. Although there is humor in most of Scorsese's films, they are predominantly dramas. In this, she felt that the different sensibility presented her with some different hurdles as an editor. "Comedy cutting is a real skill," she has said. "I learned a lot when we were doing *The King of Comedy*, from the timing instructions that Jerry Lewis was giving to other actors. The slight beat, maybe two or three seconds, before you answer a question, or the beat you put in the middle of a line, is all where comedy lies.... You have to learn how to make comedy work."[17]

In addition to being a professional mentor for Schoonmaker, Scorsese has also been a personal matchmaker. In the early 1980s, he and film producer Frixos Constantine introduced her to Michael Powell, the director of such classic British films as *Black Narcissus* (1947) and *The Red Shoes* (1948) as well as a personal hero of Scorsese's. Even though Powell was 34 years older than Schoonmaker, the two fell in love, were married in 1984, and were together until his death in 1990. "It was the best 10 years of my life," Schoonmaker later recalled. "[He] was like the sun compared to anyone else."[18]

In addition to the deep affection both Schoonmaker and Scorsese shared for Powell, the two have also been involved with preserving Powell's films and making more people aware of his contributions to filmmaking. (Sadly, Powell's career was effectively derailed after his 1960 film *Peeping Tom* was savaged by critics and rejected by audiences for its unsavory subject matter. It has since been re-evaluated, however, and many critics and film scholars now regard it quite highly.) So far, Scorsese and Schoonmaker have raised enough money to restore several of Powell's films, including *The Red Shoes* and *The Life and Death of Colonel Blimp* (1943). "I love sharing [Scorsese's] passion for my husband's films," Schoonmaker has said. "Marty says they're in his DNA. That's how important they are to him."[19]

Although the 1980s—the decade between *Raging Bull* and Scorsese's next major critical triumph, *Goodfellas* (1990)—is not widely regarded as his most fruitful creative period, he and Schoonmaker were still responsible for several fascinating films during this time. One is certainly *The King of Comedy*, a film that flopped at the box office when it was first released but has since found an enthusiastic cult following. As well as adapting her editing style to accommodate comedy, as Schoonmaker has noted, she also did an excellent job of editing in this film to simultaneously reflect and satirize the strange, choppy, relentlessly superficial nature of late-night television talk-show comedy. Another very intriguing achievement during this decade is 1989's *Life Lessons*, one segment in a three-part anthology film called *New York Stories*. (The other two segments consisted of stories directed by Woody Allen and Francis Ford Coppola.) The story of a middle-age abstract artist (Nick Nolte) who is currently sharing a New York loft with a much younger apprentice/former lover (Rosanna Arquette), it is filled with superb moments in which the images and the ways they are arranged brilliantly reflect the relationship the two share. Frequently employing Procol Harum's rendition of the song "A Whiter Shade of Pale" and other familiar pieces of popular music, the short film mixes a wide range of editing techniques from slow-motion shots and slow, sensuous dissolves to abrupt cuts and even an old-time iris-out shot to close a scene that underscore (among many things) his longing for her, her respect for him as an artist, the tension that exists between them, and ultimately the doomed nature of their relationship. Rarely mentioned in discussions of Scorsese and Schoonmaker's entire body of work, *Life Lessons* is nevertheless a marvelous short example of their work in top form.

~

With the release of the epic gangster film *Goodfellas* in 1990, Scorsese and Schoonmaker were again basking in critical acclaim. The film was nominated for six Academy Awards, including one for Best Film Editing. It also swept the BAFTA ceremonies that year, winning five awards in categories such as Best Film, Best Direction, and Best Film Editing. Since its release, *Goodfellas* has, like *Raging Bull*, consistently received mentions on a wide array of "best films" lists, and many film historians and scholars consider it one of the best films of the 1990s.

As with their best films, Scorsese and Schoonmaker used the entire chest of editing tools to achieve what they wanted to achieve in *Goodfellas*, and we see this strategy succeed in a big way. One of the most effective editing choices in this film, for example, is the use of freeze frames at particular moments to call out attention to specific points they want to make. In the opening scenes of the film, we see this repeatedly as the main character's life is summarized, serving, as film writer Justin Morrow has noted, "a kinetic, as well as narrative, function" and delivering "a visual punch and also signpost moments which Scorsese wishes to call our attention to."[20] Perhaps the most startlingly dark and ironic instance of this is the film's very first freeze frame. It's a medium close shot of the main character—just after two other gangsters have brutally stabbed and shot an already wounded man in the trunk of their car—as we hear his voice-over: "As far back as I can remember, I'd always wanted to be a gangster."

In 1995, Scorsese reunited with *Goodfellas* stars Robert De Niro and Joe Pesci to make another mob film, *Casino*, which also stars Sharon Stone. Although some people found it very much (perhaps too much) like *Goodfellas* in its style and subject matter, it was generally well received by both critics and audiences. The film is also beautifully edited in the distinctive "use-all-the-editing-tools" Scorsese-Schoonmaker style. One excellent sequence is a montage accompanied by hard-driving music that follows the flow of the money in the casino that Sam, the De Niro character, runs from gambling customers to the mob. It's handled with a dark wit and great style. Another very intriguing few moments are in the scene in which Sam first sees, watches, and (within seconds) thinks he has fallen in love with the Stone character, Ginger. Shots of him watching her at a craps table via a monitor in a security room are crosscut with shots taken right next to her at the table. Next, we see Sam continuing to watch Ginger from the casino floor itself. She gets into an argument about money with the man she has been with and throws his chips up in the air. Then we see her smiling triumphantly in freeze frame. After a couple of beats, the film cuts to a shot of the camera slowly coming in on him looking at her, thoroughly entranced, as the song "Love Is Strange" by Mickey and Sylvia comes up. The film cuts back to her (now in slow motion) walking away filled with attitude and sexy body language. We then hear his voice-over, saying: "What a move! I fell in love right there." Instantly, the film cuts to a shot of the two kissing passionately and then to another shot of him pinning an expensive brooch on her dress as the voice-over continues: "But in Vegas—for a girl like Ginger—love costs money." In just a few moments—and mostly with suggestive visual images—both the beginning and the essence of their relationship are communicated with great sizzle, vitality, and wit. It's a marvelous example of compressed storytelling, of saying a great deal very quickly and stylishly.

~

If awards and other honors are strong indicators, Schoonmaker has—since 2000—continued to outdo herself in a very big way. She has, for example, received four additional Academy Award nominations for Best Editing, winning for her work on both Scorsese's 2004 film about Howard Hughes, *The Aviator*, and for his 2006 story of police and the mob in Boston, *The Departed*.

One sequence people often refer to when discussing the editing of *The Aviator* is a spectacular air crash, when a plane Howard Hughes (Leonardo DiCaprio) is test flying develops problems and goes down over a

Beverly Hills residential neighborhood. And—from beginning to end—it is riveting, with exciting shots of airplane wings cutting through the roofs of houses, people inside those houses suddenly realizing what's happening and reacting in startled fear, and a despairing Hughes in his cockpit fearing for his own death.

Schoonmaker has acknowledged that this sequence is probably what clinched the Oscar for her that year. But, in one very insightful comment, she also cautioned against what many film critics and enthusiasts do—judging editing purely on the basis of scenes such as this plane crash, in which rapid cutting and other editing flourishes are obvious. "[T]here is so little understanding of what really great editing is," she said. "[A] film that's flashy, has a lot of quick cuts and explosions, gets particular attention. For example, [the plane crash in] *The Aviator* ... [is] so dramatic, and you can really see the editing there, but for me, and for a lot of editors and directors, the more interesting editing is not so visible. It's the decisions that go into building a character, a performance, for example, or how you rearrange scenes in a movie, if it's not working properly, so that you can get a better dramatic build."[21]

Schoonmaker has proven as good as her word here, too. Although the flourishes in Scorsese films (such as the rapid cuts, strategically placed freeze frames and slow motion moments, and other touches) get people's attention, she has, for example, also shown a great talent for revealing character through body language by cutting just at the right time. Some excellent examples of this occur in *The Departed*, especially with the three main characters, Leonardo DiCaprio's undercover cop, Matt Damon's corrupt cop, and Jack Nicholson's gangster. In several scenes, Schoonmaker holds on each just long enough (but never too long) to show the DiCaprio character's growing anxiety and fear, the Damon character's insecurity behind his bravado, and the Nicholson character's pure, often sadistic evil. In each case, she makes the point emphatically while not belaboring it.

Although she believes that editing remains a mystery to most people, Schoonmaker feels that—with the relatively recent emergence of digital editing technologies and techniques—more people are becoming aware of editing's critical importance in filmmaking. "In the last couple of years, editing has suddenly risen up into people's consciousness," she said in 2014. "I'm not sure, but maybe it's because everybody's editing their own movies now. Maybe they're understanding now what it takes and how important it is to filmmaking.... You can ruin or save a movie, make an actor's performance terrible or make it good."[22]

Still, Schoonmaker remains keenly aware of how film editing is difficult for most people to understand and appreciate. And one curious aspect of many of her interviews is a desire to describe it (and perhaps educate a bit in the process) as a poet would: through the use of metaphors and similes. "It's absolutely like sculpture," she once said. "You get a big lump of clay, and you have to form it—this raw, unedited, very long footage."[23] And, when describing the process of whittling a film down to its appropriate size, she once made a distinctively female analogy to dieting and dress size. "Until you get it to the right length, it's like a woman who's on a diet who wants to get into a dress to go to an event," she observed. "She keeps losing weight and losing weight, and finally the dress just fits perfectly."[24]

All things considered, though, Schoonmaker finds the process of editing endlessly exhilarating. "I like the creativity of it," she has noted. "You have tremendous control in editing. You're not dealing with a big set and hundreds of actors and huge crews, and you're not forced to make decisions under pressure and not get what you want and have to settle for something else."[25]

~

When asked why—despite decades of being excluded from other behind-the-camera professions such as directors and cinematographers—women have managed both to remain and sometimes to become quite prominent in the editing ranks, Schoonmaker has offered several observations.

First, she believes that editing requires certain skills that women are, generally speaking, better at. "I think that's because the men were making such a mess of it," she noted, referring back to her early experiences. "They liked editing, but they were losing everything, destroying things—I was much more organized. I do think that's a slightly female trait."[26]

Second, when asked about all the great male director-female editor collaborations from Cecil B. DeMille and Anne Bauchens to Scorsese and her, she echoes what many people, including the always-provocative Quentin Tarantino, have said. "You have to be a good collaborator with the director," she observed. "A lot of male relationships are more combative, I think, and you have to be able to not fight over a film. I know a lot of editors who are very bitter about the directors they work with. They feel they could have done a better job, and I say to them, 'Oh really? Why don't you go try—it's not easy.'"[27]

Scorsese, Schoonmaker, and the "Best Edited Film of All Time"

As Schoonmaker has noted many times, as well as being a great director, Scorsese is a great editor who has been an invaluable guide and mentor to her.

And, as noted earlier, in its 2012 survey of film editors, the Motion Picture Editors Guild named *Raging Bull* the Best Edited Film of All Time.

These two statements naturally lead to a pair of irresistible questions. First, how much of the editing genius behind *Raging Bull* (and for that matter all the films they've made together) is Scorsese's and how much is Schoonmaker's? And second, what is it about the editing of *Raging Bull* that compels film editors to rank it so highly?

The first question may very well be unanswerable. Since the 1970s, the time before he began to work regularly with Schoonmaker, nearly every Scorsese film has had a distinctly Scorsese signature attached to it. He is definitely an auteur, or the author of his films, in much the way that Griffith, Chaplin, Ford, Lang, Hitchcock, Welles, Kubrick, and other great directors have been. And, while his films vary widely in subject matter and tone, they are often consistent in their themes (such as guilt and redemption, machismo, etc.) and presentation (violence, dark humor, etc.). Beginning with *Raging Bull*, however, he has relied more on a wider range (and more extensive use) of editing techniques to bring greater subjectivity (and an often more expressionistic approach) to his films. The reason for this could be his own development as a storyteller, Schoonmaker's influence, or a combination of both. In any case, though, his reliance on Schoonmaker for more than 35 years is extremely telling. For an extended period when his collaborators have included numerous producers, writers, cinematographers, sound editors, technicians, and others, he has remained deeply committed to Schoonmaker, his "closest collaborator." She is clearly one of the most important—if not *the* most important—filmmaking partner he has. While her commitment is to help achieve his vision for each film, she, as they both readily admit, brings something of herself that gives the joint effort a character it would not otherwise have. The final edit, the final draft, of each Scorsese film has her signature on it as well as his.

The second question might be just as unanswerable. *Raging Bull* is one of the most frequently discussed and dissected films ever made. Entire books have been written about it, and any discussion of just a few pages within a book chapter will, needless to say, be incomplete.

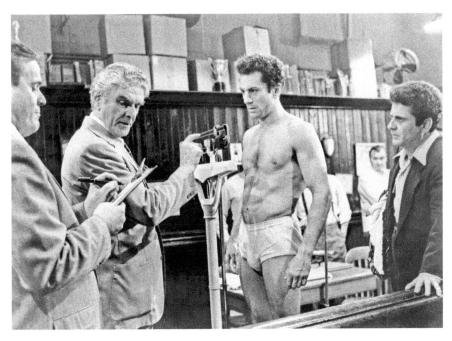

One of the most widely discussed and dissected films ever made, Martin Scorsese's *Raging Bull* (1980) has been enthusiastically praised for its highly innovative and often brilliant editing. In this scene, boxer Jake LaMotta (Robert DeNiro) weighs in (with Peter Savage checking the scale) before an upcoming bout as his brother Joey (Joe Pesci) looks on (United Artists/Photofest).

That said, why do so many people regard the art behind this film so highly?

Perhaps the most compelling reason is the combination of great discipline and great originality Scorsese, Schoonmaker, the film's cinematographer Michael Chapman, its sound effects editor Frank Warner, and others brought to the project. Beginning in the late 1960s, when editorial "flourishes" such as split screens, freeze frames, slow motion, jump cuts, unusual use of voice-overs, and other effects became more fashionable, many filmmakers ran wild with them, often using them even when there wasn't a legitimate need to do so. For example, after Arthur Penn and Dede Allen impressed millions with the slow-motion violence in *Bonnie and Clyde*, it seemed that, for the next decade or so, nearly everyone was copying the effect whether it appropriately reinforced the film's narrative or not. What Scorsese, Schoonmaker, and others behind *Raging Bull* did was to draw upon this greatly expanded palette of storytelling effects fully, often with great originality, and always with the intention of serving and enriching the narrative. And one result is the film's frequent and powerful use of expressionism, or the radically distorted presentation of the visual and auditory worlds from the personal perspective of the main character, Jake LaMotta, to achieve specific emotional effects. Beginning in the silent era, numerous films have employed expressionism, some with great success, but few, if any, have used it as effectively as Scorsese, Schoonmaker, and their team did with *Raging Bull*.

The film's expressionism is perhaps most apparent in several of the film's boxing scenes as reality is wildly distorted to mirror Jake's state of mind. This is manifested in a variety of ways. For example, sound editor Warner often used the sounds of such animals as elephants and horses very subtly but also to great effect to create the sense of bestial energy and chaos (i.e. a raging bull). He also used the noise of a de-tuned bass drum to give an even more ominous dimension to the sounds around the ring. For the various fight scenes, different size boxing rings were built, each again reflecting LaMotta's internal perceptions. For example, in the scene when he defeats Sugar Ray Robinson the ring is quite large, suggesting the grandeur of the moment for him. And, in some scenes the filmmakers even added flames to the setting, putting them at the bottoms of shots to make a not-so-subtle suggestion that the inside of a ring during a fight is truly a kind of hell. Along with Scorsese, Schoonmaker had the challenging task of integrating all these effects together with all the other shots necessary to make the scenes play credibly as well as artistically.

In addition, the actual cutting of scenes was critical to reflecting LaMotta's state of mind at different times inside the ring. In a 2014 article, film writer Justin Morrow discussed the editing strategy for the scenes depicting Jake's 1951 match with Sugar Ray Robinson, a fight that ends badly for LaMotta. Scorsese and Schoonmaker "wanted to get through the fight as quickly as possible, in terms of running time and editing speed," Morrow wrote, "both because it was a famous fight with a widely known outcome, *and* in order to highlight the brutality of the loss on LaMotta. When he is winning, the editing can be expansive and he moves around the ring with ease. When he is losing, the cutting is staccato and LaMotta's familiar working environment becomes claustrophobic, nightmarish, and unfamiliar. It is a very canny move, and the fight is edited in a horrific fashion … that doesn't reflect the reality of the ring, but the torment in LaMotta's head."[28]

The film's expressionism is also evident in the frequent use of slow motion both inside the ring and in other parts of LaMotta's life. Again, this technique is used specifically to suggest to us visually what is going on inside LaMotta's mind—to enrich the narrative. And again, it is used with great effectiveness.

Within the ring, various slow motion shots (and sounds) distort, depending on the situation, both the agony and the ecstasy LaMotta experiences at different times. When LaMotta is exultant, for example, slow motion sometimes suggests that he is savoring the moment, making it last as long as possible. When he is being knocked senseless, slow motion suggests his groggy, semi-conscious state of mind; everything has slowed almost to a stop for him. And in both cases his experience is shown as greatly intensified.

Elsewhere in LaMotta's life, slow motion is also used with great originality to fill us in on other parts of his character. In a fascinating 2013 article, "Slow Motion in *Raging Bull*," film writer Jan Stripek singled out three fascinating uses of slow motion, each to convey a different personal characteristic of LaMotta. One is to suggest the way he objectifies the character of Vickie (Cathy Moriarty) the first time he sees her. As Stripek writes: "The problem is that he doesn't see her as a person, but as individual parts (eyes, cheekbones, legs). He sees her as a sexual trophy."[29] As the film progresses, Stripek notes, slow motion is used to stress LaMotta's increasing obsessiveness, especially with Vickie. In particular, Stripek describes a scene at a dance "when we are given slow motion POV shots of Vickie and of Vickie and Salvy [Frank Vincent] as Jake looks across the room, and of Vickie and Salvy as Jake follows them from the dance and watches them drive off in Salvy's car."[30] Finally, Stripek contends, slow motion dramatically underscores LaMotta's growing paranoia. "He sees the world in slow motion and interprets every minute detail. To Jake LaMotta's paranoid mind, people's actions always require pessimistic interpretation.... His eye for detail, as shown via slow motion shots, causes multitudes of possibilities to furiously zigzag and crisscross in his mind, often causing him to suspect people of wronging him and sullying his masculinity."[31]

Raging Bull is also filled with exquisite little touches that together add to its overall impact. One touch Schoonmaker has discussed is in the segment when we see brief moments from LaMotta's home movies. The only color portions of the otherwise all-black-and-white film, they were intended to re-create the look of eight-millimeter family movies from the 1950s as accurately as possible. To achieve this accurate look, Schoonmaker used jump cuts, awkward edits, and other tricks. And there's even a story of how Scorsese, in an attempt to make the movies even more realistic, purposely used a coat hanger to scratch some of the negatives.[32]

Another is the use of "skip frames" in various scenes, an effect that gives a choppy, stuttering character to the shots. One excellent example of this is the scene when LaMotta pulverizes Gino, a fighter Vickie had once casually called good looking. The intention here was to suggest that LaMotta is literally chopping up Gino's face so he won't be good looking any more. Today, this kind of an effect can be achieved with digital editing software, but, when *Raging Bull* was made, each of the excised frames had to be taken out by hand.[33]

Still another major challenge for Scorsese and Schoonmaker (as with many of their other films) was to cut the many improvised scenes in *Raging Bull* together in ways that worked. Emotional authenticity is something Scorsese is always striving for in his films, and this has often been achieved by working with actors (such as Robert De Niro and Joe Pesci) who are great at improvising, pointing the actors in the right direction, letting the camera (or cameras) run, and hoping that this improvisation will lead to some magic moments. While these scenes are always lots of fun to cut, as Schoonmaker has often noted, they can also be incredibly complicated, time consuming, and demanding. And on *Raging Bull*, she clearly had her work cut out for her, literally pruning miles of film footage of De Niro, Pesci, and other actors improvising; selecting the best bits; and piecing them all together into scenes that appear to flow in real time.

Overall, *Raging Bull* is a strikingly innovative work—so new and (for the time) startling that it actually took several years for many film critics and viewers alike to more fully see and appreciate the great achievement that it is. With characteristic modesty, Schoonmaker has often credited Scorsese, De Niro, cinematographer Michael Chapman, and others for the film's high critical standing today. But, as Scorsese would readily and enthusiastically agree, the film would not be nearly what it is without Schoonmaker's considerable talent.

"A vital role in shaping the last four decades of American cinema"

In an article focused mainly on Schoonmaker's contribution to Scorsese's *The Wolf of Wall Street* (2013), film writer David Ehrlich couldn't resist introducing his subject with a grand declaration: "Schoonmaker's work has played a vital role in shaping the last four decades of American cinema."[34]

For just about every other film editor working today, this might seem a bit too grand, a bit too over the top. But, since the article was about Schoonmaker, no one has even come close to disputing this claim.

Since she first caught the film world's attention with her innovative editing on director Michael Wadleigh's documentary *Woodstock* in 1970—and especially since she began working as Scorsese's exclusive editor in 1979—Schoonmaker has had an enormous impact on how films and increasingly television shows are pieced together in editing rooms. More and more, filmmakers and editors are using the entire tool chest of editing tools and techniques to enrich narratives and engage viewers in a wide variety of ways. Just as Dede Allen, Verna Fields, and others created numerous new techniques and other possibilities for editors in the 1960s and 1970s, Schoonmaker—with Scorsese often at her side, of course—has taken the art several steps forward with both new innovations and further refinements in traditional editing strategies and techniques.

In the process, Schoonmaker has, through both her professional and personal example, done two very important things.

First, she has been instrumental in elevating the editor's role to new heights. Today, people are far more conscious of an editor's contribution to a film than they were when she began her career. Part of this, as Schoonmaker posits, might be due to more people working in digital and doing their own editing. But, part of this is clearly due to the many influential advances that have taken place in the editor's art over the last 50 years—many of which Schoonmaker has helped to pioneer, refine, and popularize.

Second, she has been a fabulous role model not only to female editors but also to all women who want to be the very best person at what they do for a living. As she has played "a vital role" in shaping the last 40 years of American cinema, her achievement has undoubtedly inspired many women to seek to play similar vital roles in shaping the next 40 years in their professions.

10

Quick Cuts

Nine Other Women Who've Left a Memorable Mark on U.S. Film Editing

The nine great woman editors profiled in the previous chapters are by no means anomalies, even in a profession that men have dominated since the 1920s. They represent a very subjective selection from among hundreds of women who have worked as editors on U.S.–made feature films at different times in the 100 years between 1910 and 2010. Each was chosen for several reasons ranging from her body of work to her contributions to the art of film editing, to the influence she has had on younger editors and (sometimes) younger directors, to the respect she has received from her peers and others. It would be difficult to say "cut" to any of their stories.

It would, however, be much easier to add ... and add.

For example, what about Rose Smith, who worked closely with D.W. Griffith on his epics *The Birth of a Nation* (1915) and *Intolerance* (1916) as the classic Hollywood editing style was actually being invented?

Or Dorothy Arzner, whose impressive editing in the bullfighting film *Blood and Sand* (1922) and the landmark western epic *The Covered Wagon* (1923) led to her unique role as the only woman to direct for major Hollywood studios for nearly two decades during the classic period?

Or Blanche Sewell, a "go-to" editor at MGM in the 1930s and 1940s whose wizardry was evident in, among many fine films, *The Wizard of Oz* (1939)?

Or Adrienne Fazan, who showcased her talents in such classic 1950s MGM musicals as *An American in Paris* (1951), *Singin' in the Rain* (1952), and *Gigi* (1958), winning an Academy Award for the latter?

Or Marcia Lucas, who made her mark on the 1970s filmmaking renaissance with her work on *American Graffiti* (1973), *Taxi Driver* (1976), and *Star Wars* (1977) and picking up an Oscar along the way?

Or Carol Littleton, whose highly valued work in the 1980s, 1990s, and 2000s (1981's *Body Heat*, 1982's *E.T.*, and 1984's *Places in the Heart*) made her a favorite of directors such as Lawrence Kasdan, Steven Spielberg, and Robert Benton?

Or Susan Morse, who, over a 22-year period, edited more than 20 Woody Allen films—from *Manhattan* (1979) to *Celebrity* (1998)—and for her work earned five British Academy of Film and Television Arts (BAFTA) Best Editor nominations?

Or Lisa Fruchtman, who co-edited such films as Francis Ford Coppola's *Apocalypse Now* (1979) and *The Godfather III* (1990) and also won an Oscar for co-editing Philip Kaufman's *The Right Stuff* (1982)?

Or Sally Menke, who, along with Quentin Tarantino, took filmmaking in yet another direction with her innovative, often brilliant work on films from *Pulp Fiction* (1994) to *Inglourious Basterds* (2009)?

Or any of numerous other women whose skillful editing has turned limp, listless scenes into taut, vibrant ones; given actors' performances additional nuance and depth; and made entire films more stylish and alive?

With this thought in mind, this chapter is a series of brief close-ups of nine additional women editors who made distinctive contributions to their art as they also helped create some of America's most memorable and influential films.

Rose Smith: Key Collaborator with Griffith

Like Anne Bauchens, Viola Lawrence, and Margaret Booth, Rose Smith was literally present at the creation of her art. Operating as a team with her husband James (better known as "Jimmie"), she worked directly with the master himself, D.W. Griffith, on the director's enormously innovative and influential epics, *The Birth of a Nation* (1915) and *Intolerance* (1916). Griffith considered the pair so important to the success of both projects that he worked them relentlessly, and, on the day of their marriage, reportedly allowed them only one night away from the cutting room to observe the occasion. The couple clearly made important contributions to Griffith's many editing innovations from the structuring of shots for dramatic effect within scenes to the brilliant use of crosscutting in the climaxes of both films. Just as many have called Griffith the "father of film," Smith—along with Bauchens and Lawrence—can make a strong claim to being called the "mother of film editing."

Born Rose Richtel in New York in 1897, she and Jimmie, both editors at the Biograph Company, traveled west with Griffith to assist him with his work. By 1914, they were his two principal editors, working with him not only on his two hugely influential epics but also on many other well-known Griffith films such as *Hearts of the World* (1918), *Way Down East* (1920), *Orphans in the Storm* (1921), and *America* (1924). During this time, Rose also tried her hand at acting, appearing as a dancer in *Orphans in the Storm*. Describing her early start in the film business in a 1925 article, the *Los Angeles Times* referred to her as being "a cutter for Griffith since her little girl days."[1]

As Griffith's career waned, the Smiths began working for other directors and production companies. Among Rose's later credits was her work on a very early Howard Hawks silent film comedy called *Fig Leaves* (1926) for the Fox Film Corporation, an early Raoul Walsh drama called *The Monkey Talks* (1927) also for Fox, a Marshall Neilan mystery called *Black Waters* (1929) for Herbert Wilcox Productions, a crime drama starring Marian Nixon called *The Pay-Off* (1930) for RKO, and another crime drama called *Police Call* (1933) for an independent company, Showmen's Pictures. After her last film, a drama called *Public Stenographer*, released in early 1934, also by Showmen's Pictures, she retired. She died in 1962 at the age of 65.

Jimmy continued to work, first at Paramount during the 1930s, then at the United Artists Media Group in the 1940s, and finally as an editor on such popular television shows as *Tombstone Territory* and *Bat Masterson* in the 1950s. He retired at age 65 in 1958, and he died in 1975 at age 83.

Dorothy Arzner: From the Cutting Room to the Director's Chair

Dorothy Arzner is best remembered today as a director—in fact, as the only female director to work consistently for major Hollywood studios from the late 1920s to the early 1940s—for many, the height of the classic era. Considering the industry's gender politics of the time, this was quite a feat, one that turned Arzner into a much-admired figure. "She was a remarkable woman," actress Katharine Hepburn once said. "She did what she wanted, working along quietly, and nobody thought a damn about it."[2]

Before Arzner directed, however, she distinguished herself as an extremely able editor, one who both handle difficult challenges and, in the process, save her studio significant sums of money.

Born in San Francisco in 1897, Arzner had initially wanted to be a doctor, but, after spending several months shadowing a surgeon, her interest in medicine waned and her interest in movies grew. And, in 1919, she began in the film industry at the bottom: typing scripts at Paramount for William deMille, a writer/director whose younger brother Cecil had recently coaxed him into coming to Hollywood. Soon, however, Arzner moved on to writing scripts, and then she was promoted to the cutting room at a Paramount subsidiary, Realart Studio. Since she was the only editor on staff, she was quickly given the title "Chief Editor." And during her two years in this role, she edited more than 50 films, mostly shorts.

Better known today as a director, Dorothy Arzner was one of the industry's most talented film editors during the 1920s, making her name in such films as *Blood and Sand* (1922) and *The Covered Wagon* (1923). After turning director, she also championed women editors such as Viola Lawrence and Adrienne Fazan (Photofest).

Hearing of her editing skills, Paramount's executives took Arzner out of Realart in 1922 to cut a major new Rudolph Valentino film for the mother company, a bullfighting epic called *Blood and Sand* (1922). Here, she showed her skills and resourcefulness in a number of ways. For example, one of the major challenges she faced on the project was how to insert Valentino into stock footage of an actual bullfight in Madrid. The solution—which also saved Paramount quite a bit of money on costly double exposures—was to cut three scenes from the stock footage into the scene. She then had close-ups of Valentino taken to match her longer shots.[3] Her clever idea worked, and the powers that be at Paramount were doubly thrilled—both with the excellent result and with the fact that she had saved the studio quite a bit of money.

The way she cut this scene also greatly impressed James Cruze, a leading director at Paramount who was then preparing his great western epic *The Covered Wagon* (1923). Despite her lack of experience on "big pictures" at the time, Cruze enthusiastically recruited Arzner for the project. The finished film, which holds up amazingly well today, owes a great deal to Arzner's taut, intelligent cutting and elegant pacing. Delighted with her work here as well, Cruze worked with her on other films, including his lavish 1926 historical epic, *Old Ironsides*. In addition to its share of complicated oceangoing battle scenes, the film offered an additional challenge to Arzner: it was shot in an early widescreen process called "Magnascope." And, since it was widescreen, it required the editor to rethink many of the standard editing rules used for traditional screen dimensions. It's important to note, too, that she was doing this nearly 30 years before the widescreen processes (and editorial styles) became the norm in the mid–1950s.

After *Old Ironsides*, Arzner set her sights on becoming a director. At first discouraged by various executives, she finally received her opportunity when she threatened to leave Paramount. And, for the next 16 years, she remained the only woman director working regularly in Hollywood.

During this time, she never forgot her editing roots and often insisted on working with female editors. When she worked at Columbia, as she did on films such as *Craig's Wife* (1936) and *First Comes Courage* (1943), she asked for, and got, Viola Lawrence, whom she considered *her* favorite editor. And, when working on *The Bride Wore Red* (1937) at MGM, she fought hard to have the very talented Adrienne Fazan, who had thus far been relegated to short films, promoted to lead editor on a major feature.

The reasons aren't entirely clear, but after *First Comes Courage* in 1943, Arzner, only in her mid–40s, quit feature film directing. She remained busy on various projects, though, from teaching film courses at the Pasadena Playhouse to teaching filmmaking at UCLA. She also came to the aid of her old friend and the star of *The Bride Wore Red*, Joan Crawford, directing more than 50 Pepsi Cola commercials for the company when Crawford was on its board.

During her time in Hollywood, Arzner had been linked romantically to a number of women, including several actresses. For the last 40 years of her life, however, she remained in a relationship with choreographer Marion Morgan. She died in La Quinta, California, in 1979 at age 82. For more information about her, there's a book by Judith Mayne titled *Directed by Dorothy Arzner* (Indiana University Press, 1995).

Blanche Sewell: Wizardry Behind The Wizard

Except to a handful of people well versed in film editing history, Blanche Sewell is all but forgotten today. This could be partially due to her early death in 1949 at the age of 50. But, many of the more than 60 films she edited, especially during her 24 years at MGM, will likely never be forgotten. They include Best Picture Academy Award nominees such as 1930's *The Big House*; a Best Picture Oscar winner, 1932's *Grand Hotel*; 1933's *Queen Christina*, which features Greta Garbo in one of her most luminous roles; the rousing 1940 adventure/romance *Boomtown*, with the all-star cast of Clark Gable, Spencer Tracy, Claudette Colbert, and Hedy Lamarr; and two Gene Kelly musicals, 1948's *The Pirate* and 1949's *Take Me Out to the Ballgame*. Among all the films she worked on, however, the

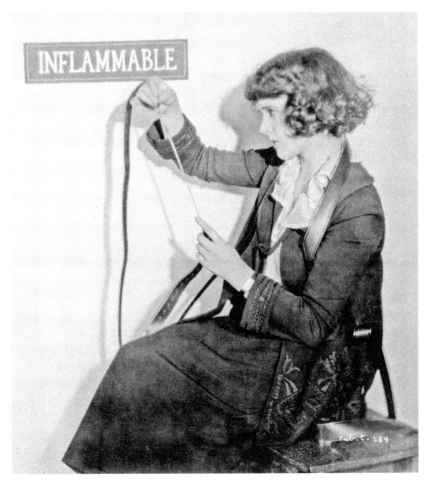

Little is known about Blanche Sewell today, but, in the 1930s and 1940s, she edited numerous MGM classics from *Queen Christina* (1933) with Greta Garbo to *The Wizard of Oz* (1939) with Judy Garland (Photofest).

one with the best chance of never fading from our collective memory is the 1939 masterpiece *The Wizard of Oz* with Judy Garland. In fact, since it became a television perennial beginning in 1956, this film—perhaps even more than the film that beat it in 1939's Best Picture Academy Award category, *Gone with the Wind*, or 1943's *Casablanca*—could be the most widely seen and appreciated film of the studio era in Hollywood. While Sewell did not have a long career, she nevertheless left her mark on many fine films.

Born in Lowe, Oklahoma, in 1898, Sewell and her family moved to Southern California, where she graduated from Inglewood High School in Inglewood, a city in southwestern Los Angeles County. Initially, she had wanted to be an actress. But, in 1921, she went to work as an assistant to Viola Lawrence on the drama *Man, Woman, Marriage*, produced by the independent company, Allen Holubar Pictures. Learning her profession quickly, she moved to MGM in 1925, where she broke in as the editor on a Marshall Neilan romance called *The Sporting Venus*, with Blanche Sweet and Ronald Colman. She quickly graduated to working with some of MGM's top directors such as Clarence Brown and Monta Bell, and she easily made the transition to sound as well as editing some of the studio's earliest sound pictures such as the romantic drama *The Single Standard* with Garbo. In the 1930s and 1940s, she was constantly in demand to work with other top directors at the studio such as Victor Fleming, Rouben Mamoulian, and Vincente Minnelli.

Watching many of films she edited, it's easy to understand why Sewell was always working. Whether she was editing a drama, comedy or musical, she had a superb sense both of getting to the essence of the action and characters and helping to make fine performances from actresses from Garbo to Judy Garland richer and more memorable. One wonderful example of her work is the famous scene in *Queen Christina*, when Garbo's queen simply walks around the room she has shared with her lover for several days, touches various objects, and says she simply wants to remember this room—every detail in it—for the rest of her life. With only a simple musical complement, the mostly wordless scene is beautifully cut to capture the intense emotion both the queen and her lover feel at that moment.

Perhaps Sewell's finest work is in *The Wizard of Oz*. Here—in addition to shaping great performances by Garland, Billie Burke, Ray Bolger, Jack Haley, Bert Lahr, Margaret Hamilton, Frank Morgan, and others through her judicious editing—she had numerous technical challenges (often involving the film's ambitious special effects) to contend with. One, for example, that has received much attention over the years is—as Dorothy (Garland) arrives in Oz—the film's innovative transition from black and white to full-blazing three-strip Technicolor. Even today, children seeing the film for the first time are mesmerized by this moment, and one can only imagine what it was like for viewers in 1939, who had rarely (or, in some cases, had never) set their eyes on a color film.

Pulling this off as effectively as the MGM technical staff and Sewell did was no easy feat. After abandoning a lengthy and costly "stencil printing" process, the technical team opted for a less costly variation. They painted the inside of the farmhouse sepia to conform to the black-and-white scenes in the film up until this point. As Dorothy opens the door, it is not Garland but her stand-in wearing a sepia gingham dress. The stand-in quickly backs out of the frame. Then, as soon as the camera moves through the door, Dorothy (played by Garland this time) steps back into the frame in a gingham dress that's bright blue, and she emerges from the house's shadow and into the bright glare of the Technicolor lighting. It's a spectacular moment, of course, and making it succeed depended on Sewell's excellent editing sense as much as any other element involved.

After working on a variety of MGM films during the early and mid 1940s, Sewell began to gravitate more toward musicals at the end of the decade. It's interesting to speculate how her contributions might have affected some of the great MGM musicals of the 1950s.

Unfortunately for Sewell, and most probably film audiences everywhere, however, she died at age 50 on February 2, 1949, in Burbank, California. Little is known about her personal life other than that she was married to a Leon Borgeau and that she had a son, Barton, who died in 1953.

Adrienne Fazan: Magnificent with Musicals

Certainly one of Hollywood's premiere film editors during the 1950s, Adrienne Fazan became, on April 6, 1959, only the third woman (after Anne Bauchens and Barbara McLean) to win a Best Editing Academy Award. Fazan received her Oscar for her work on Vincente Minnelli's musical *Gigi*. In fact, beginning in the mid–1940s with her work on musicals such as George Sidney's *Anchors Away* (1945) with Frank Sinatra and Gene Kelly, Fazan—who had already proven proficient at films from short subjects to documentaries, to feature-length comedies and dramas—quickly established herself as MGM's top editor on musicals. Among her other credits are Minnelli's *An American in Paris* (1951)—for which she received her first Academy Award nomination—and Kelly and Stanley Donen's masterpiece, *Singin' in the Rain* (1952).

Born in Germany in 1906, Fazan emigrated to the U.S. and entered the film business in the late 1920s as an assistant to Alexander Hall, who edited films at First National Pictures. By the early 1930s, she had moved to MGM, where, for several years, she worked almost entirely on short subjects.

During this time, Fazan showed both considerable talent and an inspiring work ethic. As she once recalled, "[T]he studio made a rule that we could not work overtime without special permission.... So I said, 'Oh, the hell with you.' I worked the overtime, but I didn't put in for it, because I hate that business: 'You can't do that.' What the hell! I'm working on the picture for the picture, trying to do as good [a job] as possible. Then they tell me I can't work, I have to go home when I have work to do. I didn't go for that."[4]

Despite this level of commitment, Fazan, who also had career ambitions, wanted to cut features but firmly believed that gender discrimination was keeping her back. As mentioned in the introductory section of this book, MGM's production head at the time, Eddie Mannix, had even gone on record as telling her that film editing was "too tough for women" and that women were better off at home cooking for their husbands and having babies.

Fortunately, Fazan was good friends with the one woman who had established herself as a studio director at the time, Dorothy Arzner, and in 1937—at Arzner's insistence—Fazan received her big break, the assignment to edit Arzner's *The Bride Wore Red*, an A-list feature film starring Joan Crawford. Fazan still had to make shorts for a few years after that, but she had clearly proven herself. By the early 1940s, she was working on features regularly, and, with successes in musicals such as *Anchors Aweigh* and *In the Good Old Summertime* (1949) with Judy Garland, she was establishing herself as an editor with a special talent in this genre.

Although Fazan casually noted that it was just "easier to cut musicals than dramatic films, [because] the dancers and the directors take great pains to match action,"[5] other people have offered a different perspective. Don Weis, a director who worked with Fazan on two films in the 1960s, once said, "It is not more difficult to edit a musical or a dramatic film. Both are equally difficult. Some editors are simply more talented in one area than the other. Adrienne was obviously more effective with musicals."[6]

Don Lockwood (Gene Kelly) doesn't let the inclement weather dampen his spirits in Kelly and Stanley Donen's classic *Singin' in the Rain* (1952), one of several classic musicals Adrienne Fazan edited for MGM during the 1950s. Others include *An American in Paris* (1951) and *Gigi* (1958), for which Fazan won a Best Editing Oscar (MGM/Photofest).

One of the great ongoing collaborations for Fazan was her work with Minnelli on 11 films from 1951's *An American in Paris* to 1963's *The Courtship of Eddie's Father*. In addition to Minnelli's musicals during this time (which also include 1955's *Kismet* with Howard Keel and 1960's *Bells Are Ringing* with Judy Holliday and Dean Martin), this work comprised such highly praised dramas as *Lust for Life* (1956), a biography of Dutch artist Vincent van Gogh starring Kirk Douglas.

Although many of the films Fazan edited are well known and widely respected today, perhaps the one that best qualifies for "immortal classic" status is *Singin' in the Rain*. Here, in number after number, her editing adds to the film's vitality by capturing the essence of the moment and the feelings the performers are expressing through their singing and dancing as well as acting. Just look at the contrasts in the editing between Donald O'Connor's show-stopping "Make 'em Laugh" sequence and the sweet romance of the "You Were Meant for Me" scene as Gene Kelly woos Debbie Reynolds on an empty sound stage. In the O'Connor number, the often-rapid cuts brilliantly reflect his comical, highly energetic acrobatics. And in the Kelly-Reynolds number, her cuts are far less frequent and timed perfectly to capture and lengthen the special moment the two characters are sharing. Throughout the film, too, Fazan's editing beautifully complements the distinctive directorial signature—that curious mixture of romance and sharp satire, sweetness and slapstick, and wild energy and deep feeling—that's uniquely Kelly-Donen. Everyone loves *Singin' in the Rain*, but virtually no one talks about the film's editing. That's a shame, because the editing is a significant part of its greatness.

Fazan was apparently a very private person, and very little is known about her personal life. After the 1950s, MGM and its once-thriving musical unit went into a steep decline. In 1964, Fazan was diagnosed with cancer, and about this time she left the studio. As she battled the disease, however, she continued to work as a freelancer on such films as Sydney Pollack's *This Property Is Condemned* (1966) with Natalie Wood, and Carl Reiner's *The Comic* (1969) with Dick Van Dyke until retiring in 1970. During a career of more than 40 years, she had edited more than 50 feature films, among them several enduring classics.

After 1970, Fazan lived quietly until her death at age 80 in Los Angeles in 1986. By this time, she was virtually forgotten. But many of the films she worked on will be remembered for a long while, and—considering her great devotion to the art of filmmaking—that's probably what Fazan would have preferred anyway.

Marcia Lucas: "The Forgotten Lucas"

Although the name "George Lucas" is one of the most widely recognized in all of filmdom, his wife (and in many respects his chief filmmaking partner) between 1969 and 1983, Marcia, is little known and frequently overlooked. During the 1970s—as Lucas, Francis Ford Coppola, Steven Spielberg, Martin Scorsese, and others virtually reinvented the U.S. feature film—Marcia was a major contributor to both her husband's and Scorsese's work. Along with Verna Fields, she received an Academy Award nomination for her editing of *American Graffiti* (1973). Along with editors Paul Hirsch and Richard Chew, she won an Oscar for her editing of *Star Wars* (1977), which in 2012 placed 16th on the Motion Picture Editors Guild's list of the best edited films of all time. And working alongside a young Martin Scorsese, she edited his *Alice Doesn't Live Here Anymore* (1974) and served as the supervising editor on his *Taxi Driver* (1976) and his *New York, New York* (1977).

"Marcia was a charismatic and talented woman, who had a significant—but basically unappreciated—influence on 1970s filmmaking, both directly and indirectly," wrote Michael Kaminski in his superb 2010 essay, "A Tribute to Marcia Lucas."

> In the direct sense, she was the primary picture cutter for her husband, George Lucas, as well as Martin Scorsese, in addition to the other films she edited and assistant edited. Indirectly, she was part of the social scene, as both Lucas's spouse and as a creative collaborator herself, and part of the inner circle of the influential "Movie Brats." Her opinions, her suggestions, and her interactions formed and shaped the collective movement, and her subtle influence in this respect is especially unnoticed.

She is, as Kaminski noted elsewhere in his piece, "the forgotten Lucas."[7]

What specifically did Marcia Lucas do, and why is she virtually forgotten today? Both are highly intriguing questions.

Born Marcia Griffin in Modesto, California, in 1945, her parents were divorced when she was young and she spent most of her childhood living with a single mother who often had trouble making ends meet. Then, while working by day in a bank and taking courses by night in the Los Angeles area in her late teens, she landed a job working as an apprentice film librarian. Although aspects of the job were highly technical, she mastered them almost immediately.

By the time she was 20, Marcia was working as an assistant editor for commercial companies, specializing in trailers and promos for movies and other entertainments. And, although the work could be tedious and women were still discouraged from becoming editors, she persevered. "I would have cut films for nothing because I enjoyed it so much," she observed many years later.[8]

Sometime in the mid- to late 1960s, Verna Fields—then teaching at USC—hired both Marcia and one of her promising film students, a fellow

Modesto native named George Lucas, to work on a film she was making for the U.S. Government. At first, the outgoing, emotionally open Marcia and the cerebral, introverted George seemed like an enormous mismatch. But the two shared a grand passion for filmmaking and also found that their talents complemented each other extremely well. George, for example, had a great respect not only for Marcia's editing skills but also for her ability to bring out the humanity in his stories by helping to develop engaging, well-rounded characters. They were married in February 1969.

After editing George's first film, a financially unsuccessful science fiction effort called *THX 1138* (1971), Marcia worked with him to develop *American Graffiti* (1973), a film based on George's boyhood experiences growing up in Modesto, California. For part of the editing process, Verna Fields was brought in to work with Marcia, and the two shared the Best Editing Academy Award nomination the film eventually received. But, after the rough cut (which was about an hour longer than the finished film would eventually be), Fields departed to fulfill another commitment and Marcia stayed on for many months more reworking, refining, and sharpening the material. While Fields was given shared credit with Marcia, she often noted that she felt Marcia actually did most of the work and deserved most of the credit.

Soon, other directors, seeing Marcia's work, were making her offers. And, realizing that, if she were ever to be taken seriously as an editor, she would need to prove herself on projects other than George's, she began to accept them. One of these directors was Michael Ritchie, who hired her as an assistant editor on his political satire *The Candidate* (1972). Greatly impressed, he then recommended her to his friend Martin Scorsese for the lead editor's job in Scorsese's film, *Alice Doesn't Live Here Anymore* (1974) Again, she impressed, and Scorsese quickly asked her to edit his next film, the dark character study *Taxi Driver* (1976). Marcia had viewed the dailies and was set to cut, but, because of a production delay and scheduling issues, two other editors, Tom Rolf and Melvin Shapiro, were brought in and Marcia became supervising editor. For their work, the trio received an editing nomination that year from the British Academy of Film and Television Arts (BAFTA).

Meanwhile, George had hired another editor to cut his long-time pet project, *Star Wars* (1977), and found the rough cut unacceptable. The editor was promptly fired and Marcia brought in. George and Marcia also decided to begin the editing process again from scratch, a huge undertaking for a film of this scope. So, two more editors, Paul Hirsch and Richard Chew, were brought in, and the three worked intensely for months on a completely different re-edit. During this time Marcia reordered sequences, and, in some cases, such as the film's famous Death Star trench run, ordered entire sequences re-shot. She also kept the story emotionally grounded and the characters accessible and engaging. As actor Mark Hamill, who played Luke Skywalker, recalled, "She was really the warmth and heart of those films, a good person [George] could talk to, bounce ideas off of."[9]

Star Wars opened on May 25, 1977, and the rest, as they say, is history. Not only did it quickly surpass Steven Spielberg's *Jaws* to become the highest grossing film of all time, but it also has had a profound impact both on film and popular culture ever since.

Marcia Lucas (pictured here second from left with co-recipients Richard Chew and Paul Hirsch, and actress Farrah Fawcett, after winning the Best Editing Oscar for *Star Wars* in 1978) was an influential filmmaking force in the 1970s, making major contributions to the films of George Lucas, Martin Scorsese, and others (courtesy of the Academy of Motion Picture Arts and Sciences).

At the Academy Awards the following April, Marcia also received a well-deserved honor. Along with Hirsch and Chew, she received a Best Editing Academy Award for her work on the film, becoming only the sixth woman (after Bauchens, McLean, Fazan, Coates, and Fields) to do so in the Academy's 50-year history.

After *Star Wars*, Marcia worked on several more projects for both Scorsese and her husband, from supervising the editing on Scorsese's *New York, New York* (1977) to co-editing the third *Star Wars* installment, *Return of the Jedi* (1983). In addition, she was constantly in demand to offer informal consultations on films that needed assistance with editing.

During this period, however, her marriage was becoming increasingly troubled as George focused more on developing his *Star Wars* franchise, the Skywalker Ranch in Marin County, California, and then his Indiana Jones film franchise, and she wanted to settle down and raise a family. (The two had adopted a girl, Amanda, in 1981.) They divorced in 1983, and Marcia soon stopped working as a filmmaker and married artist Tom Rodrigues. She and Rodrigues had a daughter, Amy, and in 1993, they divorced as well.

Since this time, Marcia has been a virtual recluse, refusing interviews or any contact with journalists or film historians. In fact, as Kaminski noted in his essay, her whereabouts as of 2010 were unknown. Why the life of a hermit? As usual in these cases, it's difficult to speculate. Perhaps she had simply had her fill of film industry craziness and celebrity life. Or perhaps it was the break-up from George, which just about everyone agrees was extremely painful for both of them. In any case, her desire for complete privacy has clearly contributed to her obscurity today.

Although the time she was active in film was fairly short and the number of films she worked on relatively few, Marcia's major contributions to watershed films such as *American Graffiti*, *Taxi Driver*, and *Star Wars* as well as her informal contributions to numerous other films had an enormous impact on film in the 1970s and afterwards. "She was a stunning editor, maybe the best editor I've ever known, in many ways," writer/director John Milius has said. "She'd come in and look at the films we'd made … and she'd say, 'Take this scene and move it over here,' and it worked.… And she did that to everybody's films: to George's, to Steven [Spielberg]'s, to mine, and Scorsese['s] in particular."[10]

Carol Littleton: The Touch of the Poet

One of the most respected feature-film editors working today, Carol Littleton first received widespread attention for her work on Lawrence

Kasdan's first directorial credit, the stylish (and widely imitated) neo-noir *Body Heat* (1981). Since then, she has worked on seven other Kasdan films, including the critically acclaimed *The Big Chill* (1983) and *The Accidental Tourist* (1988). In addition, she has received recognition for her work with other top-tier directors. Her contribution to Steven Spielberg's *E.T.* (1982) led to a Best Editing Academy Award nomination and a British BAFTA nomination, for example. And, among more than 25 other film projects, her work on Robert Benton's moving, evocative *Places in the Heart* (1984) and Jonathan Demme's remake of the political thriller *The Manchurian Candidate* (2004) have also received enthusiastic accolades.

One of today's most respected film editors, Carol Littleton has worked on a range of classics from Steven Spielberg's *E.T.* (1982) to Robert Benton's *Places in the Heart* (1984). She has also been a frequent collaborator with director Lawrence Kasdan (courtesy of the Academy of Motion Picture Arts and Sciences).

In addition to her mastery of the nuts and bolts of editing, Littleton has that rare ability to bring to her best work a distinctive and often poetic sensibility while simultaneously supporting and enhancing her director's governing concept for a film. "Lyrical" is another word often used to describe her work. "Her greatest achievements in structuring film images seem to fall into quiet, understated imagery," film historian Allen Grant Richards has noted. "Even with the fantastical elements of *E.T.*, ... Littleton emphasized the simple magic of the friendship between the boy, Elliott, and his alien visitor in a manner suitable to François Truffaut. While it may have been an unlikely approach to science-fiction fantasy, it surely had much to do with why audiences responded to the fable."[11]

Born in Oklahoma in 1948, Littleton had, growing up, little interest in films other than as light entertainment she saw at Saturday matinees. Then, while a student studying in Paris during her third year at the University of Oklahoma, she began watching French New Wave films and her perspective changed dramatically. "I discovered that film could be something other than escapist fare, that a great deal of art and vision was involved," she has said. "I was there studying music [and] trying to fight my way through the French language, and it helped my French to see a movie several times. Well, after you've seen a movie several times, you pick up on things other than the story. You begin to see the various elements, which constitute filmmaking style.... So I had an awakening to the notion of movies as art."[12] The clincher for Littleton was seeing Gillo Pontecorvo's war drama *The Battle of Algiers* (1966) about this time. It was, she recalls, "a pivotal event"[13] that led her to a career in film.

Between 1972 and 1977, Littleton owned her own company that produced commercials. Then, in 1977, she moved into feature film work, editing director Karen Arthur's *Legacy*. After a couple of other film projects, she and Kasdan connected for *Body Heat*, and, for the next decade, many of her films, both with Kasdan and other directors, were widely and enthusiastically praised.

Among these, an excellent example is Benton's *Places in the Heart*, a moving story of a young widow in rural Texas in 1935 who must go to great lengths to save her home and keep her family together. From the first frames of the film—as we hear the religious hymn "Blessed Assurance" and the credits are shown—we see images characterizing the community that will be central to this story: a small town standing in a vast prairie, people leaving a small church, a couple having lunch in a restaurant, another family having a meal at home, homes in town, lonely farmhouses, telephone wires spreading in all directions, an African-American eating a meal on someone's back steps and praying dutifully before he eats, a single windmill spinning at the edge of farmland, and so on. In less than two minutes, the world of this film is summed up with great simplicity and eloquence. Various aspects of this community—the rural life, the deep religious convictions of the people, the equally deep racial divide, and the relatively slow rhythms of life are all quietly revealed but still abundantly clear. As the main action begins after the director's credit fades, we know exactly where and when we are and how this story will be told to us. It's all very straightforward and understated and at the same time quite moving. Littleton continues to work in this style throughout the film, letting the story unfold scene by scene, gesture by gesture, and with great sensitivity toward the characters and their world. In a sense, her editing honors these people and their experience.

Places in the Heart was of course a collaborative effort, involving wonderful directing, writing, acting, cinematography, and other contributions as well as editing. But, as the case so often is with fine films, the editing brings it all together and ultimately gives the finished product its emotional richness. In the hands of a lesser editor, *Places in the Heart* would not have been nearly as effective a film.

Littleton herself has characterized good film editing as the ability to get to the essence of a story without drawing attention to the editing. "Simplicity is the key," she has said, "and I think that probably is the best advice for any editor. Just simplify one story to create pure life and emotion. In fact, editing is a lot like writing. You are rewriting a film. You have a script, but you're rewriting the script with the film. It's not like editing in publishing. It is not a matter of omitting and corrections. It's very different, I think. You become a writer, but you're writing with images, you're writing with music, you're writing with performances, you're writing with all the things—intangible things as well—that make an emotional event."[14]

Since the 1980s, Littleton has remained in constant demand and made important contributions to many fine films from Kasdan's *Grand Canyon* (1991) to Demme's *The Manchurian Candidate*. She has also ventured into television work, winning a Primetime Emmy for editing the 1999 made-for-TV film *Tuesdays with Morrie*.

She has had her share of misses, too. But, as Allen Grant Richards has observed, this is by no means Littleton's doing. "Even in the less-pleasing films Littleton has edited, such as *Vibes, Brighton Beach Memoirs* and the remake of *Diabolique*, critics take note of the assistance that she has given the work," he has written. "The film may not be good, but Littleton as editor has helped make it a little better."[15]

Married to cinematographer John Bailey since 1972, the two have occasionally collaborated on film projects, as Littleton has joked, "when the director's brave enough!"[16] A few include *The Big Chill, Silverado* (1985) and *The Accidental Tourist* for Lawrence Kasdan and Bailey's own film, the neo-noir *China Moon* (1994). But, perhaps more important for Littleton is the distinctive visual perspective her cinematographer-husband has given her—one that has greatly influenced her work. "I've learned an awful lot from John," she once observed. "My eye has become trained by being with him and seeing how he responds to things visually. We go to a lot of movies, art shows, photo shows, art museums, and his eye is constantly at work. And to talk about what he sees, by osmosis my eye has become trained."[17]

Susan E. Morse: Growing Up with Woody

Susan E. Morse once told a story that took place at the beginning of her career when she was an assistant on the editing of a television project in New York. She had been asked to get cups of coffee for five people who'd come to watch a screening, went to the coffee room, and couldn't find any trays to carry the cups on. For a moment, she lamented that this would mean two or even three trips carrying coffee back to the people. But then she saw some film reels, each with six circular indentations, each the perfect size to hold a cup of coffee. She put five cups into one of the reels and began filling the cups with coffee. As this was happening, the legendary Dede Allen walked in, saw what she was doing, and, with great emphasis, said: "You'll go far." Morse then added, "I think that's as great an introduction to the film industry as I [ever could have] wanted."[18]

Prescient in many matters related to editing, Dede Allen was also right about Morse. When Morse was just 24, she had been tapped by veteran editor Ralph Rosenblum to be his apprentice as he edited Woody Allen's Academy Award–winning *Annie Hall* (1977). Before the project was completed, Rosenblum had promoted her to his first assistant, and by the time Morse was 27 Rosenblum had moved on to direct and Allen had promoted her to lead editor on his classic comedy-drama *Manhattan* (1979). Then, for the next 20 years, Morse edited 20 more films for the iconic director, receiving a Best Editing Academy Award nomination for 1986's *Hannah and Her Sisters* and five Best Editing nominations from the British Academy of Film and Television Arts (BAFTA) for *Manhattan*, *Zelig* (1983), *Hannah and Her Sisters*, *Radio Days* (1987), and *Crimes and Misdemeanors* (1989). "I feel that Woody and I have grown up together...," she once recalled, "and that Ralph Rosenblum taught us both how to edit."[19]

Born in New Jersey in 1952, Morse went to Yale, where she majored in history and also served as one of the university's first female varsity captains, leading the school's field hockey team. After graduating in 1974, she enrolled in New York University's film school, where, almost immediately, she was offered a job as an intern on a PBS show directed by Roberta Hodes, who had served as a script supervisor for Elia Kazan on, among many films, *On the Waterfront* (1954). Then, on April Fools' Day in 1976, she received what she assumed was a joke phone call—a man purporting to be veteran film editor Ralph Rosenblum was asking her to be an assistant on Woody Allen's new film. The caller, of course, turned out to be the person he said he was, and the film turned out to be *Annie Hall*.

After cutting some scenes on Rosenblum's last assignment for Allen, 1978's *Interiors*, Morse stepped into the lead editor's shoes for *Manhattan*. Almost immediately, she was instrumental in organizing, developing, and refining the black-and-white film's tour-de-force opening montage of shots

With its iconic shots of New York City, *Manhattan* (1979) was the first of more than 20 films Susan E. Morse edited for Woody Allen between the late 1970s and late 1990s. Pictured here are Woody Allen and Diane Keaton in a scene from the film (United Artists/Photofest).

showing a day in the life of New York City, all keyed to Gershwin's "Rhapsody in Blue."

Clearly impressing the perfectionist Allen with her work here and elsewhere on *Manhattan*, Morse remained to edit every one of the director's films until 1998. While the two have both been quiet about why they parted ways, the *New York Times* reported at the time that Morse was apparently the victim of cost-cutting measures imposed by producer Jean Doumanian, which led to the departures of several valued Allen crew members.[20]

Part of Morse's great contribution to Allen's work during all that time was, as film writer Ally Acker has noted, providing "rhythm and cohesion" to a director's style that is essentially "anecdotal and digressive."[21] In talking about her work with Allen on *Radio Days* in particular and much of their work together in general, Morse herself has noted, "Free association was implicit in the way the script was written, and we continued this free association in the editing room." She added that in *Radio Days*, "The challenge was to create a sense of a dramatic curve in a picture that didn't have a narrative line to it … to give a sort of forward momentum to a series of anecdotes." In fact, according to Morse, the film begins with a scene in which two house burglars pick up a ringing telephone and become contestants on a radio game show—a scene that was number 72 on the shooting script. And from there, the final film goes to scene 92 to scene 10 to scene 58.[22]

All of this might suggest that editing with Allen can sometimes be a wild ride. But, as Morse said in a 2012 interview, when she compared Allen's working style with a more recent comedian-filmmaker partner of hers, Louis C.K., working with Allen could also be an extremely exhilarating experience. "[I]f they see something isn't working the way they envisioned it," she observed,

> they are both right there with a million alternative ways of expressing the same idea. There's enormous flexibility there, and creativity, and that's very helpful. Also, both are very open to discussions about things. I think that that's not the way people on the outside view them, but when you're working directly with them, they both really do want to hear what you honestly feel, and if it resonates with them, they'll take that under consideration and very much be willing to go in a different direction.[23]

Since 1998, Morse has edited more than 10 films for several different directors. One frequent collaborator is director Marc Lawrence, with whom she has worked on such films as 2002's *Two Weeks Notice* and 2007's *Music and Lyrics*. And, as mentioned previously, she has worked with Louis C.K. on his hit FX series *Louis*, taking over the editing from C.K. himself for the show's third season in 2012 and, for her efforts, receiving a Primetime Emmy nomination.

When asked if she has continued to follow Allen's work, Morse is very supportive, praising such films as 2008's *Vicky Cristina Barcelona* and 2011's *Midnight in Paris*. "I was amused by the opening montage of *Paris*," she says, "because it reminded me of conversations we had [during] *Manhattan*. That was special to me on a very idiosyncratic, personal level. It's amusing to watch things from a distance and imagine the conversations you would have had if you were working with him."[24]

Morse was married for many years to New York playwright, essayist, and novelist Jack Richardson until his death in July of 2012. Their marriage produced one child, a son named Dwight. Morse also has a stepdaughter, Emily Carter, from one of Richardson's previous marriages.

Although Alisa Lepselter has ably succeeded Morse as Allen's editor, film writer Stephen Prince nevertheless emphasizes the immense importance of Morse in Woody Allen's work during their two decades together:

"Susan E. Morse edited every Allen film of the eighties, regardless of its subject matter or visual design, and, as we have seen, Allen worked with a variety of cinematographers and production designers in those years. His insistent use of Morse demonstrates the essential nature of her collaboration."[25]

Lisa Fruchtman: From Apocalypse Now *to* Sweet Dreams

Many film editors have had "baptisms by fire," but perhaps no one has had a more fiery baptism than Lisa Fruchtman, whose first feature-film editing credit was Francis Ford Coppola's landmark epic about the Vietnam War, *Apocalypse Now* (1979). Consistently named to best-films-of-all-time lists today, the production—especially during its production and post-production phases—was often beset by problems of nightmarish proportion. And certainly many of the people involved must have felt that the film's title might also be a fitting way to describe the experience they were going through.

One of the enormous challenges was how to distill the more than 250 hours of film Coppola had shot into a running time for the finished film of about two-and-a-half hours. For this task, the director hired a team of four lead editors and an army of assistants, who worked together for more than two years. Three of the lead editors—Richard Marks, Walter Murch, and Gerald Greenburg—were all battle-hardened veterans, each with several major film credits to his name. The fourth, Fruchtman, was the youngest, and—while she had worked on major projects such as Coppola's *The Godfather, Part II* (1974) as an assistant editor—the least experienced. For her contribution to the film, she, along with Marks, Murch, and Greenburg, was nominated for both a Best Editing Oscar and a British BAFTA award. Their work has also stood the test of time. On its 2012 list of the best edited films ever made, for example, the Motion Picture Editors Guild ranked *Apocalypse Now* number three, just behind *Raging Bull* and *Citizen Kane.*

Born in 1948, Fruchtman received her A.B. from the University of Chicago in the early 1970s and began working as a film editor in Hollywood in 1973. After editing a documentary short film *Ten: The Magic Number* that year, she signed on as an assistant editor on *The Godfather, Part II*, which featured a complex flashback structure that proved to be a major challenge for its editing team. The film later received a BAFTA best editing award, and her work impressed Francis Ford Coppola sufficiently for him to promote her in 1977, making her one of the lead editors on his *Apocalypse Now*.

Looking at the film today, it's easy to understand why *Apocalypse Now* is held in such high regard. It's filled with scenes that are so original and startling in their juxtaposition of visual images and sounds that the experience of watching them one after another is stunning: the scene in which Robert Duvall's Colonel Kilgore says "I love the smell of napalm in the morning" as bullets are flying and bombs are going off all around him, the breathtaking sequence when the helicopters attack a Vietnamese village to the majestic (and chilling) chords of Wagner's "The Ride of the Valkyries," the scenes "up the river" when Martin Sheen's Willard approaches Colonel Kurtz's compound. The editing was a team effort, of course, but what the team, on which Fruchtman was a key player, produced is nothing short of mesmerizing.

In the 1980s and 1990s, Fruchtman found herself in great demand as a co-editor on several very large and challenging projects such as Michael Cimino's epic western *Heaven's Gate* (1980), Philip Kaufman's story of America's daredevil test pilots and first astronauts *The Right Stuff* (1983), and Coppola's *The Godfather, Part III* (1990). She was nominated for Best Editing Academy Awards for the last two films and won an Oscar for *The Right Stuff*.

Among these projects, the editing on *The Right Stuff* clearly stands out. Although a world apart from *Apocalypse Now* in tone and subject matter, this film is also filled with dazzling visual moments heightened by rapid, pitch-perfect editing. One

A consummate collaborator, Lisa Fruchtman was a key player on the editorial teams behind such landmark films as Francis Ford Coppola's *Apocalypse Now* (1979) and Philip Kaufman's *The Right Stuff* (1983), for which she won an Oscar (International Film Circuit/Photofest).

heart-stopper is the sequence when Sam Shepard's Chuck Yeager takes an aircraft up to the edge of space, sees the stars for one magical moment, watches as his plane fails him, tries in vain to control the plane as it plummets back to earth, and then parachutes out, appearing to be on fire. The film then cuts to people driving to the smoky wreckage of the plane. It looks grim, and then out of the smoke walks an indomitable Yeager with his parachute gathered in his arms. The cutting is handled with great intelligence, and the result is a riveting seven minutes. Again, the editing was a team effort, but, as in *Apocalypse Now*, Fruchtman was a key player on that team.

During the 1980s and 1990s, Fruchtman also proved that she could ably handle smaller, more intimate films as well. She worked as the sole editor on Randa Haines' moving 1986 romantic drama about a deaf woman, *Children of a Lesser God*, which was nominated for a Best Picture Academy Award and netted a Best Actress Oscar for its young star, Marlee Matlin. Since then, Fruchtman has edited two other films for Haines, the 1991 drama *The Doctor* with William Hurt and the 1998 drama *Dance with Me* with Vanessa Williams. In addition, she has tackled comedies, such as P.J. Hogan's 1997 film *My Best Friend's Wedding* with Julia Roberts.

After working on a variety of film projects after 2000 as both an editor and supervising editor, Fruchtman had an experience at the Sundance Institute Theater Lab in 2009 that sent her career in a new direction. There, she learned about a group of women in the genocide-ravaged African country of Rwanda. Led by playwright Odile "Kiki" Katese, the women broke a longstanding taboo in Rwanda against women drumming and joined in 2005 to form the country's first all-female drumming circle. The women, who came from both sides of the country's ethnic conflict, had come together to express both their enormous sense of loss and their hope for renewal and reconciliation.

Fruchtman knew immediately that she wanted to make a film about these women, but, although she was widely regarded as a world-class editor, she had never before made a film of her own. She then turned to her brother Rob, a veteran documentary filmmaker, and the two joined forces, co-producing, co-directing, and co-editing the feature-length 2012 documentary *Sweet Dreams*. Called "a nuanced and deftly edited film about a complex issue" by the *New York Times*,[26] the film has also received several awards and praise from numerous film reviewers.

Fruchtman, too, was delighted with the result. "By making *Sweet Dreams*, we wanted to cast a light on a visionary grass roots initiative," she noted in 2013:

It is a project of multiple goals—healing, reconciliation, women's social and financial empowerment—but it is even larger than that. And so the aim of the film is obviously not to generate more drum troupes.... It is to demonstrate the power of thinking outside the box—and of the power of seemingly small projects to generate big change. Every situation demands its own creative thinking, but the film shows what can be done even in the most difficult circumstances and inspires people to move forward in their own way.[27]

So, like Dorothy Arzner and other accomplished editors before her, Fruchtman, in *her* own way, might have found a new career for herself—as a director who addresses subjects that are especially important to her.

Sally Menke: Tarantino's "Main, Real, Truest, and Strongest Collaborator"

From DeMille-Bauchens to Scorsese-Schoonmaker, the list of close, longstanding, highly productive film director-editor collaborations over the last 100 years has become a long and impressive one. But, while other collaborations have lasted for more years and involved more film projects, few can claim to be as close or as exhilarating as the one Quentin Tarantino and Sally Menke shared between 1992 and 2010. As noted in this book's introductory section, Tarantino—a directing novice in 1992 when he set out to find an editor for his *Reservoir Dogs*—wanted a woman because he assumed she would be more "nurturing" than a man. Menke often added that he was also quite interested in someone who came "cheap." And the two clicked. Menke was hired, and the partnership, which included every Tarantino film project from *Dogs* through 2009's *Inglourious Basterds*, was electric, resulting in some of the most stylish, innovative, and vital U.S. films to appear during those two decades. Calling Menke "my main, real, truest and strongest collaborator," Tarantino has also said, "I don't write with anybody. I write by myself. But when it comes to the editing, I write with Sally. It's the true epitome, I guess, of a collaboration because I don't remember what was her idea, what was my idea. We're just right there together."[28]

Menke was born in Mineola, New York, a village on Long Island, in 1953 to academic parents. Her mother, Charlotte, was a teacher, and her father, Dr. Warren Wells Menke, was a professor of management at Clemson University. During the 1970s, she attended New York University's Tisch School of the Arts, graduating with a degree in film in 1977. After graduation, she found work editing documentaries for CBS and, in 1983, tried her hand at editing a feature film, a tepidly received comedy called

Cold Feet. In 1986, she married Dean Parisot, a film and television director whom she met at NYU, and the couple had two children, Isabella and Lucas.

In the early 1990s, Menke again turned her attention to feature-film editing, working on two very different kinds of efforts, 1990's comic-action-adventure *Teenage Mutant Ninja Turtles* and 1991's adaptation of the stage play *The Search for Signs of Intelligent Life in the Universe* starring Lily Tomlin.

Then, in 1992, when she heard about *Reservoir Dogs*, she finagled a copy of the script, read it, found it "amazing," and—hearing that actor Harvey Keitel was also associated with the project—became "more determined to get this job than ever."[29]

Once on board, Menke contributed mightily to the film's success. A highly stylized, violent, darkly comic, neo-noir with a flashback structure complex enough to rival *Citizen Kane*, *Reservoir Dogs* would have been a major challenge to a highly experienced director-editor team, but newcomers Tarantino and Menke pulled it off quite ably. "[O]ne of the enduring miracles of *Reservoir Dogs*," observed film writer Ryan Gilbey, "is its lucidity, and a control of tension that puts the audience under almost as much pressure as the hoods on screen. Menke made the shifts in tone, time, and place look entirely fluid, perpetuating the adage that editing is only bad if you notice it."[30]

Next up for the Tarantino-Menke team was the even more ambitious *Pulp Fiction* (1994). Involving multiple stories; the now-trademark Tarantino mix of violence, dark humor, over-the-top speeches, and stylistic flourishes; and an even more radical flashback structure than *Reservoir Dogs*, this film hit audiences like a bolt of lightning when it premiered at Cannes (winning the Palme d'Or) and soon reached the heights of a *bona fide* cultural phenomenon. The following year, it received seven Academy Award nominations, including one for Menke's editing. Widely imitated, *Pulp Fiction* may very well be the most influential U.S. film of the 1990s. And in 2012, the Motion Picture Editors Guild ranked it 18th on its list of the best-edited films of all time.

When people discuss Menke's contributions to *Pulp Fiction*, they most often point to "the dance scene." This is a beautifully orchestrated couple of minutes in the film when the two characters played by John Travolta and Uma Thurman dance in a night club to the Chuck Berry classic "You Never Can Tell." What's so disarming about it is the pacing. Following a great deal of rapid cutting in the scenes immediately leading up to it, this scene consists of long, leisurely, and very sensuous takes. As the two characters dance, they seem to bond in a quirky way and we see sides to them, such as the Travolta character's ease and looseness as a dancer, that seem completely unexpected. Largely because Menke lets the scene "breathe" in a way that seems so natural and in the moment, the whole experience is captivating. "Most editing is painstaking," she later said, "but this was an exciting scene to edit because it had momentum of its own and an obvious magic."[31]

This of course is only one of many standout moments in *Pulp Fiction* that were brilliantly conceived and acted and then made even more striking by Menke's editing. Another is the scene in which Samuel L. Jackson's

hit man character quotes the Bible before he shoots the terrified man he has come to kill. Still another is the scene when Uma Thurman's character is literally brought back to life with an adrenaline shot after a drug overdose. These are highly charged moments to begin with, but the way Menke cuts between characters at just the right times in the action heightens the intensity of the narrative and the suspense to a riveting, almost intolerable level. Here and elsewhere in the film her work is key in taking good material and then giving it that extra something that make certain scenes unforgettable.

Another triumph for Tarantino and Menke was 1997's *Jackie Brown*, an adaptation of Elmore Leonard's 1992 crime novel, *Rum Punch*. While not as flashy as *Pulp Fiction*, this film nevertheless includes some vintage Tarantino moments. One is a scene in which Samuel L. Jackson's and Robert De Niro's thug characters chat while watching a promotional video on TV called "Chicks Who Love Guns." First, the video is hilarious, and the cutting in it alone is a great parody of all promo videos that even remotely resemble this one. Then, as we see snippets of the video, we also watch a conversation between Jackson and De Niro and the entrance of Bridget Fonda's character. The cutting between the three characters

Until her death in 2010, Sally Menke was Quentin Tarantino's one and only film editor. Her work on such films as *Pulp Fiction* (1994) and *Inglourious Basterds* (2009) has been widely praised for its vitality, wit, and imagination (Photofest).

is often sudden and sometimes even abrupt, heightening the awkwardness and unspoken tensions that exist between them and suggesting that—with this trio—things will, in all likelihood, not end well.

In 2003 and 2004, Tarantino released his send-up of martial arts movies, *Kill Bill, Volumes 1 and 2*. One major challenge for Menke here was to align the cutting so that it effectively captured the look and feel not only of Asian martial arts and action movies but also other violent genres from Italian spaghetti westerns to 1970s "blaxploitation" films. "The thing with Tarantino is the mix-and-match," she once observed. "Our style is to mimic, not [to pay] homage, but it's all about re-contextualizing the film language to make it fresh within the new genre."[32] Although critics were mixed in their overall response to the *Kill Bill* films, they were generally positive in their appraisal of the technique involved in the storytelling, a facet of the films that depended enormously on Menke's mastery of the editing styles that are dominant in different film genres.

With the release of the very offbeat World War II film *Inglourious Basterds* in 2009, Tarantino received a level of critical praise he hadn't had since *Pulp Fiction* 15 years before. In early 2010, the film was nominated for eight Academy Awards, including ones for writing and directing for Tarantino and editing for Menke. In addition, the film received multiple nominations from the Golden Globes, BAFTA, and numerous other awards organizations. The film's big winner in the awards sweepstakes (nabbing a best supporting actor Oscar and many other honors) was German-Austrian actor Christoph Waltz for his portrayal of a charming, well-mannered, and thoroughly evil Nazi SS officer. And in one of the film's most enthusiastically praised scenes, Waltz's fine acting, combined with Menke's editing, creates several minutes of agonizing suspense.

The SS officer has come to a home in the mountains looking for a family of Jews he knows is nearby. (The people are actually hiding underneath the floorboards of the room he is sitting in.) He politely asks for a glass of milk and casually chats with another man. From time to time, the film cuts between him and close-ups of people under the floorboards huddled in terror. He then asks to smoke a pipe and calmly goes about it. The tension becomes excruciating. Although the situation may seem clichéd, the execution here is fresh and breathtaking. As Menke later said, she felt that the scene's success was due to her choice to "follow the emotional arc of a character through a scene, even if … they're just pouring a glass of milk or stuffing their pipe." She also added, "We're very proud of that scene—it might be the best thing we've ever done."[33]

Sadly, *Inglourious Basterds* would also be the last film Menke worked on with Tarantino. In September 2010, she was found dead in Bronson Canyon, a section of Los Angeles' Griffith Park. It had been as hot as 113 degrees that day, and, according to the police report, Menke had apparently become disoriented while hiking in the heat, passed out, and died. She was 56 and was survived by her husband and two children.

Hearing of Menke's death, film editor Joan Sobel, who had been an assistant to her on four films, said, "She was a brilliant editor.... She had the ability to see the point of a scene and to see the bigger picture simultaneously." Sobel added that Menke was also "innovative," "funny," "opinionated," and "definitely a role model to editors and certainly to me. I learned a lot from Sally. She just loved editing and loved working with Quentin. They had a truly unique relationship."[34]

And Still More...

Again, this is an incomplete list.

During the studio era, for example, even as women were being pushed out of editing jobs, several other women managed to survive and have notable careers. Among them were Irene Morra (1893–1978), who began with D.W. Griffith as a negative cutter in the 1910s and, before her retirement in 1958, had amassed 76 editing credits that included such films as 1953's *Calamity Jane* with Doris Day. Another was Jane Loring (1890–1983), who edited at least 23 films for Paramount and other studios from 1928 to 1936, including 1929's *The Saturday Night Kid* with Clara Bow and 1935's *Alice Adams* with Katharine Hepburn. Still another was Monica Collingwood (1908–1989), the fourth woman ever to receive a Best Editing Academy Award nomination (for her work on 1947's *The Bishop's Wife* with Cary Grant and Loretta Young).

Since the 1970s, as the list of women editors continues to grow, more and more women have distinguished themselves in various kinds of films. For example, Lynzee Klingman (1943–) won an Oscar for her work co-editing (with Sheldon Kahn) 1975's *One Flew Over the Cuckoo's Nest*. Mary Sweeney (1953–), a frequent collaborator with director David Lynch, received a BAFTA Best Editing award for her work on Lynch's widely praised 2000 film *Mulholland Drive*. Dody Dorn (1955–), who has worked with Christopher Nolan on several films, received an Oscar nomination for her work on Nolan's *Memento* (2000), a film that also placed 14th on the Motion Picture Editors Guild 2012 list of the best edited films of all time. Dana Glauberman (1968–) has received Eddie nominations from

America Cinema Editors for her work with director Jason Reitman on his fine films *Thank You for Smoking* (2005), *Juno* (2007), and *Up in the Air* (2009). And Alisa Lepselter (1963–), who has edited every Woody Allen film since 1999, has received Eddie nominations for her work on both 2008's *Vicky Cristina Barcelona* and 2011's *Midnight in Paris*.

No doubt there are many other highly deserving woman editors who have not been included here. And, to those who have strong feelings about certain omissions, both sincere apologies and an enthusiastic invitation to make the cases for them in future books and articles.

Conclusion

Contributions Worth Noting—and Celebrating

In most respects, the story of women in the U.S. film industry is typical of women in virtually every other segment of society. Gender discrimination has been—and in many places remains—apparent. Although Kathryn Bigelow became the very first woman to win a Best Director Oscar in 2009, for example, she remains one of only a handful of women directors working on mainstream feature films today. And cinematography—a field that has always been a virtual male monopoly—remains extremely difficult for women to enter, let alone succeed in.

In a pair of important respects, though, the U.S. film industry has been different. First, for a brief period during the 1910s and early 1920s—most of those years occurring, incidentally, before they were granted full voting rights—many women working in Hollywood had enormous power, distinguishing themselves as producers, directors, writers, and editors; proving—beyond the shadow of a doubt—that they could do it all. And second, while the "gendering" of roles in the 1920s and afterwards pushed women out of producing, directing, editing, and other jobs, a small but significant number of female editors remained and, in hundreds of films, reaffirmed their immense value to the industry. In the process, they earned the respect of many of Hollywood's most powerful figures, received a large share of industry-wide recognition and praise, and inspired new generations of women at mid-century and afterwards to enter the profession. Several of these women have, in turn, been instrumental in extending and enriching the art of editing and, by doing so, giving it far more prominence and prestige in the film world.

202

The contributions of *all* these women editors are worth noting—and celebrating. In recent years, of course, more attention is being paid to Dede Allen, Verna Fields, Anne V. Coates, Thelma Schoonmaker, and other female editors who emerged in the 1950s and 1960s as both filmmakers and film historians acknowledge the innovative, enduring impact of their work. Yet, while much more certainly needs to be said about them, the work of the female editors who preceded them—the giants on whose shoulders they have stood—needs to be more fully and enthusiastically acknowledged as well. Scarcely known outside of tight-knit film circles in their time and virtually forgotten today, Anne Bauchens, Viola Lawrence, Margaret Booth, Barbara McLean, Dorothy Spencer, and others were once towering figures in their field. Often working in semi-anonymity, they supplied "the final drafts" of countless films, routinely turning diamonds in the rough to superbly cut gems.

Clearly all of these women have directly or indirectly inspired many other women to become film editors and sometimes even aspire to other key filmmaking roles such as producers and directors.

And clearly their examples can inspire a far wider audience as well. This certainly includes women in any profession who aim to succeed in spite of major hurdles. And it can include anyone, woman or man, who must face major obstacles in any personal or professional endeavor. These women showed, often ingeniously, that it could be done. And they proved that—despite odds that can sometimes be formidable—capable, focused, and tenacious people can not only succeed but also inspire others and shape the course of their professions.

Ten Books About Film Editing

For those who would like to learn more about the art of film editing, there are literally dozens of books, documentaries, and other sources to choose from. Here is a list of 10 popular and frequently recommended books on the subject:

1. Edward Dmytryk, *On Film Editing: An Introduction to the Art of Film Construction* (Waltham, MA: Focal Press, 1984).

2. Don Fairservice, *Film Editing: History, Theory, and Practice* (Manchester/New York: Manchester University Press, 2001).

3. Norman Hollyn, *The Film Editing Room Handbook: How to Tame the Chaos of the Editing Room, Fourth Edition* (San Francisco: Peachpit Press, 2009).

4. Sidney Lumet, *Making Movies* (New York: Vintage, 1996).

5. Walter Murch, *In the Blink of an Eye: A Perspective on Film Editing*, Second Edition (Los Angeles: Silman-James Press, 2001).

6. Gabriella Oldham, *Final Cut: Conversations with Film Editors* (Berkeley/Los Angeles/London: University of California Press, 1992).

7. Michael Ondaatje, *The Conversations: Walter Murch and the Art of Editing Film* (New York: Knopf, 2004).

8. Bobbie O'Steen, *The Invisible Cut: How Editors Make Movie Magic* (Studio City, CA: Michael Wiese Productions, 2009).

9. Richard D. Pepperman, *The Eye Is Quicker: Film Editing: Making a Good Film Better* (Studio City, CA: Michael Wiese Productions, 2004).

10. Ralph Rosenblum and Robert Karen, *When the Shooting Stops ... the Cutting Begins* (Boston: Da Capo Press, 1986).

Chapter Notes

Introduction

1. Monika Bartyzel, "Girls on Film: How Women Were Written Out of Film History," *The Week*, August 30, 2013.
2. Ally Acker, *Reel Women: Pioneers of the Cinema, 1896 to the Present* (New York: Continuum, 1993) p. 18.
3. Anthony Slide, *Early Women Directors* (New York: A.S. Barnes, 1977) p. 51.
4. Karen Ward Mahar, *Women Filmmakers in Early Hollywood* (Baltimore: The Johns Hopkins University Press, 2006) p. 2.
5. *Ibid.*, p. 201.
6. Acker, p. *Xxv.*
7. John Anderson, "The 'Invisible Art': A Woman's Touch Behind the Scenes," *New York Times,* May 25, 2012.
8. Wendy Apple (producer), "The Cutting Edge: The Magic of Movie Editing," Starz Encore Entertainment documentary, 2004.
9. Scott Feinberg, "Top Directors Reveal How Female Film Editors Shaped Their Movies," *Hollywood Reporter*, December 11, 2013.
10. *Ibid.*
11. Anderson.
12. *Ibid.*
13. *Ibid.*
14. Carolyn Giardina, "Hidden Key to Thesps' Success: Editors," *Variety*, December 10, 2009.
15. Anderson.

Chapter 1

1. While William used the family's traditional "deMille" as his last name, the more egocentric Cecil opted for the slightly showier "DeMille" with a capital D.
2. Scott Eyman, *Empire of Dreams: The Epic Life of Cecil B. DeMille* (New York: Simon & Schuster, 2010) p. 76.
3. Constance Sharp Sammis, "Film Editor Indefatigable," *Christian Science Monitor*, February 11, 1957, p. 4.
4. *Ibid.*
5. *Ibid.*
6. *Ibid.*

7. Ally Acker, *Reel Women: Pioneers of the Cinema, 1896 to the Present* (New York: Continuum, 1991) p. 263.

8. Donald Hayne, *Cecil B. DeMille, the Autobiography* (Englewood Cliffs, NJ: Prentice-Hall, 1959) p. 119.

9. Kevin Lewis, "The Moviola Mavens and the Moguls," *Editors Guild Magazine*, March-April 2006 (vol. 27, no. 2).

10. Eyman, p. 510.

11. Eyman, p. 92.

12. Lewis.

13. *Ibid.*

14. Eyman, p. 502–503.

15. Barbara Sicherman and Carol Hurd Green, editors, *Notable American Women: The Modern Period: A Biographical Dictionary* (Cambridge: Harvard University Press, 1986) pp. 65–6.

16. Mordaunt Hall, "Claudette Colbert, Warren William, and Henry Wilcoxon in C.B. Demille's *Cleopatra*," *New York Times*, August 17, 1934.

Chapter 2

1. I.S. Mowis, "Viola Lawrence Biography," Internet Movie Database (IMDb).

2. Harold Heffernan, "Viola Lawrence, Famed Film Editor, Has Worked for Studios for 49 Years," *The Milwaukee Journal*, October 17, 1960, p. 30.

3. *Ibid.*

4. Charles Higham, *Orson Welles: The Rise and Fall of an American Genius* (New York: St. Martin's, 1985).

5. *Ibid.*

6. It wasn't until the 1960s that American audiences were able to see the film with the "Swanson Ending." It was shown on television with Swanson herself hosting and providing her version of events. After additional scenes, long considered lost, were found, a more complete version—and one closer to von Stroheim's original concept—was assembled by Kino Video in 1985.

7. Michael Koller, "Erich Von Stroheim's Damned *Queen Kelly*," *Senses of Cinema*, Issue 44, August 2007.

8. Heffernan.

9. *Ibid.*

10. *Ibid.*

11. Karen Ward Mahar, *Women Filmmakers in Early Hollywood* (Baltimore: Johns Hopkins University Press, 2006) p. 201.

12. Heffernan.

13. *Ibid.*

14. Fiona Villella, "Shadows on the Horizon: In *A Lonely Place*," *Senses of Cinema*, November 2000.

15. Curtis Hanson, "*In a Lonely Place*: Revisited"; documentary, Meg Staahl, producer; Columbia Tristar Home Entertainment, Inc., 2002.

16. Patrick McGilligan, *Nicholas Ray: The Glorious Failure of an American Director* (New York: Harper-Collins, 2011) p. 187.

17. Villella.

Chapter 3

1. Sidney Lumet, *Making Movies* (New York: Knopf, 1995) p. 151.

2. *Ibid.*, p. 153.

3. Claudia Luther, "Margaret Booth, 104; Film Editor Had 70-Year Career," *Los Angeles Times*, October 31, 2002.

4. Graham Daseler, "Cutters Way: The Mysterious Art of Film Editing," *Bright Lights Film Journal*, Issue 78, November 2012.

5. Dennis Gomery, "Margaret Booth," filmreference.com/writersandproduction artists.

6. Kevin Brownlow, *The Parade's Gone By* (Berkeley and Los Angeles: University of California Press, 1968) p. 302.

7. Wendy Apple (producer), "The Cutting Edge: The Magic of Movie Editing," Starz Encore Entertainment documentary, 2004.

8. Brownlow, p. 302.

9. *Ibid.*

10. *Ibid.*

11. Luther.

12. Brownlow, p. 303.

13. *Ibid.*

14. Luther.

15. Kristen Hatch, "Cutting Women: Margaret Booth and Hollywood's Pioneering Female Film Editors" (Columbia University's Women Film Pioneers Project) https://wfpp.cdrs.columbia.edu/essay/cutting-women/.

16. *Ibid.*

17. Ally Acker, *Reel Women: Pioneers of the Cinema, 1896 to the Present* (New York: Continuum, 1993) p. 221.

18. Kevin Lewis, "The Moviola Mavens and the Moguls," *Editors Guild Magazine*, March-April 2006 (vol. 27, no. 2). http://www.editorsguild.com/v2/magazine/archives/0306/cover_story.htm

19. Apple.

20. Lewis.

21. Luther.

22. Acker, p. 222.

23. Luther.

24. Gomery.

25. Luther.

26. Acker, p. 221.

27. Lewis.

28. Ronald Bergan, "Margaret Booth: Veteran Film Editor from Hollywood's Golden Age," *The Guardian*, November 15, 2002.

29. Luther.

30. Bergan.

31. Luther.

32. Apple.

33. Lewis.

34. Luther.

35. Brownlow, p. 305.

36. Frank Miller, "Mutiny on the Bounty," TCMDb Archive Materials http://www.tcm.com/tcmdb/title/15288/Mutiny-on-the-Bounty/articles.html.

37. *Ibid.*

38. *Ibid.*

Chapter 4

1. J. E. Smyth, "Off the Cutting Room Floor: Hollywood Editor Barbara 'Bobbie' Mclean," www.womensfilmandtelevisionhistory.com, November 11, 2014.

2. Kevin Lewis, "The Moviola Mavens and the Moguls," *Editors Guild Magazine*, March-April 2006: Volume 27, no. 2.

3. George F. Custen, *Twentieth Century's Fox: Darryl F. Zanuck and the Culture of Hollywood* (New York: BasicBooks, 1997) p. 181.

4. Smyth.

5. *Ibid.*

6. Custen, p. 181.

7. Smyth.

8. Custen, p. 277.

9. Susan Ware and Stacy Lorraine Braukman, *Notable American Women: A Biographical Dictionary Completing the Twentieth Century* (Cambridge: Harvard University Press, 2004) p. 435.

10. Monstergirl, "*Nightmare Alley* (1949) in the Cutting Room with Editor Barbara Mclean. See the Descent of Man, the Human Condition Up Close, and Throw in a Geek, Please." *The Last Drive In*, November 26, 2012.

11. Lewis.

12. *Ibid.*

13. Adrian Dannatt, "Obituaries," *The Independent*, April 13, 1996.

14. Smyth.

15. *Ibid.*

16. Lewis.

17. Dannatt.

Chapter 5

1. Dorothy Spencer, "The Film Editing," *American Cinematographer*, November 1, 1974, p. 1316.

2. *Ibid.*

3. Peter Flynn, "Dorothy Spencer," FilmReference.com.

4. I.S. Mowis, "Dorothy Spencer," IMDb.

5. Kevin Burns and Brent Zacky, "*Cleopatra*: The Film That Changed Hollywood." American Movie Classics, April 3, 2001 (*Variety* review quoted).

6. Matt Thrift, "*Cleopatra* Review," *Little White Lies*, July 7, 2013 (website).

7. Spencer.

8. Flynn.

Chapter 6

1. Mark Harris, *Pictures at a Revolution: Five Movies and the Birth of the New Hollywood* (New York: Penguin Books, 2008) pp. 326–327.

2. *Ibid.* p. 327.

3. Hope Anderson, "Considering Dede Allen: The Editor as Revolutionary," Under the Hollywood Sign.wordpress.com, January 2012.

4. Claudia Luther, "Dede Allen Dies at 86; Editor Revolutionized Imagery, Sound and Pace in U.S. Films," *Los Angeles Times*, April 18, 2010.

5. Kevin Lewis, "No Wincing Allowed: Dede Allen, the Director's Editor," *Editor's Guild Magazine*, 2007.

6. Michael Horton, "Dede Allen: The Lost Interview, Part 1," YouTube, 2006.

7. Lewis.

8. *Ibid.*

9. Horton.

10. *Ibid.*

11. Lewis.

12. *Ibid.*

13. *Ibid.*

14. Horton.

15. Lewis.

16. Greg S. Faller, "Dede Allen," FilmReference.com.

17. Lewis.

18. Anderson.

19. Faller.

20. *Ibid.*

21. *Ibid.*

22. Anderson.

23. Ally Acker, *Reel Women: Pioneers of the Cinema 1896 to the Present* (New York: Continuum, 1993) p. 225.

24. Lewis.

25. Acker, p. 225.

26. *Ibid.*, pp. 225–226.

27. Lewis.

28. "Past Recipients," Woman in Film, wif.org.

29. Luther.

30. Roger Ebert, "*Bonnie and Clyde*," *Chicago Sun-Times*, August 3, 1998.

31. Luther.

32. Allen frequently credited her assistant, Jerry Greenberg, with the cutting of this scene, but, while this might be so, she played a major role in the scene's design and creation. Her "Editorial Signature" is clearly on it.

33. Harris, pp. 286–287.

34. Luther.

Chapter 7

1. Neil Harvey, "30 Years of *Jaws*," *The Roanoke Times*, June 13, 2005.

2. *Ibid.*

3. Wendy Apple (producer), "The Cutting Edge: The Magic of Movie Editing," Starz Encore Entertainment documentary, 2004.

4. Harvey.

5. Eric Vespe, "Steven Spielberg and Quint Have an Epic Chat All About *Jaws* as It Approaches Its 36 Anniversary," *Ain't It Cool News*, June 6, 2011.

6. Leonard Maltin (ed.), *Leonard Maltin's 2004 Movie and Video Guide* (London: Penguin, 2003), p. 715.

7. Ian Freer, "*Jaws* Filmmaking 101: A Closer Look at the Camera Work, Dolly Zoom, and Editing of the Movie," *Empire*, 2012.

8. Gerald Peary, "Hollywood's Mother Cutter," *The Real Paper*, October 23, 1980.

9. *Ibid.*

10. *Ibid.*

11. *Ibid.*

12. *Ibid.*

13. Bill Warren, "Review of *Targets*," *Audio/Video Revolution* (archived by WebCite from the original, February 26, 2008).

14. A reference to Picasso's famous painting depicting the chaos and anguish of the Spanish Civil War in the 1930s.

15. Vincent Canby, "Real Events of '68 Seen in *Medium Cool*," *The New York Times*, August 28, 1969.

16. Roger Ebert, "*Medium Cool*," *Chicago Sun-Times*, September 21, 1969.

17. Apple.
18. Peary.
19. Paul Rosenfield, "Women in Hollywood," *Los Angeles Times,* July 13, 1982.
20. Entry on Crystal Award from Women in Film website.
21. Peary.
22. Joseph McBride, "The Editor: Verna Fields," *Filmmakers on Filmmaking: The American Film Institute Seminars on Motion Pictures and Television, Vol. One* (J. P. Tarcher: Los Angeles, 1984), pp. 139–149.
23. Craig Bloomfield, "Oscar Horrors: A Shark in the Edit Suite," *The Film Experience,* October 24, 2012.
24. Freer.
25. Susan Korda, "We'll Fix It in the Edit!?," Lecture transcript from 2005 posted at the website of the Berlinale Talent Campus.
26. Freer.
27. Bloomfield.

Chapter 8

1. Steven Spielberg, "*Lawrence of Arabia*—Conversation with Stephen Spielberg," YouTube (https://www.youtube.com/watch?v=OX3bqRemW8U).
2. Ian Jefferys, "The Most Famous of Edits," YouTube (https://www.youtube.com/watch?v=Ypul7nPcMII).
3. Trevor Hogg, "Cutting Edge: A Conversation with Film Editor Anne V. Coates," Flickering Myth.com, August 24, 2011.
4. Susan King, "Editing Is the Splice of Anne V. Coates' Life," *Los Angeles Times,* October 14, 2009.
5. Hogg.
6. *Ibid.*
7. Gabriella Oldham, *First Cut: Conversations with Film Editors* (Berkeley and Los Angeles: University of California Press, 1992) p. 154.
8. Hogg.
9. Oldham, p. 158.
10. *Ibid.*
11. *Ibid.*, p. 159.
12. *Ibid.*
13. Walter Murch, "Walter Murch Interviews Anne Coates," EditorsNet, May 2000 (http://www.editorsnet.com/article/mainv/0,7220,121767,00.html).
14. Oldham, p. 156.
15. Kevin Lewis, "Coates of Many Colors: The Varied Career of Anne V. Coates," *Editors Guild Magazine,* March-April 2010 (vol. 31, no. 10).
16. *Ibid.*, p. 164.
17. Lewis.
18. Jeff Stafford, "Interview with Anne V. Coates, Oscar Winning Film Editor for *Lawrence of Arabia,*" TCM Film Site (http://www.tcm.com/this-month/article/67245%7C0/Interview-with-Anne-V-Coates-Oscar-winning-editor-.html).
19. *Ibid.*
20. Murch.
21. *Ibid.*
22. *Ibid.*
23. *Ibid.*
24. Lewis.
25. Oldham, p. 155.
26. *Ibid.*, p. 154.

27. Mick LaSalle, "Clooney Breaks Out/*ER* Star Finally Makes a Show of It in Crime Caper *Out of Sight*," *San Francisco Chronicle*, June 26, 1998.

28. Wendy Apple (producer), "The Cutting Edge: The Magic of Movie Editing," Starz Encore Entertainment documentary, 2004.

29. Roger Ebert, "*Out of Sight*," *Chicago Sun-Times*, June 19, 1998.

30. LaSalle.

31. Kenneth Turan, "*Out of Sight*," *Los Angeles Times*, June 26, 1998.

32. Hogg.

Chapter 9

1. Noel Murray, "Thelma Schoonmaker Talks to the *Dissolve* About Her Collaboration with Martin Scorsese," *The Dissolve*, March 24, 2014.

2. Hamish Anderson, "The Woman Behind Martin Scorsese," *Elle*, November 22, 2011.

3. *Ibid.*

4. *Ibid.*

5. *Ibid.*

6. *Ibid.*

7. *Ibid.*

8. *Ibid.*

9. Nancy Tartaglione, "Venice: Thelma Schoonmaker on Working with Martin Scorsese, *Silence* & Preserving Michael Powell's Legacy," *Deadline Hollywood*, September 2, 2014.

10. Daniel Aloi, "Scorsese's Film Editor, Thelma Schoonmaker '61, Talks of *Raging Bull* and Michael Powell," Cornell University *Chronicle Online*, November 29, 2005.

11. *Ibid.*

12. Roger Ebert, "*Woodstock*," *Chicago Sun-Times*, May 3, 1970.

13. Terrance Rafferty, "His Girl Friday," *Village Voice*, November 30, 1982, p. 83.

14. Murray.

15. Leo Robson, "Thelma Schoonmaker: The Queen of the Cutting Room," *Financial Times*, May 9, 2014.

16. Lan N. Nguyen, "The Last Temptation of Thelma," *IVillage Entertainment*, March 15, 2005.

17. Murray.

18. Anderson.

19. Tartaglione.

20. Justin Morrow, "A Look at the Influential Editing Techniques of Martin Scorsese and Thelma Schoonmaker," *No Film School*, August 28, 2014.

21. Nick Pinkerton, "Interview: Thelma Schoonmaker," *Film Comment*, March 31, 2014.

22. Tartaglione.

23. Eric Hynes, "Thelma Schoonmaker and the Art of Editing Long Movies," *The New York Times*, January 17. 2014.

24. *Ibid.*

25. Rafferty, p. 83.

26. Anderson.

27. *Ibid.*

28. Justin Morrow, "Legendary Editor Thelma Schoonmaker Breaks Down *Raging Bull* at the Tribeca Film Festival," *No Film School*, April 21, 2014.

29. Jan Stripek, "Slow Motion in *Raging Bull*," *Cinema Shock*, January 21, 2013.

30. *Ibid.*

31. *Ibid.*

32. Morrow, April 21, 2014.

33. *Ibid.*

34. David Ehrlich, "Legendary Editor Thelma Schoonmaker Reveals the Process of Cutting 'The Wolf of Wall Street,'" Film.Com, December 23, 2013.

Chapter 10

1. Jane Gaines, Radha Vatsal, and Monica Dall'Asta, eds., "Rose Smith." Women Film Pioneers Project. Center for Digital Research and Scholarship. New York: Columbia University Libraries, 2013. https://wfpp.cdrs.columbia.edu/person/rosesmith/

2. Ally Acker, *Reel Women: Pioneers of the Cinema, 1896 to the Present* (New York: Continuum, 1993) p. 21.

3. Jay Carr, "Director Arzner: A Mind of Her Own," *Boston Globe*, April 22, 1984, p. B-2.

4. Don Knox, *The Magic Factory* (New York: Praeger, 1973) p. 64.

5. Acker, p. 237.

6. *Ibid.*

7. Michael Kaminski, "In Tribute to Marcia Lucas," *The Secret History of Star Wars* http://secrethistoryofstarwars.com/marcialucas.html.

8. *Ibid.*

9. *Ibid.*

10. *Ibid.*

11. Allen Grant Richards, "Carol Littleton," *Film Reference, Writers and Production Artists* http://www.filmreference.com/Writers-and-Production-Artists-Kr-Lo/Littleton-Carol.html.

12. Gabriella Oldham, *First Cut: Conversations with Film Editors* (Berkeley and Los Angeles: University of California Press, 1992) p. 65.

13. *Ibid.*

14. *Ibid.*, p. 64.

15. Richards.

16. Oldham, p. 73.

17. *Ibid.*

18. Manhattan Edit Workshop, "Susan E. Morse, A.C.E., Talks About Dede Allen, A.C.E." YouTube (https://www.youtube.com/watch?v=QvUwK09M3nU).

19. Acker, p. 230.

20. Bernard Weinraub, "Deconstructing His Film Crew: Woody Allen's Longtime Staff Is Hit by Cost-Cutting Efforts," *New York Times*, June 1, 1998.

21. Acker, p. 230.

22. *Ibid.*

23. Zach Dionne, "Louis C.K.'S New *Louie* Editor Susan E. Morse Compares Him to Her Old Boss, Woody Allen," Vulture.com, May 21, 2012.

24. *Ibid.*

25. Stephen Prince, *A New Pot of Gold: Hollywood Under the Electronic Rainbow 1980–1989 (Volume 10, History of the American Cinema)*. (Berkeley and Los Angeles: University of California Press, 2002) p. 197.

26. Miriam Bale, "A Little Shop of Possibilities," *New York Times*, October 31, 2013.

27. Rahim Kanani, "Exclusive Interview with Lisa Fruchtman, Director of *Sweet Dreams*, Skoll World Forum, April 9, 2013.

28. Ryan Gilbey, "Sally Menke Obituary," *The Guardian*, September 29, 2010.

29. *Ibid.*

30. *Ibid.*

31. Ben Walters, "Sally Menke: The Quiet Heroine of the Quentin Tarantino Success Story," *The Guardian*, Wednesday 29 September 2010.

32. *Ibid.*

33. *Ibid.*

34. Dennis McLellan and Andrew Blankstein, "Sally Menke Dies at 56; Editor on Quentin Tarantino's Movies," *Los Angeles Times*, September 29. 2010.

Bibliography

Acker, Ally. *Reel Women: Pioneers of the Cinema, 1896 to the Present*. New York: Continuum, 1993.

Aloi Daniel. "Scorsese's Film Editor, Thelma Schoonmaker '61, Talks of *Raging Bull* and Michael Powell." Cornell University *Chronicle Online*. November 29, 2005.

Anderson, Hamish. "The Woman Behind Martin Scorsese." *Elle*. November 22, 2011.

Anderson, Hope. "Considering Dede Allen: The Editor as Revolutionary." *Under the Hollywood Sign*. January 2012.

Anderson, John. "The 'Invisible Art': A Woman's Touch Behind the Scenes." *The New York Times*. May 25, 2012.

Apple, Wendy, producer. *The Cutting Edge: The Magic of Movie Editing*. Documentary. Starz Encore Entertainment, 2004.

Bale, Miriam. "A Little Shop of Possibilities." *The New York Times*. October 31, 2013.

Bartyzel, Monika. "Girls on Film: How Women Were Written Out of Film History." *The Week*. August 30, 2013.

Bergan, Ronald. "Margaret Booth: Veteran Film Editor from Hollywood's Golden Age." *The Guardian*. November 15, 2002.

Bloomfield, Craig. "Oscar Horrors: A Shark in the Edit Suite." *The Film Experience*. October 24, 2012.

Brownlow, Kevin. *The Parade's Gone By*. Berkeley and Los Angeles: University of California Press, 1968.

Canby, Vincent. "Real Events of '68 Seen in *Medium Cool*." *The New York Times*. August 28, 1969.

Carr, Jay. "Director Arzner: A Mind of Her Own." *Boston Globe*. April 22, 1984.

Custen, George F. *Twentieth Century's Fox: Darryl F. Zanuck and the Culture of Hollywood*. New York: BasicBooks, 1997.

Daseler, Graham. "Cutter's Way: The Mysterious Art of Film Editing." *Bright Lights Film Journal*. Issue 78, November 2012.

Dionne, Zach. "Louis C.K.'s New *Louie* Editor Susan E. Morse Compares Him to Her Old Boss, Woody Allen." Vulture.com, May 21, 2012.

Ebert, Roger. "*Bonnie and Clyde*." *Chicago Sun-Times*. August 3, 1998.

_____. "*Medium Cool*." *Chicago Sun-Times*. September 21, 1969.

_____. "*Out of Sight*." *Chicago Sun-Times*. June 19, 1998.

_____. "*Woodstock*." *Chicago Sun-Times*, May 3, 1970.

Ehrlich, David. "Legendary Editor Thelma Schoonmaker Reveals the Process of Cutting 'The Wolf of Wall Street.'" Film.Com. December 23, 2013.

Eyman, Scott. *Empire of Dreams: The Epic Life of Cecil B. DeMille* New. York: Simon & Schuster, 2010.

Faller, Greg S. "Dede Allen." FilmReference.com.

Feinberg, Scott. "Top Directors Reveal How Female Film Editors Shaped Their Movies." *Hollywood Reporter*. December 11, 2013.

Flynn, Peter. "Dorothy Spencer." FilmReference.com.

Freer, Ian. "*Jaws* Filmmaking 101: A Closer Look at the Camera Work, Dolly Zoom, and Editing of the Movie." *Empire*. 2012.

Giardina, Carolyn. "Hidden Key to Thesps' Success: Editors." *Variety*. December 10, 2009.

Gilbey, Ryan. "Sally Menke Obituary." *The Guardian*. September 29, 2010.

Gomery, Dennis. "Margaret Booth." filmreference.com/writersandproductionartists.

Hall, Mordaunt. "Claudette Colbert, Warren William, and Henry Wilcoxon in C.B. Demille's *Cleopatra*." *The New York Times*. August 17, 1934.

Hanson, Curtis. "*In a Lonely Place*: Revisited." Documentary, Meg Staahl, producer; Columbia Tristar Home Entertainment, Inc., 2002.

Harris, Mark. *Pictures at a Revolution: Five Movies and the Birth of the New Hollywood*. New York: Penguin Books, 2008.

Harvey, Neil. "30 Years of *Jaws*." *The Roanoke Times*. June 13, 2005.

Hatch, Kristen. "Cutting Women: Margaret Booth and Hollywood's Pioneering Female Film Editors." Columbia University's Women Film Pioneers Project.

Hayne, Donald. *Cecil B. DeMille, the Autobiography* Englewood Cliffs, NJ: Prentice-Hall, 1959.

Heffernan, Harold. "Viola Lawrence, Famed Film Editor, Has Worked for Studios for 49 Years." *The Milwaukee Journal*. October 17, 1960.

Higham, Charles. *Orson Welles: The Rise and Fall of an American Genius*. New York: St. Martin's, 1985.

Hogg, Trevor. "Cutting Edge: A Conversation with Film Editor Anne V. Coates." Flickering Myth.Com. August 24, 2011.

Horton, Michael. "Dede Allen: The Lost Interview, Part 1." YouTube, 2006.

Hynes, Eric. "Thelma Schoonmaker and the Art of Editing Long Movies." *The New York Times*. January 17, 2014.

Kaminski, Michael. "In Tribute to Marcia Lucas." *The Secret History of Star Wars* http://secrethistoryofstarwars.com/marcialucas.html.

Kanani, Rahim. "Exclusive Interview with Lisa Fruchtman, Director of *Sweet Dreams*." Skoll World Forum, April 9, 2013.

King, Susan. "Editing Is the Splice of Anne V. Coates' Life." *Los Angeles Times*. October 14, 2009.

Knox, Don. *The Magic Factory*. New York: Praeger, 1973.

Koller, Michael. "Erich Von Stroheim's Damned *Queen Kelly*." *Senses of Cinema*. Issue 44, August 2007.

LaSalle, Mick. "Clooney Breaks Out / *ER* Star Finally Makes a Show of It in Crime Caper *Out of Sight*." *San Francisco Chronicle*. June 26, 1998.

Lewis, Kevin. "Coates of Many Colors: The Varied Career of Anne V. Coates." *Editors Guild Magazine*. March-April 2010 (vol. 31, no. 10).

_____. "The Moviola Mavens and the Moguls." *Editors Guild Magazine*. March-April 2006 (vol. 27, no. 2).

_____. "No Wincing Allowed: Dede Allen, the Director's Editor." *Editor's Guild Magazine*. 2007.

Lumet, Sidney. *Making Movies*. New York: Knopf, 1995.

Luther, Claudia. "Dede Allen Dies at 86; Editor Revolutionized Imagery, Sound and Pace in U.S. Films." *Los Angeles Times*. April 18, 2010.

_____. "Margaret Booth, 104; Film Editor Had 70-Year Career." *Los Angeles Times*. October 31, 2002.

Mahar, Karen Ward. *Women Filmmakers in Early Hollywood*. Baltimore: The Johns Hopkins University Press, 2006.

Maltin, Leonard, ed. *Leonard Maltin's 2004 Movie and Video Guide*. London: Penguin, 2003.

McBride, Joseph. "The Editor: Verna Fields." *Filmmakers on Filmmaking: The American Film Institute Seminars on Motion Pictures and Television, Vol. One.* Los Angeles: J.P. Tarcher, 1984.

McGilligan, Patrick. *Nicholas Ray: The Glorious Failure of an American Director.* New York: HarperCollins, 2011.

McLellan, Dennis and Blankstein, Andrew. "Sally Menke Dies at 56; Editor on Quentin Tarantino's Movies." *Los Angeles Times.* September 29, 2010.

Miller, Frank. "Mutiny on the Bounty." TCMDb Archive Materials.

Morrow, Justin. "Legendary Editor Thelma Schoonmaker Breaks Down *Raging Bull* at the Tribeca Film Festival." *No Film School.* April 21, 2014.

_____. "A Look at the Influential Editing Techniques of Martin Scorsese and Thelma Schoonmaker." *No Film School.* August 28, 2014.

Murch, Walter. "Walter Murch Interviews Anne Coates." EditorsNet. May 2000.

Murray, Noel. "Thelma Schoonmaker Talks to the *Dissolve* About Her Collaboration with Martin Scorsese." *The Dissolve.* March 24, 2014.

Nguyen, Lan N. "The Last Temptation of Thelma." *IVillage Entertainment.* March 15, 2005.

Oldham, Gabriella. *First Cut: Conversations with Film Editors.* Berkeley and Los Angeles: University of California Press, 1992.

Peary, Gerald. "Hollywood's Mother Cutter." *The Real Paper.* October 23, 1980.

Pinkerton, Nick. "Interview: Thelma Schoonmaker." *Film Comment.* March 31, 2014.

Prince, Stephen. *A New Pot of Gold: Hollywood Under the Electronic Rainbow 1980–1989.* Volume 10, *History of the American Cinema.* Berkeley and Los Angeles: University of California Press, 2002.

Rafferty, Terrance. "His Girl Friday." *Village Voice.* November 30, 1982.

Richards, Allen Grant. "Carol Littleton." *Film Reference, Writers and Production Artists.* http://www.filmreference.com/Writers-and-Production-Artists-Kr-Lo/Littleton-Carol.html.

Robson, Leo. "Thelma Schoonmaker: The Queen of the Cutting Room." *Financial Times.* May 9, 2014.

Rosenfield, Paul. "Women in Hollywood." *Los Angeles Times.* July 13, 1982.

Sammis, Constance Sharp. "Film Editor Indefatigable." *Christian Science Monitor.* February 11, 1957.

Sicherman, Barbara, and Carol Hurd Green, eds. *Notable American Women: The Modern Period: A Biographical Dictionary.* Cambridge: Harvard University Press, 1986.

Slide, Anthony. *Early Women Directors* New York: A.S. Barnes, 1977.

Smyth, J.E. "Off the Cutting Room Floor: Hollywood Editor Barbara 'Bobbie' Mclean." www.womensfilmandtelevisionhistory.com, November 11, 2014.

Spencer, Dorothy. "The Film Editing." *American Cinematographer.* November 1, 1974.

Stripek, Jan. "Slow Motion in *Raging Bull.*" *Cinema Shock.* January 21, 2013.

Tartaglione, Nancy. "Venice: Thelma Schoonmaker on Working with Martin Scorsese, *Silence* & Preserving Michael Powell's Legacy." *Deadline Hollywood.* September 2, 2014.

Turan, Kenneth. "*Out of Sight.*" *Los Angeles Times.* June 26, 1998.

Vespe, Eric. "Steven Spielberg and Quint Have an Epic Chat About *Jaws* as It Approaches Its 36th Anniversary!" *Ain't It Cool News.* June 6, 2011.

Villella, Fiona. "Shadows on the Horizon: In *A Lonely Place.*" *Senses of Cinema.* November 2000.

Walters, Ben. "Sally Menke: The Quiet Heroine of the Quentin Tarantino Success Story." *The Guardian.* September 29, 2010.

Ware, Susan, and Stacy Lorraine Braukman. *Notable American Women: A Biographical Dictionary Completing the Twentieth Century.* Cambridge: Harvard University Press, 2004.

Weinraub, Bernard "Deconstructing His Film Crew: Woody Allen's Longtime Staff Is Hit by Cost-Cutting Efforts." *The New York Times.* June 1, 1998.

Index

Numbers in *bold italics* refer to pages with photographs.